THE TOUCH

A novel by

Ronald T McMillan

ISBN: 1500309419
ISBN 13: 9781500309411
Library of Congress Control Number: 2014911584
CreateSpace Independent Publishing Platform
North Charleston, South Carolina

Acknowledgment

I am grateful to the people who have supported my writing, especially my wife, Rohini, and my grown children, Sean, Aaron, and Rani Page.

Especially fond of any new manuscript of mine was Roy Dhanda, my father-in-law. Roy read my stories enthusiastically, and gave me clear insight on what he thought. He was a scholar and a great writer, and I was always honored to have him as a reader.

Lastly, thank you, Rachel Cartwright, for your good advice and keen editorial skills.

CHAPTER ONE

Sometimes I feel like it's all too much, this business.

At the end of the day, I'm often too wired to sleep, too exhausted to think. But not ready to stop. If I'm close, very close, to revealing the illusion that's been skillfully rendered, I'm in an uproar.

When someone does something wrong and desperately wants to hide it, they yearn for camouflage. They move hastily along dark sidewalks; they stop looking up. They develop a plastic smile. There is a darkness trailing behind them that makes me shudder. They walk among us.

Maybe I should explain. I have this talent. It's gotten me into trouble, but it also pays the bills. It's a curse, and it's a blessing. It fills me with doubt. I often hate it because of the way it makes me feel.

I solve murders.

Early on, I felt like a freak. I heard things that weren't there. I saw occurrences that shouldn't have been possible. I knew details about unfamiliar events. I had no idea what was wrong with me. I never told my folks, nor anyone else. That is, until I was seventeen and drunk and blurted it out to a quiet woman who was my first love. She said I was a rare one who could see the other side of the world. I was gifted. It confirmed my darkest fears. She never spoke to me again.

The first time I saw a dead body was in Black Mountain, North Carolina, where I grew up. It was only for a moment because the swarming police shooed me away. The scarlet rhododendron blooms washed over her half-submerged face like a garland from the devil. She was twisted around a sycamore root, and her swollen expression whispered silently to me.

Three months later, I awoke in a sweat and drove down to the creek and waded in to the place where she was found, sank my head underwater, and saw the buried, glinting handcuffs the sheriff had missed. They traced them to William Phillips, a rich man whose property covered half of Rattlesnake Mountain. He'd played rough for years. Too rough, that one night. He was my first conviction, in a way.

After that, the dead woman's face haunted me. I had discovered something about myself that was too much for a young man to contend with. Criminal justice was not my calling yet. Dead bodies—and all their insanity—were the last thing I wanted to associate with. But there was this thrilling notion I kept feeling. It was too clear to ignore. I had found out something that others had overlooked.

When I was younger, on cool autumn coon-hunting nights, I was known as a keen shot with my uncle's .22. The baying hounds and blood frightened me and excited me. Dad slung the warm, dead raccoon over my back for me to brandish. It felt good to have him against me. I felt that same way when I found those handcuffs. That hunt, though, was for a different kind of animal—a killer. I began to sense that I could be in the thick of this other hunt in a way I had never been in the woods. Game are predictable. Flush them, run them, tree them, shoot them. Humans, definitely are not.

At least, that's what I thought then. Now I know a little bit more about such things. The smell in the air when someone has been harmed exists. It's real to me. There are other things, too. There's a shock wave in a crime scene that bounces around for a while. Like the palm of one's hand striking bathwater, it sloshes over everything, and if I arrive early enough, I can feel it.

I'm rarely so lucky to have such clues when I'm on an investigation. I don't really have a system like the other homicide detectives on the Buncombe County police force here in Asheville, North Carolina. They are very systematic. They have bulletin boards and photos arranged neatly, and arrows pointing all over the place. I don't write anything down. I have no photos other than the images in my head.

Yes, I have a degree in criminology, but I don't follow the textbook investigative procedure. I wish I could. It would make it a lot easier. I don't have such intellectual desires.

I do have a touch.

I'm not in North Carolina at the moment. I'm in Washington, DC, at the request of a very frustrated homicide detective named Sammy Chung. Chung's a big Hawaiian with white hair who always finds the bad people. He's perfectly connected. He loves the Redskins and sits in the exclusive boxes at the games. Plays racquetball with members of Congress. They steam afterward and talk shop and swear. He takes pride in his work and lets everyone know it.

He's silent now.

I got the call from him three weeks ago. A well-known young woman had vanished, and DC police were under enormous pressure to find her. An attractive college student, she disappeared after entering a Chinatown nightclub one evening. Her convertible was still in the parking lot in the morning. No evidence of foul play existed. Absolutely nothing about her existed at all.

Our conversation had stalled. Chung bore down when I grew quiet. "John, I know you're just settling down in Asheville. I know you want to establish yourself."

"Yes, I do," I replied.

"You're probably wondering why I think I need you."

"Yes."

"Because," he said, "DC police know you've got a good nose on you. Especially on this kind of case."

"More good cops up there than down here, Sammy."

"Good cops all over, Mr. Wiley."

"How long she been missing?"

"One month tomorrow."

"Disappearances are a heartbreaker," I replied. "She may have run off with her boyfriend. She might have been abducted, or worse. We both know the files are full of these types. Thousands go unsolved each year. Sure she didn't just run away from it all, Sammy?"

"It's been ruled out. She had everything right here. All good, no bad."

"So you're asking me to come up for a routine missing persons case, Sam. What's the real reason?"

"She's a close friend's daughter," he said.

"So you need a favor?"

"Yeah."

"Do I owe you one?"

"No, but your father does. I bailed him out of jail the night before finals in his sophomore year at Wake Forest. He told me if I ever needed a favor from him, his roommate ever again, for any reason, for the rest of my life, I could always ask him."

"You're lying, Sammy."

"Call him up."

"I will," I said, though I'd heard that sorry story since I was a kid. My godfather, Sammy Chung, DC's finest, fat homicide cop, was cashing in after thirty years. "Let me think about it, Sammy. I'd have to clear a leave of absence with my precinct captain. He's a bastard. I haven't been here long, so no way he'd go for it."

"Already been arranged, John."

"I'm green at this kind of thing. I've heard big-city precincts are a nightmare. I don't do rules very well. I guess you've heard."

"I have. You're being brought in as a crime-scene specialist. You'll have more freedom than ever. Anything you need—FBI lab access, remote sensing data, DNA up the ass. All yours, John."

"You know I don't work that way, Sammy."

"I know you don't. You're a special one. That's exactly why we need you. We've exhausted all resources. We've interviewed hundreds. Combed through every landfill for any bit of evidence. Checked every hard drive in the city. Even used the bloodhounds. She's vanished."

"What's her name?"

"Elizabeth Hartner, and she's nineteen years old."

My neck hair stood bristle straight. I'd seen FBI files the week before on Senator Jack Hartner's missing daughter. Up till then, it had been a discreetly handled investigation, at the senator's request. Now it was going public. The press was going to gorge on this one.

"There's another thing I should mention," he added.

"What?"

"Tomorrow the senator is announcing a one-million-dollar reward for information leading to her recovery."

It was sad the way my attitude changed. I can't say that didn't sway me, because I would be lying. "Where will I stay?"

"On my sofa," he said.

CHAPTER TWO

When I first saw a picture of Elizabeth Hartner, it reminded me of all the other thousands of pictures I've seen of missing persons. They all look completely happy. Most of them are high school pictures or sections from Olan Mills family portraits the parents gave police. A better shot of the missing person would be one with a bloodied face and greasy hair and swollen eyes. That's the way they usually look when they're finally found. If they're found at all. That's the picture we ought to circulate on the milk cartons.

Hartner had long, dark hair, dark eyes, a clean, straight nose, and a fairly sensuous mouth. I could see Rosetta Hartner, Elizabeth's pure–Cherokee Indian mother, mixed in her features. Sammy gave me so much background data on the missing girl; I took it all back to his white-brick home in the northwest part of the city and sat on his screened porch and read.

Elizabeth Hartner had been seen with three friends entering a popular dance club on Fifteenth Street, about eleven thirty on a blustery March night. Though she didn't have a wristband announcing she was old enough to drink, she was soon drunk, and loud. A bitchy little alcoholic, as she often described herself. Her friends, all roommates at George Washington University, admitted they bribed older men to get them drinks if their own fake IDs failed. Clubbing meant drinking, and, when the mood struck them, drugging.

I wanted to trace her steps.

But what were the steps she took? After stepping onto the dance floor with a huge group of friends, she'd disappeared. They searched the restrooms, the two other floors of the club, the parking lots.

Nothing. No struggles with a drunk boyfriend or horny patron to go outside. No "I'll be right back."

All the interviews from witnesses were pointing toward one thing— a scene where everyone saw a slightly different version of reality, but not a complete one. Which is what happens all the time anyway. That dance floor was a scene of confusion. The house music was pounding, the lights were blinding, the air was thick, and the bodies tight. She could easily have walked out, and no one would have noticed. But why would she walk out? Only two reasons. Fear, or lust.

After reading further, I put my money on lust.

The last thing on Elizabeth Hartner's mind was her academic major at school: political science. She rarely studied. She was nearing academic expulsion. According to pulled transcripts, she'd barely passed her freshman year, and now, as a sophomore, she was falling fast. Daddy had probably stepped in and bought her another semester. But it wasn't going to help. She was two months away from flunking out of school.

Sammy's notes indicated her real major was partying. The only child of Jack and Rosetta Hartner, Elizabeth had led an easy life. They spoiled her as all only children are spoiled, but they also disciplined her with equal force. That force came from her father. The senator's stomach churned constantly at his daughter's behavior. She was out of control, and increasingly a political embarrassment. Her rebellious behavior ran as deep as her father's own conventional ideas.

Her mother was the peacemaker, the soother, and the spoiler. Her daughter would receive only the best of everything. Pain and struggle would be diverted from her life. According to her interview, Rosetta felt she must shelter Elizabeth from the nasty political world her father worked in. Living in DC and swirling in the political establishment was not normal. It was full of treachery and backstabbing and power mongering. It was all about money in the end. So, to help things along, the Hartners bought their daughter the silver BMW 540 convertible. It didn't have the therapeutic effect they had hoped for.

The BMW came equipped with a potent V-6 engine, but that wasn't enough for Elizabeth. Friends in the import-racing scene soon convinced her to modify her car for street racing. The Maryland New Carrolton Metro Line stop was twenty minutes away. For years it had been the East Coast's most enduring spot for quarter-mile showdowns. After midnight, hundreds showed up to race, show off their rides, and drink and drug. It was instantly appealing to her.

The records showed she maxed out three Visa cards at a nearby speed shop in Fairfax, Virginia, within the month. Turbo charger, headers, performance exhaust, nineteen-inch rims, and racing Pirellis. Computer chips for tuning all the go-fast goodies. Two weeks later, she installed nitrous oxide. When spurted into the fuel injector, NOS is like strapping on a jet engine. It's dangerous for two reasons: One, it's super flammable, and two, its seductive little red button is a tricky proposition for poor drivers like Elizabeth Hartner was.

Everyone realized it—she was over her head with that car. Those close to her realized she was also over her head with her life.

I shower in the extra bath at Sammy's house and shave close. It is 5:00 p.m. My image in the fogged mirror looks childish to me, as usual. My hair is short and my body very lanky. I slip on a crisp white shirt, pressed khakis, and hand-shined loafers. Dressing this way makes me feel mature. But I also love a starched shirt because it means order in the crazy world I inhabit. I do silk ties, but not tonight. Undercover cops are so grungy these days; no one thinks the kid with the button-down polo shirt is actually a detective.

I ease my old Toyota Land Cruiser out onto Wisconsin Avenue and head south, into town. I've read enough case data for the moment. I've been introduced to all the law enforcement personnel on this case. I've spoken with the DC chief of police, Harris Willis. I've been assigned a tattered desk down the hall from Sammy's office at the Georgetown precinct.

What I need to do now is what I always do. Get out here. Get out and see all the places Elizabeth Hartner saw before she vanished. A warm spring night is ahead of me, and I wonder, as I pull through the

GW campus, overflowing with pastel cherry trees, why this city feels so cold.

Crime scenes are what I thrive on, and this case doesn't have one. Hartner might be in Vegas or L.A., or who knows where. I need to find where the violence took place, if it did at all. Maybe I'll drive around and sniff the air and study the flight of birds like I do, and the trail will stay dry as a bone. Maybe she's living happily with a sugar daddy who'll keep her in the good life.

But she was a home girl.

Sweating in the evening's stickiness, I walk the whole GW campus. It sprawls in and out of this neighborhood called Foggy Bottom, without clear boundaries. Side streets are dark, and sleepy, and quiet. Traffic sounds far away. Elizabeth must have been bored living on campus. Interviews with friends never mentioned it, but I can feel her restlessness as she stands here, staring up at her dorm window on the third floor.

On that last evening she went out, what would she be thinking about? Running freely down these steps to her car, I read she'd worn black slacks, sandals, and a low-cut white blouse. Carolina Rodriguez, her best friend, claims Elizabeth had no enemies. No one who wanted to wish her any harm. In my pocket is a picture given to police of Elizabeth Hartner taken on the dance floor that night. This last known shot of her will surely make the news. She's smiling at the camera, looking attractively drunk. Hair pulled up, with splashy diamond earrings.

I'm contemplating hitting the dance club but remember it won't roll till midnight. In Asheville, North Carolina, we're asleep way before that. Those Blue Ridge breezes sucker one into bed early every night, the sheets so cool and damp. By dawn, with the windows open, even on a summer night it's time for double blankets. I can still hear my mother's coffeepot perking to life as the sun comes up, and right here on this street, I can smell its aroma.

I picture Elizabeth Hartner moving past me into the night, and it strikes me very clearly that she was in love that evening. It also strikes me that she might be dead.

Within moments of that dark thought, Sammy rings my cell. He picks me up on the campus ten minutes later.

"We can get there quicker in my car."

"Where?"

"Verizon Center."

"What are we looking at?"

"A young woman's decomposed body."

"Hartner?" I'm breathless.

"Clothing is close," Sammy says. "But it's hard to tell. She's in bad condition. The body's bent over, stuffed down in a window well. Maintenance guys were clearing out leaves when they uncovered her."

A half-dozen squad cars are already there. As soon as I step out of the car, it starts pouring rain. We move through the yellow tape, past a dozen huge Dumpsters, down a ramp, and along the back of the center. Rain splatters everything. Floodlights are set up over the woman. Off to one side, a big man stands by himself, his billowy white jumpsuit whipping in the blowing rain. White sneakers gleam on his feet. He is even taller than I am. His stance is one of sorrow, as if he were attending a funeral. Even with his sunglasses, I can tell I've seen that face before. He looks at me sadly, then strolls away, vanishing into the rain. Two people accompany him.

I turn back. The window well is roped off, and I can see the dead woman's illuminated figure down in there. She looks caved in. One last expression is etched on the woman's face: it's screaming, *I'm so tired.*

The legs are drawn up, as if she was trying to stay warm. Her black hair is matted and muddy and frozen, like a collar around her neck. The steel grate over top stripes her in shadows. But then photographs are snapped, and the illumination brightens her, making her more alive, yet more dead. Sammy's moving around frantically. He's teary-eyed. Praying it's not her, it will kill him if it's her. He's connected more deeply than I thought. He and Senator Jack Hartner are close, it's a personal thing. He's got to find her alive, find her before his friend's daughter is murdered.

Three hours later, we receive the news from the forensics lab.

It's not Elizabeth Hartner.

CHAPTER THREE

At ten the next morning, Sammy and I walk up the front steps of Senator and Mrs. Hartner's Tudor on Reservoir Road. We are escorted through a big foyer and toward the back of the house. The senator and his wife are waiting for us in a bright library. It has a sliding oak ladder that gets to the high, expensive books. Rosetta Hartner looks at me intently as we are introduced. We sit; all of us talk for some time, and I don't hear a thing. The senator's wife is more beautiful than I thought. It unnerves me. We discuss the dead woman's body that was discovered last night two blocks from the club. Rosetta Hartner eyes me more often than she should for a senator's wife. I don't react because this is serious, and I'm far younger than she is, and besides, I know I'm completely wrong.

I've just been asked a question by her, and I'm not sure what to say. She's told me how much she appreciates me coming up to help them find their daughter. She wants to know if I would like to look over Elizabeth's room for clues. Although it was examined by detectives weeks ago, she suggests that maybe they missed something. She says she knows about my success in law enforcement, which makes her feel better already.

"Yes," I answer. "I'd like to see her room."

Sammy smiles; we all rise, and she leads me out of the library. The senator glances at us. A curving staircase takes us upstairs and to Elizabeth's room, the first on the right. We enter, and it smells clean and unused, like the Holiday Inn. Mrs. Rosetta Hartner is dressed in tight, faded jeans and a soft black sweater, lower cut than it should be. I haven't the courage to follow the sight of her cleavage as it vanishes down into the cashmere. I'm still on her eyes. They are big, dark, knowing brown eyes, and they are cradling me like a baby.

I focus on the room and turn away. The bedroom's a sterile place, with no posters, no overflowing dressers. Elizabeth couldn't have stayed here much. The dressing table is tidy. Gold hoop earrings, all very similar, hang neatly by their stems on a rack. I open the closet and see it's too well organized. Everything's been buffed over.

"Is this the way Elizabeth actually kept her room?"

"No, Mr. Wiley. We cleaned it up a couple of weeks ago. Liz was super messy. I suppose we should have left it alone, but we wanted it neat in here in case she comes back." She's silent. Painted red toenails seem lonely, down in her sandals.

"Then the clues are all stale, Mrs. Hartner."

"Mr. Wiley, call me Rosetta."

"Call me John, Rosetta."

Her smile is soft. She touches my arm.

"Did you talk with her the day she disappeared, Rosetta?"

"I hadn't spoken with her in a week."

"Did Senator Hartner speak with her?"

"No, not in some time."

"Why?"

"He's very busy…as a senator."

"When you did talk with her, who called whom?"

"We called her. Liz was a typical teenager, and talking with her parents was not her top priority."

"Were you and she close?"

"Very," Rosetta Hartner says. "Though going off to school and living in the dorm weakened the bond between us."

For some reason I walk over to the bed, bend down, lift the heavy bedspread, and peer under the bed. It's a habit I developed as a kid. Underneath it's full, crammed tight with shoes, lacrosse sticks, clothes, books, stuffed animals. Cobwebs.

"John, that's…" she starts.

"What?"

13

"Liz's dump. Senator Hartner and I didn't want to disturb it. She couldn't throw out anything important. It's kind of her memorial—hidden under the bed."

Rosetta Hartner begins tearing up. I peer in deeper; it reminds me of underneath my own childhood bed. A full underside gives one good protection from monsters looking for a residence. I rise and thank her.

"Don't you want to take it all out and look it over?" she asks me. "Detective Chung never even discovered it."

"No, thanks, Rosetta. I'm sure it's fine just the way it is."

She seems relieved. We move out of the room together. At the door I pause and look back one more time at the rows of gold earrings on the dresser.

"Your daughter likes hoops."

"Yes. That's all she wears."

I pull out the photo of Elizabeth taken on the dance floor that last night. On her ears are diamonds. "Were these new?"

She's surprised. "Yes, I guess they were."

"But they are not really her style?"

"She never wore diamonds. She thought they made her look too grown up."

I put the photo away and follow Rosetta Hartner back down into the library. Her long black hair hangs down her back, shining sadly.

I spend the afternoon talking with the missing girl's roommates at the GW Hudson Hall dorm on O Street. Sitting with three of them in their room, I see Elizabeth's corner bed sitting empty and well made. Her belongings here seem more real. She is a rock fan in the worst way, with mementos from concerts plastered over her dresser and desk. I tell them there are no suspects up to this point, and no one on campus is currently under suspicion. No evidence of a crime has even been discovered. For encouragement, I tell them most of the 98,000 missing-person cases in this country end with the person being found, or with them simply returning home. I avoid telling them that a small fraction of those people are dead.

That afternoon, on my way back to the Hartner residence, I hear on the radio news of the one-million-dollar reward money being offered. As I pull up to their home, I feel like a mercenary. Neither of the Hartners is home, but the help allows me in, per the Hartners' instructions. Actually, I don't want to talk to them. I am escorted to the south end of the house, where I move through a mudroom and then out into a spacious three-car garage. It is empty except for one vehicle. The 540 BMW convertible sits there with a layer of spring pollen over its silver body, its top up. It has already been dusted for fingerprints, sniffed by dogs, and thoroughly examined by crime lab guys. The "thorough" part is what excites me. There really is no "thorough"—there is only one point of view. Maybe I can look things over and dig a little deeper.

Sammy rings my cell. "Where are you, John?"

"In the Hartners' garage, underneath Elizabeth's Beamer."

"See anything unusual under there?"

"Not yet, Sammy. I just got here."

"You don't see a young, female, black detective there in the garage?"

"Right."

Sammy says, "She's been assigned as your partner, John. Name is Ginger Woods. Told me she's already arrived there." He pauses. "Look around, Sherlock. You see a pair of high heels standing around somewhere?"

I groan and twist my head all about, seeing nothing. Wait, there they are, black, spiked pumps, thirty feet away, standing silently together. My eyes, rising up from the shoes, can see a few inches of her toffee-colored calves.

"Yeah, I see her now," I reply.

"Funny, you, of all people could have missed her." He hangs up.

The heels start moving toward me with a cold, precise click that sounds like trouble. I slide over and pop my head out a few inches. I don't like working with anyone, normally. Actually, ever. I'm too disorganized, and too antsy for most cops. I see her turn by the corner of the car. It's going to be a long day. I'll piss her off quickly.

A short, taut, young black woman looks down and smiles widely. She is wearing a cheap business suit, holding a big purse, and she has long, orange fingernails. Short ringlets of peroxided hair frame an oval face that is too childish-looking to be in this business.

She's still smiling.

"This isn't going to work, Miss..."

"Woods. Ginger Woods." She extends her hand briefly, waiting for me.

"Sorry, I'm very busy." I scoot back underneath the car and started looking at the oil pan. The high heels just stand there. I spend five long minutes and find nothing down there at all. I emerge and stand up, realizing she is no more than five feet tall, almost a foot and a half shorter than I am.

She extends her hand again patiently. "Nice to meet you, Detective Wiley."

I shake her hand. Mine's covered with grease.

She opens her purse and pulls out a clean white handkerchief, handing it to me. Ass-kissing already. I take it and wipe my hands off and give it back. She uses another one for her hands.

"Well, nice meeting you." I walk toward the door. She instantly follows me. I stop, turn around, and see her smiling.

"Are you going somewhere?" she asks.

"I was."

"Can I join you?"

"No."

I move out of the garage, down the hall, into the foyer, then outside to my car. I sit in the Toyota for a long while, watching for her to come out. Nothing. To hell with it. I walk back inside the house, back into the garage, and see her still standing there.

"Are you waiting for me?" I inquire.

"Yes."

"Why?"

"I've been assigned to help you."

"I don't need help. I need space. Lots of it," I inform her.

"Oh, me too. I won't get in your way, I promise. My purpose is to aid you with your investigation," she says.

"The best help you can give me is to vanish."

16

From down there, she looks at her orange nails, then slowly back up at me. She smiles nervously. "Please, give me a chance, Detective Wiley. I need this opportunity badly. I'm a rookie from out of town. Just give me a few hours. If I don't cut it by tonight, I'll back off. Okay?"

"Fine," I say.

She brightens. "Good, where do we start?"

I look her square in the eyes. "You tell me?"

She looks perplexed. "Well, let's see..."

I'm losing patience. "Are you acquainted with this case, Mrs. Woods?"

"Yes," she says. "And it's 'Ms.' Woods. I'm up on everything. Ask me anything."

"Whose name is this automobile registered in, for starters?"

"Mrs. Rosetta Hartner."

"Why?" I ask her.

"Elizabeth Hartner couldn't get her own insurance. She already has six points on her DMV record."

"For what?" I ask.

"Reckless driving. Ms. Hartner was issued a citation for racing her father's Mercedes last fall. Eighty-six in a thirty-five-miles-per-hour zone."

"So they bought her her own car to race instead?"

Detective Woods smiles. "Crazy, huh?"

"What's Elizabeth's blood type. Got any idea?"

"Type O."

"And the dead woman behind the Verizon Center?"

"AB positive."

I switch gears. "You arrived here before me. Have you examined the car?"

"Yes."

"What's the most curious thing you came across?"

She pauses.

I'm comfortable now. We know who's in charge, finally. Maybe I'll teach her a few tricks, if she's nice. I move back over to the car, open the driver's door, and examine the driver's seat position. All the way back. I climb in and spend a few minutes just sitting there. Standard, fancy car. The keys are in the ignition. I start it up, and it roars to life, howling powerfully. I recall it's been heavily modified. I know nothing about the latest in-car hookups.

Woods announces, "She's running about 385 hp after all the mods. And still street legal."

"Yeah." I snoop, open the glove box, flip down the visors, play around with the radio a bit. I get out. I pop the hood and study the big turbo charger and the fat, red ignition wires. The engine compartment is wall-to-wall gismos, packed with stuff I've never seen. I linger, pretending to know what I'm looking at. The detective is standing close, watching me.

I turn to her. "See anything significant?"

"Well, half the FM stations are set on 'country' and 'easy listening.'"

"Yes, they are," I reply. "Why?"

"Someone else changed them. Elizabeth's preferences were pop and rap."

"Then her parents changed the stations after the car was brought home from forensics?"

Detective Woods shakes her head. "They've not driven it at all. It hasn't moved since the day it was driven back here by Officer Johnson on April fourth."

"Then the officer changed them?"

"Almost impossible. He knows not to tamper with evidence."

"So, your conclusion is…?"

"The preset stations on the car radio were changed the night Elizabeth disappeared."

She's sharp.

"She changed them before she went into the club?" I ask.

"No. None of her friends would have stomached that."

"So, the station changes were made…when?"

Detective Woods says, "Sometime between when she entered the club at 11:30 p.m. and the next morning."

"How might that occur?" I ask.

"Someone else was in her car who liked those kinds of stations."

"Why do such a thing?"

"For enjoyment."

"Then whoever changed those stations wasn't nervous or in a rush. It takes a while to preset six stations," I say.

"Yes. That's true," Woods says.

"So, your conclusion is?"

"She slipped out of the club that night to spend the evening with someone who happens to like that kind of music."

"Bingo."

"Someone older," she adds.

"Why older?"

"No one under thirty tends to go for that stuff."

I laugh. "All of this theorizing, Detective Woods, is hypothetical. We can't prove any of this until we ID all fingerprints pulled from the radio. We can't run with anything yet, correct?"

She nods in agreement. "No. But maybe we can run with that."

She points down, into the engine block. Dangling way down, lodged in a sea of wires and chrome, is a sparkling diamond earring.

CHAPTER FOUR

Detective Woods is good. I'll admit that. But there's more to her than that. She instantly worked with me in a way no one ever had. Finding the earring was a nice touch. But even if she hadn't discovered it, I would have approved of her. And approving of her is going to be a problem for me. I don't like taking suggestions. She gave none. She gives me space, and that is cool. She is professional, and that is a relief. At least, for the moment. As with most young, attractive female police officers I've known, one thing will happen. Sooner or later, she'll get under my skin, become a huge distraction, and then, I'll be screwed.

The Hartners go nuts over the earring. So does Sammy and forensics. I give the credit to Detective Woods, who found it in the first place. Within hours, the lab guys sweep the car again but find nothing further. The dusted fingerprints—initially lifted from the radio buttons in the BMW—belong solely to Elizabeth Hartner.

Pulling fingerprints from the earring is not so easy. No clean ones can be obtained. The crime lab is obsessed with running DNA tests and fluoroscope tests to detect tiny blood smears on the jewel.

I am more interested in the earring itself than who has touched it. It is hardly a normal earring. The setting of the gem is a circle of water-white, half-carat stones clustering a center, full-carat bluish diamond. Each jewel is held in place by six carved golden prongs, and all the stones are perfectly color-matched. The setting is fabricated of twenty-two-carat gold. Typically, nothing like it is made in the States. On the inside ridge of the gold is stamped the symbol "*."

I take the earring, sealed in plastic, from the lab three days later, and slide it in the front pocket of my slacks. The minute I do so, I feel a shiver of lust run down my legs. It reminds me of a feverish love I've known only once, when I was in college. It was a reckless, forbidden association, and this sensation feels the same way for me.

The Hartners feel the earring itself is a total fake. After questioning Elizabeth's friends at GW, Sammy concludes she did not borrow such jewelry from them. They say Elizabeth had worn the earrings for the first time the night she disappeared. After running a stolen property search of local estate jewelry thefts, Sammy determines that the earrings aren't hot.

Detective Woods picks me up in a rented Ford Focus, and we visit three well-respected jewelers in the city; owners and on-site goldsmiths are highly impressed with the earring. It is not an imitation. The center stone of the earring contains a cobalt-tinted diamond of considerable value. The craftsmanship is first class, as is the design. Estimated value of the single earring: $27,000. As to who sold such jewelry, no one could say. It was probably custom-mounted in Dubai, where much of the best twenty-two-carat gold jewelry in the world is made. The blue stone looks like DeBeers quality, from Antwerp. The asterisk stamp mark on the back of the earring is a mystery to everyone. Possibly the jeweler's signature stamp. There are no laser-inscribed ID numbers on any of the stones. This brand of goodies is beyond even the resources of Elizabeth Hartner's own purchasing power.

So, we can run background checks on all the rich men she's had any association with—who also like country music—and we should be halfway home. Detective Woods is solid on that, and gets to work reviewing all witness interviews and case profiles for a match.

With reluctance, Sammy does some background on Elizabeth Hartner's love life. This is the senator's daughter, and that topic is a bit too close for comfort for the senior detective. Not much shows up, though. She was a big-time flirt on campus, yet an almost impossible girl for anyone to date. She preferred dark-haired upperclassmen at GW, but she rarely saw anyone steadily. She hung with the girls more than anything. She had two casual boyfriends early in high school, but hasn't seen either of them in years. I keep flashing on her being infatu-ated at the time she vanished, but with whom?

After six weeks of one vanished Elizabeth Hartner, the DC police de-partment nervously announces there is not a single valid suspect con-nected with the case. There are no solid leads. There's not even proof of a crime being committed.

There are twenty individuals heading the list of people she regu-larly associated with. None had reason to make her disappear, and all have good alibis. There are several dozen other people with whom Elizabeth had occasional contact, and their whereabouts that night and motives are also clean. Even close family was looked at. There are older male figures that she occasionally associated with, such as her GW professors and associates of her father's, but none ever came onto her or had the wealth required for sugar-daddy status.

Focusing now on Elizabeth Hartner's 540 BMW, we drive out to Fairfax, Virginia, and visit the speed shop where the automobile was tuned for street racing. A half-dozen cops have already come by the big, well-lit shop named Speed Trenz since week one of her disappear-ance. Wilhelm Goshen, a silver-haired gentleman, did most of the work on her automobile. He is programming a lime-green Honda Civic with splashy decals when we stroll up.

His handshake is too firm. "I wish I could tell you something else about that poor young girl, but..."

"In my day, we slapped baby moons onto Chevy wagons and called it a day," I say, looking over the flashy import he's working on. "Now, it looks like big bucks to play this game."

"You look too young for such old-fashioned cars as station wagons, son."

"It was my father's old bomb from college, actually. It was a total embarrassment for me to drive."

"What year?" Goshen asks.

"A sky-blue 1966 Impala, with a 350 and a four-speed automatic."

"Tell your papa I'll buy it from him right now."

The old fart has been breathing too many exhaust fumes. "I'll ring him up tonight and let him know you're interested."

"Please do," he says.

Detective Woods is impatient. "Mr. Goshen, just a few questions if I could. What made Ms. Hartner suddenly decide to customize her new car?"

"Modifying one's automobile is a huge craze right now. The after-market parts available for boosting horsepower are plentiful. Once the speed bug bites, it'll keep you up at night. Like a lot of people, Ms. Hartner was addicted to the street-racing scene."

"Did she regularly race?"

"She couldn't handle the car in its stock version, much less after we got done with it."

"Then why spend all that money?'"

"Bragging rights," the mechanic says.

"So she never went out to Metro or over to Manassas for night racing?"

"She did, but someone else raced that car. And brutally hard, too. Spark plugs and tread were wasted in two months flat. She was always complaining it wasn't fast enough. I knew she wasn't the one running the car."

"Who was?" Detective Woods asks.

"I've been asked that question a dozen times. I don't have any idea. She always came here alone."

"Did she ever go to the track?" I ask.

"No. As quick as her car was, she probably would have lost there. Even she knew never to enter a race you weren't certain you could win. The street was the only place for her machine."

"Mr. Goshen," Detective Woods asks, "what's your specialty in automobiles?"

"BMW, of course. I was trained at the factory in Stuttgart, Germany, many years ago. Today, I'm forced to tune these Japanese toys out of necessity. They're not real automobiles in the finest sense."

Woods pauses. "Since you're an expert on German cars, I've always wondered, what's the blue-and-white checkered BMW insignia stand for? Do you know?"

Goshen smiles and turns away. "Folks, I'm very busy. Call me later if you have any more questions."

We walk out. Wilhelm Goshen returns to his work, turning up the radio beside his computer. I can barely make out Garth Brooks's voice singing, "Long neck bottle, let go of my hand…"

I dream at night of finding Elizabeth. Every few days, it deepens in complexity, like a mix of daytime data, whipped together to run in my head at night. I do a lot of thinking at night when I'm asleep. Sometimes I awake exhausted, as if the night's not been a time for rest at all, but a time for investigation. Those mornings, I'm grateful to just spend the day not thinking at all. I fear one day all my nights may turn into those frantic thinking spells.

I know much of my success in police work has been because of hunches I have followed. But I don't discount what I gather at night. It's not something I share with members of my precinct. Sometimes, that nighttime stuff spills out into the day, and for a few moments, I'm dreaming as I'm awake. It makes me comfortable, as if I can see the real world for a moment. But I don't want to see too much.

I sense elements of Elizabeth's abduction in my dreams. She was down by the river that night. For a while, my dreams of her center on a city chase, racing from block to block, leading nowhere. But last night, I sensed something critical about the Potomac. A single thread. A thread that can be pulled. If it doesn't snap, it will lead to the tapestry of what happened.

I know that now.

I like paddling this birch-ribbed canoe on this wide, dark-green river. It reminds me of the sleepy waterways back home. The Potomac has some major white water upstream that's best suited for kayaking, but down here, in the shadows of Georgetown, it's still. The green willows and poplars crowd the shores as I slowly paddle upriver, away from Key Bridge and the low-cut, monument-filled city downstream. There are three islands, really just small rocky shoals that lie ahead, called the Three Sisters. The outfitters have told me that many people have drowned there. It looks too serene for that.

This river has not been dragged for the body of Elizabeth Hartner, but it will be, tomorrow. An obsession has been building in this city concerning her whereabouts. TV news and talk shows are chewing on the story of her disappearance like old jerky, relishing each day that passes without her. It's almost a perfect story because it may never end. If she is never found and a suspect doesn't get charged, it could command our attention for months or years. The fact that she's a well-known senator's daughter, wild and pretty, means big-time media attention. A local radio station asked me to come by for an interview. I have nothing to say.

I don't think I could find her out here, just paddling along. A river like this can hide a corpse forever, churning it along the bottom, twisting it down under rock and tree limb. Or it can drive that body downstream, underwater, for many miles, finally sliding it up into a shallow glen where picnickers might be cooking out. The flesh will give way to bone within a few months, and the bones may crack and splinter as the body is spun around. She could disintegrate into shards down there. I don't really know if this place was where she met her fate, but it's a place where my imagination is very curious.

My cell phone vibrates irritatingly against my pant leg.

"Where are you this morning?" Detective Woods asks.

"Paddling up the Potomac."

She pauses, surprised. I haven't told her about my Elizabeth dreams, or anything about the river.

"Working out all the stress?"

"Yes," I say.

"I've got two pieces of info that may interest you," she announces. "Can you join me for lunch, ASAP?"

"No." I paddle smoothly by the Three Sisters islands, using a steady J-stroke, so I don't tip over and die. "What have you got?"

"Hartner's personal trainer at the GWU gym on Twenty-Third Street needs talking to again. He's been giving slightly erratic accounts of his relationship with her each time he's interviewed."

"How do they vary?"

"First," she begins, "he says they never ate together...then says they did, once. He's fuzzy about how often Elizabeth came in to work out with him. He's not sure what kind of machines she liked, or what her workout consisted of. He's lying about something."

"Or has a bad memory," I add. "What else you got?"

"Elizabeth's mechanic at Speed Trenz, Wilhelm Goshen, never actually graduated from the BMW mechanics' school in Germany like he said. He's done a lot of work for shops all over the metro area. Never stays too long anywhere. Temperamental, it seems. As far as I can tell, he was never certified anywhere as a mechanic."

"Why lie about it?" I wonder.

"To appear sophisticated, and worldly. Apparently, he's neither. I'm going back out to talk with him today."

"Don't," I say. "If we pin him down on that, he'll clam up on whatever else he's hiding, which may be considerable. I don't want him to know we're thinking about him."

"What should I do?"

I look upriver and see its course curving around the green Virginia hills. I want to keep paddling. I need to keep looking. But Woods may have something, and she could easily run it into the ground.

"I'll meet you in a half hour at the deli on L and Twentieth," I say.
"Got it."

"Woods, what made you suspect the mechanic was lying?"

"Everybody well associated with BMW knows they made aircraft engines for Germany during World War II. Their auto insignia today is still a propeller against a cloud-filled blue sky."

"Sharp, Woods. Where'd you get that one?"

Her laugh is harsh, and short. "My grandfather was a fighter pilot in World War II in the Pacific. He used to tell us lots of stories."

CHAPTER FIVE

Before Woods and I can move to follow up on Goshen's evasion, Sammy invites me to the Hartners' for a big dinner party. I put on my only suit, twist on a raw silk tie, and Sammy and I drive over and walk up the steps to the senator's home.

"The senator and his wife give this party every year," he says, ringing the worn mother-of-pearl doorbell. "They're not in the mood tonight, obviously, but feel they must keep up a positive facade. It's always been an important occasion in the past."

Inside the home, it's warm and noisy. Waiters move smoothly, serving complicated food. Sammy gives me a rundown on the who's who of the DC political establishment as of late. This is a Republican fundraiser, but it's also a mandatory gathering of some of the top Senate leadership on the Hill. I feel completely out of place. Sammy chats with a large group of dark-suited gentlemen, and I am soon introduced to a number of important people who seem very interested in me. Yet, I notice they appear equally interested in all others they meet. Senator Hartner is particularly warm with me, escorting me around like a new terrier.

"Mr. Wiley," inquires one bearded, red-eyed senator, "are you close to making any revelations on Elizabeth's disappearance?"

"No."

"It's a tragedy every parent dreads. There's no way to prepare for it, and, equally distressing, no way to live with it."

I nod, then see Mrs. Hartner across the room in an elegantly tight dress. It seems to be growing around her body, like new spring foliage. She shoots me a few polite smiles during the next few hours. She does not come over.

I'm restless and move into the foyer, where I am stopped by an old, well-known *Washington Post* reporter. She tugs at my sleeve. Her perfume reminds me of my dead grandmother. "Give me your exclusive story up till now, Mr. Wiley," Gloria Sullivan asks me. "I find you fascinating. I guess you know that this city is very taken with you."

"I wasn't aware," I say.

"It's true. But beware of false motives and selfish needs. There will be great amounts of money to be made around this investigation of the senator's daughter. Guard against revealing too much to too many people."

"I'll be careful," I tell her.

As I walk out from the warmly lit foyer, Gloria Sullivan reminds me, "The one who has taken the poor child will want to keep track of you, you know. They will draw close at certain times, as a moth does toward the flame."

"The perpetrator must always return to the scene of the crime?" I ask.

"No. The good ones never do, and whoever is involved in this is very good. They left us without a sliver of evidence. That's the mark of a professional. No, I don't think that they will ever return, but by the nature of their own neurosis, they will be incapable of not following the story—and you, Mr. Wiley, are increasingly part of the story. They will find out about you, and sooner or later, come to observe your movements. That's all I'm saying."

With wine glass in hand, she walks away. I tell myself to keep her words in mind. But right now, I have other priorities.

I move up the staircase, bounding quickly, and reach Elizabeth's room. I slip inside, flick on the lights, and exhale. I had a recent dream of her room. It's time to see if it's true.

If I were caught lying here, on the missing girl's bed, with my shoes off and my arms behind my head, it would not be good. But I am gathering information of the kind that would not ordinarily be accessible any other way. I felt it the first time I pulled up the covers and peered under Elizabeth's bed, with Mrs. Hartner looking on tearfully. I'm feeling it now. Elizabeth Hartner was in this bed the night she disappeared. I'm sure of it now. I shut my eyes. I see them.

It's the middle of the night, and they're giggling; they sneaked into the quiet Hartner house through the pantry, up the back steps, and into her room. I see and feel such passion. It's churning my gut; it's spinning my head. He's dark haired. Or maybe not, because his short-cropped hair is bare against his pale skull and it's rubbing redness across her neck and lips. They're not in love as much as insane with each other. This is not the first time he's been here, but he's much more in command this time. There is no stopping him tonight. She's reluctant. But she wants him with an angry ache that won't go away. It's rage more than lust that's brought them both here. It has to be here, because here, in her father's house, it is forbidden. Take that, Daddy.

She's using the young man, I can see that now. He's growing more frustrated; they're panting in the dark on this bed, their naked chests heaving. Their clothes are pulled off. She's still holding back, and he's going crazy. He can't stand it. It's hard to figure out who's more enraged now. Who's using whom. She's upset, and now he has rolled off her and is swearing. She leans toward him, kissing his hand, but he pulls it away. She wants to make love now, but he's furious. Not about her, though. About something else, much deeper. They are drunk. Maybe that's it. But he's obsessed about why he's actually seeing her. He can't hold back the self-hatred anymore. He slaps Elizabeth with an incredibly hard, open palm that pops into the darkness. Shocked, she leans up, her naked body full of wrath; she slaps him back even harder.

It's gone. The whole scene that was just here, gone. I open my eyes and rub my face. I must have fallen asleep for a while after what I saw. It was so clear; now, it's so fuzzy. I must remember it before it fades in my head. I need to verify that Elizabeth was actually here with him. Lots of things I see are not truly accurate. I've learned that the hard way. I must verify it went down like that. I think back to the lovemaking scene. How to identify her lover? Lean, wiry body. I see him slap her again, and I roll back my eyes in my head, and the scene draws sharper in my mind. His face is long, dark browed, with deep-set eyes. His pants are slung halfway off the bed. Khakis, it looks like, cuffed, with a dim silver belt buckle. I see, on the floor, sandals—hers, black, open-toed, lying on their sides. I see another pair: flat, low-cut leather sandals, with a toe ring and narrow foot strap connected by a braided leather strip. I search the room for evidence, running through the scene in my mind, back and forth, again and again. Exhausted, I open my eyes and look straight into the quizzical expression on the face of the senator's wife, who is standing in the doorway, staring at me.

"What are you doing here, Mr. Wiley?"

"I came back up to have one more look around. I hope you don't mind?"

She has both hands on her hips. "And what did you hope to discover this time?"

"I never know till I see it."

Her arms abruptly drop by her sides. Then, they slowly come together in a knot against her breasts. Tears I've not sensed splash on her wrists.

"I feel so crazy, Mr. Wiley...I don't know what to do about Elizabeth. I miss her terribly," she sobs. "Help me, please ..."

She reaches out a shaky hand toward me. She holds it out in space. I move swiftly, not ready for this. I take her hand in mine, and she shuts the door. It clicks closed, and she pulls me to her. As I put my arms around this woman, I know instantly that she is only a distraught mother, made insane about the loss of her only child.

She whispers, "I saw you earlier and I wanted to come over, but..."

I put my hand more firmly around her.

"I couldn't be seen with you," she says softly. "My husband is very jealous of you."

"Me?"

"He suspects I'm attracted to you."

"Mrs. Hartner..."

She looks down now. "Mr. Wiley, I shouldn't have said such a thing to you. I know you're a professional. I know you're doing all you can to find Elizabeth. You have no idea how much confidence I have in you. I shouldn't have disturbed you up here."

Her brown eyes look up at me in a way that makes me feel very competent. She is falling deeper in my arms. She is holding me very tight. I gently push her back till there's a space between our bodies.

"I saw your daughter on this bed, Mrs. Hartner. I had a very clear vision of her in my mind."

She is dead quiet.

"I saw Elizabeth with a young man. They were here that last night together. I'm sure of it." I pause. "Is that possible, Mrs. Hartner?"

She searches my expression for a while. "Yes."

"Do you have proof?" I ask.

"No."

"Then, what makes you say yes?"

"The bed covers were disturbed the next morning when I came into her room. I smoothed them over. I never mentioned it to anyone."

I ask, "Why didn't you tell Sammy? He could have dusted the bedroom for prints. He could have pulled fibers and DNA evidence from the bed. He could have pushed this whole investigation miles farther down the road. Why didn't you tell anyone?"

"Because then the senator would have known she was in this house without our knowledge. It would have driven him insane, discovering she was here that last night with someone. I know it's crazy, but you don't know him. It's better he knows nothing about this." She pauses. "How did you manage to see what you saw?"

"Mrs. Hartner, I had a vision of them after I lay down on her bed for a while."

Her eyes widen. "You are like they say, Mr. Wiley, after all. What did he look like?"

I run through the scene for her, from start to finish. She nods when I mention the sandals. Moving quickly to the closet, she walks in and retrieves something. Sandals, exactly like the ones I described. "I found them under the bed that morning," she says.

I move out to my truck, and when I step inside it, it doesn't feel right. Sammy is still inside at the party, but I had to get out. For the first time since I came to DC, I want to leave and return to Asheville. I feel a huge, sad burden, one ready to spill down on the Hartners and me. It is more than I have encountered before during any other case. There is this chilling certainty that I feel about her suffering. Perpetrated on her by a powerful and very evil force. I don't believe in the devil, but I do believe in the power of overwhelming ignorance. But this is different. It feels downright diabolically clever.

I don't want to stay, and I don't want to drive away, either. Elizabeth's disappearance has grown too close to my gut.

I have crossed over the forbidden line that separates a professional from one who's gotten too close, and thus, too emotionally involved. She and her mother are mixing in my mind in a joyous, frightening, provocative, horrid spin that is nearly making me ill. And, now, here I am, sitting in my car, feeling disturbed about something else. I look on the seat, in the back, as if someone were back there. No one. But something's spooked me now. I turn on the radio and get ready to pull away from here, and perhaps, from the whole case. There are too many moving parts, too many expectations, and way too many creepy images for me to sort through. I don't care if she's been wronged. I want away from here.

That's when it hits me. Something in my truck is actually tormenting me. It's that feeling I got when I first sat in the car. I look on the floor with the light on. I get up and look under the seats to see if something hideous is down there. I'm clearly irritated by something, and it's more than the case itself. What the hell is it? I get back in the seat, take a deep breath, and think about starting the car.

I can't do it.

Is there a bomb in the engine, I wonder? I pop the hood, crack it gingerly, and peer in the engine compartment. I know every nook and cranny in that old motor well, and all looks fine. Back in the cab, I peer under the dashboard. I see something foreign under the dash. I see now what's been bothering me—it's a bug in my car. Way up inside the dash near the steering column. Facing the driver's seat. A remote microphone.

I'm being monitored.

I suddenly feel much better. I know instantly what the problem is. It's been in my subconscious for the last week. I sensed it before, as if someone had sprayed a funky room deodorant in my Land Cruiser. I feel a subtle shift in my attitude clink into place. I won't be leaving this case after all. Not after this. I've gotten too close. They're afraid of me. I start the car and drive away, reminding myself to sweep all other areas in which I operate.

I'm closer than I thought.

CHAPTER SIX

From Francis Scott Key Park in Georgetown overlooking the Potomac River, I see police boats dragging the water in slow, systematic movements. They are looking for the young woman's body. It's a cold and unemotional kind of work. Their haul might just as well be shrimp or yellow fin from the movements they're making. Up on Key Bridge arching above them, there's a small crowd peering down. Some are lunchtime joggers, some tourists, some simply curious. They stop a moment and watch the boats on the river below. They pause to look, just in case her body rises up at that instant.

I'm starting to isolate myself. Today, I've decided not to answer my cell, or attend the afternoon briefing with Sammy and his precinct detectives, or chat with the forensics guys in the hallways at the Wisconsin Avenue Police Station. I'm making this tiny park my observatory today. The bench I'm sitting on is cold, but a midmorning sun is at work. Way down, deep in my belly, I'm as curious as those gawkers on the bridge. Yesterday, when the dragging for Elizabeth Hartner began, it seemed the whole city was in attendance. But finding nothing, many, including dozens of DC cops, have gone back to work.

After a couple of hours, I walk over and pump the parking meter beside the Ukrainian Embassy where my truck is parked. The steep cobblestone street dead-ends right above Georgetown's old C&O Canal. The canal's ancient thoroughfare momentarily distracts me, and I lean over and study it, passing below. What was big time technology two centuries ago, today is a stagnant green ribbon. As I turn, I glimpse a tiny reflection flashing from across the Potomac. I walk back up and sit and watch the river. I see the flash again. It's on the Virginia side. A News 5 chopper flies up and hovers over the river, watching for the body. It flies away impatiently when no corpse emerges.

I walk from the park and then down across Key Bridge, and join the small crowd watching the activities on the river below. A small girl, clenching her mother's hand, whispers, "Please...don't let her die."

I keep walking across the bridge toward the Virginia side and toward the spot where I saw the reflection. I see, way off to one side, a cameraman shooting with a long lens on a tripod. He's aiming across the river at the dredging boats. But he's also aiming at my little park. I approach the end of the bridge and pass behind a grove of blooming Shademasters. I move around the abutments and onto a knoll above the river. No one's there now.

I linger, seeing three depressions in the new spring grass where the tripod was removed. Down along the bank, I glimpse someone moving away, along the street back into Rosslyn. A small dark man in a white cap and jogging suit. Why shoot pictures when you're just out for a run?

I'm walking along the C&O Canal footpath now, away from the city, staring at the old waterway. Beyond, out through the bare woods, the Potomac shimmers warmly. Scullers are streaking by in eight-man boats, barely a foot wide, sixty feet long. I'd like to join them and pull a few thousand meters, my crew skills faintly alive in my bony shoulders and thighs. The sand crunches behind me as a cluster of mountain bikes passes by in tight formation. The last rider looks back at me, then pedals away with the others. I sit for a while by the canal and gaze downriver. Far away, I see them, pulling their nets in search of Elizabeth.

I begin to ponder: exactly who was Elizabeth's angry boyfriend, the one with her that last night at the senator's house? My imagination, or actual fact? He's not a profile I've ever read about. She knew him secretly. Surely he operated beneath radar for a reason. His concealment doesn't make sense unless she'd only known him for a short time. He'd eventually make the light of day with family and friends. If he's not connected with her disappearance, why doesn't he come forward? His existence must be proven.

I'm feeling irritated by the swollen breeze that's carrying a swirling spring pollen. I sneeze, and my eyes twitch. Back home I'm a mess in the spring. Here in DC, it may be the same. But it feels different today. The atmosphere down by the river feels annoying. That can mean the beginning of insight.

I look down the path and see a young woman walking toward me. She's been looking at me but now looks away. She's dressed in a plaid skirt and open-neck blouse and sensible flats. With books in hand, her eyes are down. She looks up at me briefly.

I grin. She smiles.

"Hi, there…" I say.

"Um, hi."

I'm rising now, as if I'm walking in her direction anyway.

"Where's your jogging suit?" I ask, reaching for something to say.

A nervous laugh comes out. "Well, I'm not really prepared to sweat today." She has violet eyes, medium-length dark hair, and flawless skin. Half-Chinese, I guess. Somewhere deep in my gut I'm feeling wildly vulnerable.

"Me neither," I say, "but it looks like everyone *else* is getting in shape." Runners are approaching, sustaining me.

She's looking awkward, not sure what to say.

"I'm new in town. My name's John Wiley. Nice to meet you."

"Nice to meet you. I'm Tara Chin. I'm heading to my study group." She looks seriously at her books.

"You're a student at GWU?" I ask.

She frowns. "I'm at Georgetown." She points back through the woods.

"The campus is right here, is it?" I lie.

"You *are* new in town."

"Very new."

We're both silent for a dozen steps. The discussion is close to meltdown. "What brings you to DC?" she blurts out.

I hesitate. "I'm a cop from North Carolina. Just up for a bit of an internship."

Her eyes widen. "Oh."

"How about you, what are you studying?"

She beams. "Environmental sciences. I'm working on my master's thesis on endangered watersheds in the Blue Ridge Mountains."

"I know those hills down south, in Asheville, at least."

"Well, this is my group," she announces, pointing to an oak bench ahead. Other students are approaching.

I take her in one last time. She's tall, with interesting curves. Pretty hands. I catch her eyes. "Bye, Tara."

"Good-bye, John."

She joins her friends, talking animatedly. I look back as I walk away and see her smile at me.

I'm back the next day by the river, and it's cold. I'm surprised by the change in weather. T. S. Eliot said April is the cruelest month. It seems true.

The search for Elizabeth continues downstream. I should be down where they're dragging the river near the Kennedy Center, but instinctively I stay nearer to Key Bridge. All the fair-weather athletes have moved inside, and I stroll down the canal towpath alone.

Last night I read up on Senator Hartner's bright career in the US Senate. As the senior Republican from Arizona, his conservative leanings were popular on the Hill. Conservatives had a majority in the Senate and the backing of a growing countrywide shift to the right. Passivity was on the run. America was fighting terrorism, defending itself overseas, and finally calling a spade a spade. The Republican president, James Mendel, often chose Senator Hartner as a sounding board for his own agenda. Working hard, paying your own way, aiming high, believing in God Almighty—these were concepts both men held high. Hartner could have been President Mendel's vice-presidential running mate during the recent elections had Hartner possessed stronger name recognition in the country. Instead, the aged Senator Tuck Johnson of Tennessee was tapped because of his Gulf War career and his big jaw. Tuck Johnson's politics were farther to the right than Hartner's, and in the end, his GOP basics pulled in critical Midwest support that helped James Mendel slip into office.

But Hartner had worked tirelessly to campaign for Mendel, and the newly elected president soon rewarded his friend with more power than that wrought from being a one-dimensional VP. Senator Hartner's recent Lawsuit Reform Bill contained thoughts right out of the president's playbook. Its passage brought Hartner more visibility and the president higher poll numbers. Hartner soon gained the chairmanship of the Judicial Committee. He sat on the yellow sofa in the Oval Office when the president was in a jam and needed the advice of his senior advisors. He drove golf balls with Mendel at Army Navy Country Club across the river. He was ripe for a big-time political career.

Then his daughter disappeared.

The impact on him was subtle at first. Senator Hartner wanted the investigation carried out without fanfare or publicity. When both objectives collapsed and the story broke, his face was on the nightly news for weeks. It grew weary looking. His poll numbers shot up in sympathy. His colleagues on the Hill admired the way he carried on: calmly enduring the burden on the outside, darkly tormented on the inside. There was other, deeper agonies going down in the senator. How ironic that he was so powerful, and yet, now, so powerless. He controls political destiny in the Senate, but the twisted rules of abduction or murder don't care. It takes so long to build up a person's life, yet no time to take it away. The paradox of this powerlessness drives Hartner to rely on Sammy Chung and compels Sammy Chung to lean on me. The only thing I have to count on at the moment is myself.

Making the Hartners happy again isn't what drives me. What haunts me is the inequity of those who tear down the world—never to be held accountable for it.

Is there a link between Hartner's political connections and his missing daughter? No ransom note has been delivered. No blackmail threat has been uncovered. If Elizabeth was harmed, was it because she was the daughter of one of the most powerful men in the country, or simply a girl in harm's way?

In my reverie, I miss her coming toward me on the path. In the shifting cold wind by the river, I don't hear her footsteps running in the sand. Today, Tara Chin is in a black sweat suit and gloves and a hat. Bright running shoes, and no books. I know it's her because her violet eyes are even more brilliant in the morning sun. She looks embarrassed that I'm in her way again today. I can see it in her shy smile as she slows her run, then walks toward me. "Hello, again."

"Good morning," I reply.

"How are you?"

"Fine. No study group by the river today?"

"No, thank God. It's my day off." She looks me over. "Obviously no jogging for you today?"

"Some of us have to work," I say.

She winks. "You don't look like you're even breaking a sweat."

"It's all up here," I say, tapping my temple.

"Impressive," she says, then waves a gloved hand good-bye. "See you."

I watch her run down the sandy trail. I hear a tiny voice in my head say, *Forget her now—you're so easily side-tracked. Focus on what's in front of you. You are nearing a breakthrough if you will just stay down here by the river. Here is where you feel the connection with Elizabeth Hartner. Stay today, and think.*

Ten minutes later, I've cleared my mind, sat on an empty bench by the canal, and made some calls. I'm meeting Detective Woods this evening. She insists I look over her research on William Goshen, Elizabeth's lying automobile mechanic.

Woods has made a connection, though a tenuous one, with Goshen and the blue diamond earring found in Elizabeth's car. Goshen worked in the faceting department of a gem cutter in Germany when he was young. Could he have fabricated a piece like that? I ask. She's not certain.

Sammy's worried I'm out of the loop these days. He's buying me early breakfast tomorrow. There's much I've not told him. He has not realized he's got to stay in touch and keep me focused.

I see Tara Chin running toward me on her return trip. Her feet are shuffling in the sand. She's tired, and her gloves and hat are in her hands. She's looking down at the trail. A light sheen of sweat is on her face.

Stay within yourself. Don't get caught up.

It's obvious the girl can't hang. She's overdressed and overheated. I look up at her in sympathy. "You want to get some lunch?" I ask.

She's exhausted. "Sure."

We walk back up into a blossom-filled Georgetown, careful not to drive my Toyota. The microphone is still in my truck. I want them only to hear what I want them to hear. We stroll down M Street, and she wants to go to Clyde's. We sit in the tiny window seat, and I fiddle with the tablecloth. She stares at me and then out the bright window to the brisk passersby. She's hungry but won't admit it until the macadamia-crusted broiled shrimp arrive, and I see her smile as she pierces the big prawns with her long fork. I get the chicken club, and she eats half of it.

"How's the food at school?" I ask.

"It's gotten old," she says.

"So, you live off campus?"

"I live in a basement of a townhouse owned by a lady named Agnes Sloan. She's a block off campus, and she loves to gab. Mr. Sloan left her a fortune, but unfortunately, no one to talk to. She's like an old nosey auntie, on my butt constantly because I'm always late."

"Late?"

"I party a little," she says, ordering pie a la mode and two forks. "How about you, Mr. Wiley? You like to go out at night?"

"I'm a bad dancer, amateur drinker, and a morning person."

"We don't have much in common."

"Well, I know one thing," I say. "Neither of us is a runner."

Tara Chin flushes. "I'm starting my spring training today. You just happened to be there, that's all."

"I'm lucky I was," I say.

She pays the bill with cash.

Normally, I don't wake up in the middle of the night. I'm a sound sleeper. But then, this is not a normal evening. Yes, I know how far off track I've gotten. But it was for a good cause. Tara Chin swore she wouldn't let me drink too much. She told me the only way to go clubbing was in a blurring, drinking, dancing orgy, and it must be done spontaneously. I agreed only after we had spent lunch and dinner together. Before I knew it, it was 3:00 a.m. and I was high-fiving her friends good-bye in a cold parking lot. Because of my condition, she drove us home.

Now I wake up, and the room is dead quiet. An unfamiliar hallway light is on. My head spins like a top, and I realize this isn't Sammy's extra room.

Tara's sheet-covered naked body is against me. Her breathing is slow and steady. Out the window is a distant, gray dawn. Wind swirls against the French doors, blowing dandelion spores in nauseating eddies. Our figures lie together like two people who know each other. She's tucked in close, and I feel a strong temptation to pull her even tighter, close my eyes, and fall asleep. Another part of me says get the hell out, now. I don't know where my truck is, or even where I am. But I'm a detective. I'll improvise.

I lean up, then sit on the bed and realize the full extent of my injuries. Cold vodka shooters and Heineken are never coming my way again. I find my clothes, peek in the mirror, and see that in one night a full year has been added to my face. I lean down and plant a kiss on her bare shoulder. It's just as well she's asleep.

What I'm going to do is not for the faint of heart.

Ducking out her townhouse basement door, I move up the steps and into a tiny, dumpy backyard. I see my truck's dark profile in the alley beyond. This must be Tara's place, because down below and across the jumble of trees lies the thin sheen of Canal Road. I'm within walking distance of the river. I've forgotten my coat, but a spring morning is in the air.

Five minutes later I'm standing in the woods, looking at the Potomac River, wondering why in hell I want to jump in now. It's not a recommended activity in my state. On the bank, I strip, walk down to the river's edge, and plunge in. The water is colder than I imagined. It crushes the air from my lungs. I swim hard out into the slate colored current, turn on my back, flutter my big feet, and try to relax. I scan the river. It's deserted in all directions. The night is fighting dawn, and soon I'll be a very visible naked man, swimming in the river. Time to move.

The waters are swifter than I thought, so I swim hard upstream. It's a vast, jostling world I find myself in. The foliage along the banks undulates, its grays merging to morning greens. Key Bridge yawns beyond me like a waking sea monster. A living river soul is in charge of this place, and it's not sure who I am. Underneath me, at the bottom of the river, I know there are things I can't see. But I can feel them up here. When I arrive on the Virginia side, I kneel in the sand and pant.

It's then I see flashlights whipping in the darkness on the opposite side of the river, where I dived in. Headlights of bounding ATVs soon close in on the same position. Park police are moving about. Then, just as quickly, they all move away onto the canal towpath and vanish. Shivering and swearing, I slide back in the river and begin the brutal swim back across. My toes are numb, and I'm growing sick from the river water I've swallowed. A glimmer of fear begins to grow inside me—telling me this is how people drown. I think back to when I was a kid and got sucked out to sea by a Kitty Hawk riptide. All I did then was relax, and I made it. But now my legs are cramping in violent knots. My arms aren't far behind. I submerge, and am sucked underwater in pain. I can't remember why I needed to do this. I drift by one of the Three Sisters rocks and hang on for a second. The current whips me like a hungry serpent, dragging me away now. I focus, swimming like a crazy man, my breaths rasping like an asthma attack. I hear my own panicked prayers in my head.

Then, I feel the sudden certainty of sand underfoot.

Coughing and crawling up onto the shore, I'm shocked that I actually made it. Boot prints in the pale mud are all over the place. I stagger on the bank, dress quickly, and stand up in relief. Downriver, a pink Washington morning is growing in the sky. Mission accomplished. I instinctively know this much now: Elizabeth Hartner is not in this river.

CHAPTER SEVEN

"All communication to me must be verbal from now on. No more e-mail, cell phone calls, or hard-copy anything. Understood?"

Sammy's unshaven face is inches from me. Steam from his pancakes is fogging his glasses.

"Why?" I ask.

"Never mind why. 'Why' doesn't get answered in this town. The operative question is when. As in, 'when do we start?'"

"When do we start?" I ask.

"Yesterday. We started yesterday, but you missed your third daily briefing in a row, and ducked Detective Woods again. What's up with you—you flaking out on me?"

"It's always a possibility. But no. I'm okay. Just doing my thing like I always do. I told you, I'm not the gold standard for following directions."

Sammy gently lays down his fork. He wipes his mouth with the paper napkin and exhales for a long time. I sense his blood pressure peaking. "John, let me explain something to you. Even though you're a guest here, you've got to stay in the box with the rest of us. Especially on this case. Lots of shit's coming down. There are layers to this thing I don't even know about, but believe me, it's involved. The sudden clampdown on communications is for security purposes. There's a growing fear that the senator and his family are at risk. We know nothing about what happened to his daughter, and because we know nothing, we're widening the net as to who might be involved. That means international personalities are being looked at."

"Makes sense."

"That also means other departments of the US government are moving into the investigation."

"Like?"

"I don't know, but the FBI isn't calling all the shots anymore. The new focus is on the Middle East at the moment. Now, half the town's spooks are poring over this."

"So, Elizabeth Hartner's disappearance is part of a bigger problem?"

He ponders his response. "Perhaps."

"Then tell me what I need to know to do my job correctly, Sammy."

"I wish to hell I could, John. It's not in the equation right now. Maybe later. Just keep doing what you're doing, but play ball with us, okay?"

"Sammy, I ought to tell you, my truck's bugged."

He sighs. "I know it is. Or, was. I had it removed. Sorry about that."

"Why, Sam?"

"We went through a lot of paranoia at first. No one was beyond a deep background scan. Don't worry. You passed."

"Why bring me up here if I wasn't trusted?"

"You were, and you are." Sammy pauses. "So much so, the senator wants to talk to you personally, John, right after we're done." He points out the window. Down the narrow brick-lined street, double-parked beneath a wide maple, is a long, black Lincoln.

Sammy eyes me before I go. "How'd you learn about the bug, John?"

"Just got lucky."

Shortly, I step into the senator's vehicle, and once I'm inside, it glides away impatiently. Jack Hartner is clean-shaven. He's dressed in a dark suit and yellow tie. His face is angular, yet vaguely out of focus. His eyes are drained, and his mouth set with great will. He's looking like most people do normally. Not like famous guys on TV look when they're on camera. It disarms me.

"You need anything…soda, coffee?" He gestures toward the limo's bar.

"No."

He removes a fresh pack of Lucky Strikes, tamps them, peels the seal and foil away, and lights one. "How was your swim last night?"

"Swim?"

Senator Hartner says, "You know, across the Potomac at five in the morning, naked?"

"Cold."

"Find out what you needed to know?"

"Definitely."

He smiles finally, letting go a little. "What did you conclude?"

"I don't think she's in the river, Senator."

"Mr. Wiley," he says, leaning forward, "you're a real mystery to me. I know everything you've done since you've gotten here. I will know everything you do until you leave. You don't act like any cop I've ever known in my life, and I've known many. And, because of that, I need to know something. Do you really care about finding Elizabeth?"

"Very much so."

"Why? Is it the reward money?"

"No, it isn't."

"Then, what? What's driving you? I need to trust you, but can't unless I'm certain you're who I think you are."

"You mean, am I honest?"

"Yes."

"Well, no. I'm not honest. I probably lie a dozen times a day. Usually about stupid things—hiding parts of me I'd rather people not know about. As for me being who you think I am, I'm just a regular detective who works in law enforcement. We ache, and the only way to cure the ache is to keep chasing the bad guys."

"You're not interested in adding my daughter to your list of professional successes? There will be a great deal of publicity if you locate her, Mr. Wiley. Isn't that part of it too?"

"True. I can't deny that. This one's big."

46

"Big, indeed." He exhales the last draw of his cigarette through his nose, then crushes it forcefully in the side ashtray. He reaches into his pocket and removes a small cell phone.

"Mr. Wiley, this is for your use and no one else's. It will ring me any time of day, any place in the world. It cannot be traced or detected. I need to know what's happening in your investigation. I'll be honest. I don't trust you. But I need you. Get my daughter back, Mr. Wiley, and I promise, you can write your own ticket after that. I can make it happen for you, you know that."

"That's not necessary, Senator. I don't draw strength from that kind of offer. In fact, those kinds of expectations only confuse me. I'm better off just keeping it simple. I don't know what I'd do with your reward money, anyway."

"No?"

"You have to understand something. I don't know *why* I've been given the gift I have. When I was young, I was in constant fear of the unique things I could see and feel. I prayed they would leave me. I made elaborate deals with God at night. It never went away. Instead, as I grew up, my perception only got more acute. And my anxiety grew with it. In fact, it wasn't too long ago that I finally found peace with myself and my abilities."

"What happened?"

"I solved my first murder."

As if to please the DC police, I'm riding the sandy canal towpath on one of their own mountain bikes. I'm spending time here again, and no one seems to mind. There are no other leads more important. After being in the river the other morning, I'm sure that Elizabeth isn't out here. But something is.

Cycling by my side is Detective Woods, who by her own admission is not mountain-bike capable. She barely stays even with me. Her rich makeup is damp, and she is trying her best not to tell me how much she hates this. As we approach Fletcher's Boat House, she says, "Elizabeth Hartner's diamond earring is not new. Did you know that?"

"No, I didn't. When was it made?" I wonder.

"Eighty-five years ago."

"How did you determine that?"

"Elizabeth's earrings were part of a necklace and earring set owned by an Austrian opera singer named Gertrude Sal, during World War I. The set was given to her by a Saudi Arabian prince who grew mesmerized by her voice."

"How do you know it's the same jewelry, Woods?"

"The earring we found in Elizabeth Hartner's car is absolutely identical to Sal's. I digitally enhanced old photographs of the original set. They're a perfect match."

"They may look identical, but Elizabeth's earrings could be a copy."

"Elizabeth's earring was just examined by the city's best antique jeweler, who also curates at the Smithsonian. He claims the stones in her earring were cut in the early twentieth century because of their slight facet inaccuracy. Stones today are polished by more precise methods."

"How does that help us?" I ask.

"We can trace the Sal set over the last seventy-five years and see who last owned it."

"Okay, why don't you do that?"

Woods's peroxided hair is sparkling in the sunlight. Her long amber fingernails are on the verge of fracturing as she grips the handlebars. "I already did, Detective Wiley. Want to hear my results?"

"You're going to tell me, somehow, Elizabeth's mechanic, Wilhelm Goshen, got hold of them at a local yard sale, then enticed her out for a midnight drive with the jewelry and murdered her."

Woods is not amused. "Goshen still has a lot of inconsistencies. But he has no clean connection now that we've established the earring is antique."

"Then what's the earring's history?"

"The jewels stayed in the Sal family as an heirloom until the set was stolen, along with a number of Picasso pencil sketches, from their home in Vienna, Austria, in 1998."

"How did you dig that one up, Woods?"

"I used the FBI's database designated for the Hartner investigation. It's unstoppable. I pulled up an insurance claim made by the Sals. It contained diamond certification, provenance, and recent photographs of the set. Same earrings."

"So, the earrings were hot after all," I say.

"Probably got fenced on the European black market the next morning after the robbery."

"So, then..."

Doubt crosses her face. "Well, tracing stolen goods is more difficult, but not impossible. The matching necklace was not worn by Elizabeth, so what became of it? The same curator at the Smithsonian swears he actually saw it last year, claims it was the exact same design as the earrings."

"How did he come across it?"

"It was part of a large group of rare jewelry he appraised for a private estate."

"Who was the client?"

"The jeweler claimed confidentiality at first. After I threatened him with a subpoena, he admitted the people were part of a large organization that occasionally came to him for appraisal work. They are secretive, organized, and all their gemstones were documented."

"Their name?" I ask.

"Vishava."

We ride our bikes up onto Chain Bridge and then cross over the Potomac itself, looking west. A wide river valley spreads before us, with sprawling homes sunk in the steep Virginia cliffs. The south side of the river runs more rapidly by a narrowing of its course, and beneath us, a massive pond has claimed part of the river for itself. The pond's stillness contrasts with its bordering white water. I look below and see a beaver dam, and farther out in the pond, a rugged beaver lodge. Great blue herons are wading in the distance. Dark-backed seagulls are teasing the turkey vultures high above us.

I think about the name Woods just mentioned, Vishava. It resonates in me, blending river and cliffs, and the uncertainty of the word itself.

"You're going to tell me who Vishava is?" I ask.

Woods is silent. She doesn't know.

It's after midnight, and I'm standing on that same Chain Bridge by myself now. Somewhere down below me, in that water, is trouble. I felt it all day. Should I demand the river draggers come up and work these rapids? Should I wade down into the beaver pond now, like I'm tempted to do?

Earlier, I was with Tara Chin at a club on New York Avenue. Its tiny front door was a zoo, and inside, it was loud and tight and exclusive. At her townhouse she wanted me to come in, but I passed. I've let certain expectations come my way, and tonight, I needed to find a way to fill them.

Not knowing what Vishava was all about killed Woods. I expect she'll find me out here within a few minutes to tell me what she's found. Her skills are not mine, and mine are not hers. On paper, they should probably keep her and send me home.

The wind is warm tonight, and the moon is luminous. Tonight, something big is coming down. I study the rippling waters of the pond below. I don't know what the hell I'm looking for, yet my skin crawls.

The senator's phone rings in my pocket. It shatters my focus. I stop breathing. "John, it's Sam. Where the hell are you?"

"Up on Chain Bridge...what's going on? How'd you get this number?"

"Get over to Senator Hartner's home, ASAP."

"Did they find her?"

"In a way, yes."

I'm searching the water in disbelief. This river isn't part of Elizabeth Hartner's disappearance at all. "What happened to her? Is she alive?"

"Just barely, John. The Hartners just received a videotape of their daughter. She's begging for someone to help her. Her wrists are bound, and she's utterly tormented. There's no one else on the tape. She appears unaware she's being filmed. It's insane."

"What do they want?" I whisper.

"That's what doesn't make sense, John. There are no demands with the tape at all. They don't want anything. They just want us to know that she's in hell.

CHAPTER EIGHT

There is absolute silence in the Hartners' vast library. On the TV screen in front of us is the frozen image of a girl I've been looking for for weeks. Seeing her alive, even in this state, is very moving. She's tougher than I thought. She's not dealing well with where she is or what has happened. But something about her tormented, whispered words, right at the end, gives me hope.

A white-gloved forensic specialist stands motionless by the tape player and looks to the senator and his wife. It is the third time he's played the half-minute tape for me. A dozen times for the rest of the numerous people in the room.

There is no consensus about what to do. Certainly, the tape and its images will soon be scrutinized like no other piece of criminal evidence has ever been. A transcript of Elizabeth Hartner's every word, whimper, cry, and head bob will be written up and analyzed. But there is a growing fear within the Hartners that no other communication will ever come forward. They're panicked.

Sammy disagrees. "The existence of a motive in a criminal act as premeditated as this one, Jack, is a certainty. We don't know what they want, but I guarantee you, they want something."

Police Chief Harris Willis nods affirmatively. "This is only the second move in a long chess match, Senator. Unfortunately, they have made the first two moves to our none. It's no accident they waited this long to contact us. They could have sent this tape earlier, but then its impact would have been less potent. After all these weeks of Elizabeth's continued disappearance, it grabs us. Good strategy."

"Strategy?" Rosetta Hartner utters in disbelief. "These people have no soul or any intellect to form a strategy, as far as I'm concerned. Their aim is simply to terrorize and nothing more. And they've succeeded."

Jack Hartner grips his wife's hand firmly. They're frozen to the sofa, like shell-shocked soldiers, stunned that they've actually seen the enemy.

"Soulless, yes, but stupid, no, unfortunately, Mrs. Hartner," Chief Harris says. "But now that we know Elizabeth is alive, I know she will stay that way. Their motive was never murder. We can all thank God for that."

The Hartners nod.

"Now that the kidnappers have exposed themselves, even in this vague way," the chief continues, "a window onto their activities is cracked open for us. We can shift resources. We can work with renewed hope that our search is not in vain. A new, special task force will be assembled immediately, Senator. This will continue to be the top priority for my police department. We will recover your daughter safely, Mrs. Hartner. And we will prosecute those who have done this to her."

I study Detective Woods, standing by my side. Even though it's three in the morning, she's completely focused.

Mrs. Hartner has been avoiding my eyes, but now holds them and searches my expression. "Detective Wiley, we haven't heard one word from you. You must have many thoughts about this. In a way, we're more desperate now than before we saw this wretched film. What do you feel?"

"What I sense tonight, I may throw out tomorrow," I reply. "I've not had time to form a theory yet. I feel, like the rest of you do, that this tape represents both a huge relief and a huge resentment, all rolled into one. The good news is, you can sleep tonight, knowing at least she's alive. Hope is what we've all been seeking. And your daughter's fighting spirit delivers the hope we need. I sense that much."

"Thank you, Detective Wiley," Senator Hartner says quietly. "We needed to hear that."

Before I leave their home that night, I am pulled aside by Senator Hartner. "We need to talk."

We move down the dark-paneled hall into a copper and steel-bathed kitchen. The senator pours us two cold beers and sits at the center island across from me.

His eyes are bloodshot. "Rosetta told me about your revelations in Elizabeth's bedroom. How detailed and insightful they were. She says you think Liz was here with someone that last night before she disappeared."

"Other than a pair of men's sandals," I say, "we don't have any real evidence about his existence. But I think she was here with someone, yes." I pause. "I haven't been able to verify it. There's no one currently under investigation that matches the kid's description. I could have imagined it—it's always a possibility. For me, verification is the key. But that proof has been slow to come. The river has sidetracked me more than I want to admit."

"Don't deny your hunches about anything, Detective Wiley. From what I can tell, they're merited. That's why I'm talking to you now. Rosetta said the bedcovers in Elizabeth's room were disturbed the next morning after she disappeared, which means you're probably right about them being in the house. I have to come to terms with the fact that she was here. So now we need to find this man. What do you need to make that a possibility?"

"Time."

"Anything else?"

"Luck."

Senator Hartner laughs darkly, watching the bubbles float up his beer glass. "Luck is something this family has always had an abundance of. Luck in finance, politics, and power. But our luck is exhausted now. Good fortune means nothing to us without our daughter. Perhaps divine intervention would be a better commodity."

He eyes me intently. "Why was she here that night with him? What did you feel about the two of them?"

"Deception."

Senator Hartner is shocked. "Deception? Not lust?"

"Oh, lust was part of it, Senator. But they were fighting in her room more than loving."

"About what?"

"They'd been drinking. In the end, their own hidden fears spoiled it for them," I say.

Hartner is stunned. "So there was no lovemaking?"

"No."

"Why was her friend angry?"

"He was ashamed about why he was actually seeing her. Enough apparently, to dampen his own desires."

"And Elizabeth?"

"She was nervous about his real intentions."

"Was there any real affection between them?"

I've pondered that for a long time. Elizabeth's infatuation that last night surely must have been for him. "Yes, I think there was."

The senator stands, drains his beer, and then begins to walk out. "I believe every word you're saying. Find him, Mr. Wiley."

A few hours later, Sammy and I are sitting with a criminal sketch artist down in the basement of the Northwest precinct. We are rendering a portrait of Elizabeth's mystery man. If we can approximate his features, we can run his portrait through the FBI's facial scan analyzer and catch matches within its huge database.

The problem is, my mental images of his appearance are not clear. All I see is a lean, young crown of his head, with small ears, a long face, and a slim nose. His nationality is uncertain to me, perhaps Euro-Mediterranean, but with fairer skin and short-cropped, fine hair. The eyes are the biggest problem, because I can't see them in my head. Take the eyes away, and I cannot define an individual. Within a half hour, we have a working charcoal sketch. But the face is too wide, so we lengthen the chin. The brow is too clean, so we give it more mass. The mouth is too full, so we back off of it. Try as I may, I cannot define his eyes.

We run with a moderately accurate portrait. The technician digitizes the drawing, loads it in the database, then runs a facial recognition program. Within minutes we have several thousand matches. I spend four hours scanning arrest photos of people all over the country, then, from all over the world. At the end, I'm no further ahead in defining who he is. No one yet looks like the kid I saw in my dream.

Sammy's leaning way back in his chair, chatting on his cell to his wife. He's tired, and after a long night at the senator's, going home early. I'm left there alone in the lab. Finally, Woods comes in and sits with me.

"Let me take over for a while, Detective Wiley. You look like you seen far too many mug shots." She's colored her short hair even blonder. Her nails are a honey hue now.

"Yes, please do, Woods. Call me if you find him."

I walk outside to a fine Washington afternoon and know where I should go. Shortly, I'm ringing Agnes Sloan's doorbell at her Georgetown townhouse. Her big, blue, old-person hairdo gets a generous compliment from me.

"Thanks, honey. Tara's downstairs, go on down."

I see Tara Chin sitting on the sun-dappled bed by the French doors. She's cross-legged and buried in textbooks. Papers are all over. She smiles in surprise, leans up, and gives me a hug. I lie down beside her and curl up in fatigue. She kisses my mouth warmly. I kiss her back, and then pull my ball cap over my eyes. Her fingers trace my lips. I realize I'm exhausted. I sleep.

I open my eyes and see Tara's striking face studying mine. She's just told me something. She's holding up my cell phone. I sit up.

"Yes?"

"It's Detective Woods. Sorry to wake you, Detective Wiley, but I thought you'd want to know. I may have found him."

"Found who?" The sun is low. The clock reads five hours later.

"Elizabeth's mystery man. Perhaps you didn't imagine him. He's real. But only you can say for sure. Can you come over?"

I move quickly out the back door, not sensing Tara's disappointment.

CHAPTER NINE

His photo is not what I expected. Or what I hoped for. It's too vague compared to the image in my head. But as I study the front and side views of the man's face, a thought stirs in me. I now see something I'd forgotten about. The kid with Elizabeth had a scar on his left nostril. So does the nose of the young man on the video monitor. As if a razor had cut him deeply, then healed, but not cleanly. We 3-D render both charcoal drawings and arrest photos, rotating both side by side on the computer. They're damn close. The nose scar does it for me.

"I think you've got him, Detective."

Woods beams. "He was picked up in a standard Immigration and Naturalization Service raid last year in the basement of Mid-East Market in Arlington, Virginia. Deported three months later, back to Egypt. His name is Raul Gutab, and he's nineteen years old."

"No green card or visa?"

"None. Some of his cohorts admitted they came in illegally through Quebec."

"What became of them?" I ask.

"Two were actual legal immigrants; the other two were eligible for work permits. All the others were escorted out of the country."

"INS is aggressive lately?"

"Got to be," Woods says. "Too many undocumented people walking around makes Homeland Security guys nervous. They're sweeping out hundreds, and I'm not just talking Mexicans. For a while INS's main target was criminal aliens, but now workplace raids are back in vogue."

"So Raul Gutab came right back into the country," I say. "Sneaking back in carries extra risks. Must have been something here more compelling than just groceries."

"Compelling like Elizabeth Hartner?"

"Perhaps," I say.

"You think she was his reason for returning to the US?"

"First, find out just exactly who this outfit named Vishava is. They had possession of the Sal diamond necklace set soon after it was stolen. Elizabeth Hartner was seen wearing those same earrings the last night she was in Mr. Raul Gutab's company." I smile at her. "And notify Sammy what we've found. It's another gold star for you."

"For you," Woods says. She moves from the room like a woman possessed. "Watch out, Vishava," she whispers.

I usually don't reveal what I've sensed about a victim. I rarely even speak of it as a source of information in my investigations. Not that I'm ashamed of my feelings. But it appears to put solving criminal investigations in the hands of some unconscious talent rather than in the sure grip of an up-and-coming detective. How good would I be if I'd never conjured images about the crimes I solved? Would I be able to gumshoe my way through case after case the old-fashioned way? No. I'd be selling insurance or running a mill. What I do is because of what I am. If my perceptions leave me one day, I'll be a very available, unemployed young man.

After physically holding the kidnapper's videotape, the suffering of Elizabeth Hartner is battering at me. It's locking me down, and I must be free of it. I dare not share what I'm feeling. I've learned from experience not to reveal details to family or friends. When I get too close to the dead or suffering, their pain must be quickly forgotten—or I'm worthless.

Can I stay so cool about her torment? The video only scratches the surface of the hell I believe she's in. Without an apparent motive or demand, we can't do much but wait for them to come to us. Finding her is critical, yet I have no insight as to where she is.

From the moment the existence of Raul Gutab was confirmed, I've been consumed with his role in Elizabeth's disappearance. And so, this evening, from my truck, I'm watching the Mid-East Market, where he was arrested last year. I'm not a great stakeout guy, often missing the obvious while looking for the unobvious. But Chief Harris has ordered massive law enforcement personnel out in search of Raul Gutab. Three detectives, well-placed along the street, have joined me.

Earlier today, undercover cops in search of Raul Gutab raided the Mid-East Market, this big, disorganized grocery store on Wilson Boulevard. The store owner claimed he hasn't seen Gutab since his deportation. The kid, he says, was hired to do grunt work, and he kept to himself. The proprietor was cooperative, acknowledging he hadn't always checked for green cards. Sammy questioned him for an hour and left. That was enough time to place a clean tap on the Mid-East Market's phone lines.

Within two hours, a series of calls is made to various locations around the world from that office phone: one to Cairo, to an unlisted number; one to Zurich; one to Amsterdam; one to Sierra Leone, in West Africa; and, locally, three to Old Town, Alexandria. The numbers all correspond to wholesale suppliers of extremely exotic foodstuffs that help the Mid-East Market cater to the local Muslim population in Northern Virginia. All legitimate outfits. Perhaps we caught him on a busy day. But local distributors handle those kinds of items more quickly and cheaply these days.

Raul Gutab's sandals contained skin fragments that FBI forensics guys are examining now. His DNA and fingerprints will be forthcoming. Holding the sandals in my hands reveals absolutely nothing for me to ponder, as if a void about his existence were frozen within its smooth, tanned surfaces. Judging from the size of the foot imprint within the sole, he is five-nine and 145 pounds.

The senator's private phone rings in my pocket. It's Sammy. He has this private number now. "John, Elizabeth Hartner's kidnapping video just broke on the evening news."

"Christ, so quickly? Who leaked it?"

"We don't know, but somehow, they got a copy. Her face will be all over the papers tomorrow. We're under strict orders not to talk to any reporters. Got it?"

"Yes."

"Sit tight and enjoy the evening. Make us all proud. Bring Raul in tonight, okay?"

"Right away, Sammy."

I feel, suddenly, that no one in DC law enforcement was responsible for leaking that tape to the media. Another copy was sent to the *Washington Post* on purpose.

This time of the night, before dawn, is a bad one for me. It reminds of the fear that haunts people's psyches right before death. There's no inkling in their mind that an amazing event is overtaking them. Now, just like them, I worry the sun won't arrive.

It's still and quiet here in Arlington. A cardinal's voice echoes in the darkness. From the obscurity of my truck, I've seen nothing to indicate this market stakeout is going to produce anything other than a wasted night.

I'm alone now—the other detectives have left. News bulletins have remarked darkly about Elizabeth's kidnapping tape, now circulating on the local TV news shows. It's likely to be a long day for the Hartners, battling the press. The media will resume its total obsession with her disappearance.

An untrimmed forsythia hedge, splaying yellow in the darkness, has held my subconscious attention for hours. Breezes have brought many of its best blossoms down.

When I first notice him, it's because he impatiently moves past those saffron blooms without regard, knocking more of them to the grass beneath his work boots. He's crossing under the streetlights, calmly passing by, thirty yards in front of my parked truck, then down the block into the alley next to Mid-East Market. I didn't see any sign that he might have been someone who was opening up the place early. He could be completely unconnected with the store. It was a very unremarkable event.

It's not until I'm on my way back to Sammy's that I realize I know his stride from somewhere. A man's gait is a subtle body signature, and I study it. But where had I seen his before, and what difference would it make, anyway?

He begins to interest me again when I lie down and stare at the stippled ceiling in Sammy's guest room. His boots, clomping heavily on his feet, the uneven cadence of his shoulders, the awkward swing of his arms.

How is it possible I knew the look of this stranger's walk? I must have studied it somewhere. But I had never been to that area by the market, so it was elsewhere. I think way back to the first day I was in town, then move up in time across each day's moments until I remember. I saw a stride like his the first day I watched the river dragging from Francis Scott Key Park. I saw him when I walked over Key Bridge in search of a flash of light. The flash turned out to be his camera's lens filter. He'd been photographing the dragging of the river from the Virginia side. Or, perhaps, me. I only saw him from behind. But it was the way he was walking that I remember. Not the stride of a true jogger that day in Rosslyn and, this morning, not the true stride of a workman on his way to work. His was more the stride of an aristocrat. Even if his cap was on backward.

I sleep a few hours, then shower, dress, and drive back to the market. Sammy's guys are on the street, so well positioned I can't spot them at first. I set up far back down the street and wait. It's improbable I will see him again. But within an hour I see a well-dressed, bald gentleman exit a dark Lexus convertible, walk down the street, and step into the market. His stride looks damn similar to the man earlier this morning. He's dressed differently. First time I've seen him without a hat.

He's out within ten minutes with a bag of produce, carrot stems spilling from the top. He gets in his car and whips away too quickly for me to react. "I'm out of here," I radio to Detective Argent, the stakeout supervisor.

"You got something, Wiley?"

"Probably not. Just a hunch."

"We know about your hunches. Need backup?" he asks.

I hesitate. "Let's don't create a commotion. I'm not sure it's anything."

"We'll be here."

I drive down the street quickly, nearly losing the Lexus. The black convertible turns down a side street, then moves through a quaint neighborhood. We move into downtown Rosslyn together. He hasn't seen me, watched his mirrors, or shown any suspicion. But then, he quickly turns before Key Bridge and whips down onto the GW parkway, vanishing up the highway along the river. I wish like hell I had a faster truck. He's gone.

I keep driving until I pass an overlook area a few miles down the parkway. He's there, sitting in his car with the top down, talking on his cell, staring across the river from the overlook. I pass by. A hundred yards down the road I pull onto the shoulder and lock the truck. Creeping back down toward him in the woods, I move along the steep bank, high above the river. I advance along a narrow trail till I'm ten feet directly below his parked car. I can hear him speaking angrily on his phone.

Another car quickly pulls up beside him.

They are arguing for a few tense moments. Doors slam. Then, both cars back out, pull away, and roar down the parkway. I bound up from my perch below them, run across the parking lot and see, far ahead, the Lexus slowing as it approaches my parked truck beside the highway. Behind it, honking cars force him to move on. His Virginia tag is TYX-4354. Beside me are the discarded groceries he's thrown to the pavement.

From my truck I call Woods; she runs the convertible's tag for me. The vehicle's owned by a car rental firm in McLean named Auto Exotics, a high-end outfit catering to celebrities in town. She finds that the

Lexus was returned thirty minutes before she arrived to question the car rental firm.

Over the next week I stake out the Mid-East Market for another glimpse of my man, whom I've named "Chameleon." He's vanished completely. No new disguises, no midnight strolls, nothing. Not one fingerprint came from his discarded grocery bag. All international calls from the market have stopped. Selected patrons of the grocery store have been followed for days without incident. Background checks on the store owner are clean. All traces of evidence, what little there were, have dried up. As if we were growing too close to something, were detected, then pushed away from the truth.

Raul Gutab's whereabouts still occupy the thoughts of a great many people in DC law enforcement. An even greater number are involved in analyzing Elizabeth Hartner's kidnapping tape. Police Chief Willis Harris has held exhaustive news conferences. The Hartners have gone into seclusion, peeking out their windows at the press camped on the street outside their home.

Detective Woods has found absolutely nothing about Vishava. It doesn't exist in any form as a corporate entity. A massive search of the name on the fastest computer around reveals no matches. This is a stage that most investigations arrive at, and many stay at permanently. These dead ends have smashed the optimism of last week. Senator Hartner calls me almost daily. His tone is defiant, yet bleak.

I find myself spending more of my evenings at Tara's. When I come to her at night, all I want are her soft lips, fragrant hair, and no problems. She supplies them. Not many days ago I was achy and feverish when I arrived. She put me to bed, nurturing me without hesitation. Something in her body was good for me.

She's fascinated with the Hartner case, asking good questions, making interesting suggestions. Tara has a sense about Elizabeth Hartner that is so different from mine. She's been positive about her survival all along, even before the tape arrived. Her intuition seems genuine.

She's convinced me to leave town for the weekend, spend time with her in Little Washington, Virginia, by the Blue Ridge Mountains. Her research often brings her there. She's booked her favorite bed-and-breakfast. We swim the serene Rappahannock River. Tara talks river systems, tributaries, watersheds, and wetlands. I grow at ease, happy to think about something other than Elizabeth Hartner. I don't dream about anything. But I know it's bad, this sudden easiness. She pleads with me to stay through the week. It feels wrong. I am dulling any edge I've honed.

Driving back into DC, alone, I see the familiar green Potomac, and I don't know why, but I suddenly think of home and our Jack Russell from hell, Max.

CHAPTER TEN

The Jack Russell is not law enforcement's first choice for a tracking dog the way a Basset hound is. K-9 units rarely use this tiny breed. What this little white-and-brown powerhouse lacks in nose power, he makes up for in intelligence. Russells are fierce, aggressive foxhunting dogs, primarily for use underground. They will dig out any quarry and cause it to bolt. I've used Max twice before in cases where human power failed to locate hidden evidence.

Max, my father's old walking companion, is a very valuable canine. At first, I hesitate to call Ben Wiley, but not because he would say no to Max's involvement. (Like all really great fathers, in the end, he gives in to his child's requests.) More worrisome to me is Max's age. He's thirteen, white muzzled, and showing his years. But I change my mind after talking it over with Dad. Give him a whiff of a person's garment, and he will still scent-track across hill and dale, and even across pavement, until a match is found. Perhaps it's a result of Max's direct bloodline to the immortal Trump, the first strain of this working breed.

Sammy, aware of Max's abilities, runs it by Police Chief Willis, who calls the Hartners. Without hesitation, they have the little Jack flown up from North Carolina on first class under police escort. Max, possessive and intolerant, is not impressed.

Growing up with this little white dog was a lesson in patience for me. He needed to run hard, be contained, and be in charge. Only when we took him along on those cool evening coon hunts did we realize his potential. He could race up the trunks of squat trees, chasing petrified raccoons right off the limbs. When bored, he would invent games or dig like a front-end loader. He killed dozens of hare and mice on our mountain property, and brutalized every cat in town.

He's exactly what this investigation needs.

Max arrives at the Hartners' residence around lunchtime, prancing along in front of a DC police K-9 handler. Waiting are the senator, Mrs. Hartner, Sammy, Detective Woods, and a few curious cops. Max sees me standing on the front step and greets me with a high bound, landing squarely in my arms. His stubby tail is wagging furiously. He's comfortable now. He realizes all this extra motion was just so he could come play with me.

"One helluva dog, Detective Wiley," says the handler. "He had the whole airplane charmed within ten minutes. Especially the females."

I reply, "I've never seen him pass up a lady's affections."

Max jumps down from my arms, then runs full speed around in the Hartners' lush front yard three times. He races back up to me and sits by my side. Our family loves Max's brindle markings—especially because the AKC doesn't. I smile. "He's ready."

The Hartners look downright content.

"Shall we proceed, John?" Sammy says.

I'm not an expert in scent tracking like a real dog handler is. But I do have a technique with Max, having worked with him since he was a pup. In his case, it's all about reward. In my pocket is a baggy of cooked filet mignon pieces. Max already knows that he will soon be receiving lots of it. The game we play is about finding things and then getting fed. It's almost that simple. Another part of Max lives just to please us by doing what he was born to do—hunt. So, the hunt and the game and tenderloin all mix in his sharp little brain to form one big thrill.

We move inside the Hartners' home and walk around for a while. There are lots of scents to come across, and lots of rooms to move around in. I tell everyone to relax, talk for a while, and let me and the dog just cruise. Woods is trailing me, already in love with Max after he affectionately licked her fingernails.

Within ten minutes, we have covered the whole house, and I introduce Raul Gutab's sandals to Max. They have been placed on their side on the kitchen floor with a little meat underneath them. Max eats, plays with the sandals, and starts to rip one apart, when he hears me say, "Find more, Max, find more." We play a bit more, then I pull the sandals away and instruct him again. He spins, barks, then races around in the kitchen, nose to the floor, in a focused, determined trot. We finish with the kitchen, move out down the hallway, and soon cover the entire ground floor of the house. Max catches a scent in the mudroom, scratches the walls a bit, then races back down the hallway and up the back staircase. Within ten seconds, he's scratching at Elizabeth's bedroom door.

Woods is astonished. "Is he for sale?"

"You couldn't afford him," I reply, opening the door, and I watch Max move in for the kill. He makes several passes across the carpet, then runs straight into the closet where Mrs. Hartner originally hid the sandals. He stands still, looks up at me, and barks. "Good dog, Max. Well done." I toss him a sizable chunk. He gulps it down, snaps down one more, then moves out of the closet and leaps up onto Elizabeth's bed. Max rolls around, sniffing covers and pillows and headboard. All these scents are months old, but for him they're clear and pungent. He barks twice, leaps down, and then vanishes under Elizabeth's bed and into her personal junk pile. Woods and I wait, surprised. Max worms his way all around underneath there for a while. He emerges, with his butt wagging hard. He has something.

In his clenched teeth is a cobweb-covered leather wallet. I praise Max, give him another chunk, stand up, and open it up.

I'm shocked. It's Raul Gutab's billfold. Woods slips on vinyl gloves and examines the contents. Inside is a Virginia driver's license, two credit cards, and some folded papers containing phone numbers.

"Didn't DC cops search this room months ago?" Woods asks.

"Sammy did. He missed searching Elizabeth's private dump under there. So did I."

"Raul left a lot of stuff around. Why?"

"Maybe he left in a hurry."

"Maybe he left so fast he couldn't do anything but run," Woods says.

We move downstairs, and Woods goes toward the library to show everyone what was found. I start to follow her, then pause.

There's one more place to search.

I escort Max the other way, down the long hallway that leads out into the garage. We move toward Elizabeth's BMW. I open it up and Max moves right in, sniffing the seats and floor mats. He's happy. He smells Raul Gutab again. He's now in the backseat but not so happy. He's nosing into the crevasses of the leather cushion, burying his nose again and again. He's jumping up and down and barking.

"What, Max?"

Everyone has walked in and is watching Max. I reach down and pop the rear trunk release. Max leaps out, circles the car, and dives in the trunk, barking happily. His bounding profile appears and disappears with each leap.

I move around and look into the trunk.

There's nothing there. Nothing but the smell of Raul Gutab.

"So, what have we got?" Sammy asks us. "I'll tell you what we've got. We got the edges of the jigsaw puzzle forming. Maybe even a corner piece. I can feel it, can't you, Johnny?" In rare moments he calls me Johnny.

"What's a corner piece?" Woods wants to know. We're tucked in a tight booth at The Tombs in Georgetown, eating one of the biggest burgers made in the city.

"The corner piece is Gutab's wallet. It verifies his name, his connection to Elizabeth, his scent trail in the house, and his scent trail in the BMW. Big piece of the puzzle."

"What's a side piece?" I ask.

"A side piece is the bullshit kidnapping tape they sent to the Hartners. It's not a clean piece of evidence. It's sterile, as far as I'm concerned. These guys are on top of their game. Yet, they didn't plan on Gutab leaving evidence around."

"Surely he confessed he dropped his wallet in her bedroom."

"Probably doesn't know where he dropped it," says Woods.

"That's preferable. They will not suspect we're catching up."

"We're catching up?"

"Stay positive, Johnny. You've made a big contribution. I mean, your dog has."

Woods sees my disappointment. "That's right, Detective Wiley. Max certified what you worked so hard to discover in the first place. The existence of Raul Gutab."

"Gutab is probably just a side piece," I reply.

"The more pieces we discover, the closer we are," she says. "We don't need all the pieces to find her."

"True," Sammy agrees. "The wallet revealed Gutab's credit card records have been dormant since the night Elizabeth disappeared. His post office box in Arlington is overflowing. He left town after his assignment ended."

"So, he was certainly in on her abduction?" I ask.

"Definitely," Sammy says. "His fake Virginia driver's license was first class. He was her setup guy."

"So, where is he now?" Woods asks.

"Maybe he's one of her captors," Sammy says.

"Part of me agrees," I say. "Part of me thinks he cared too much for Elizabeth to betray her."

Sammy says, "Care or not, he had an assignment, and obviously carried it out that night. She's probably sitting in a cold Kashmiri cave. Any day, a big-time ransom note is going to arrive at the Hartners' home."

"Then it's all about money?" I ask.

"It's always about the money. What else could it be?"

"If Vishava is behind the jewelry Gutab gave Elizabeth, then money is not necessarily their prime interest. They have big resources."

"International celebrity kidnapping is a huge business, John. That jewelry was one of their props to entice her. The network for snatching famous people is well established. She could fetch ten million. A couple dozen tricks a year and you've suddenly got real income."

"True, she's obviously an attractive target."

"And the senator's got connections to raise all the cash to pay them," Woods adds.

"Did," Sammy says. "If he's lucky, he'll soon be broke and back in the possession of his daughter."

"You're pessimistic about Elizabeth's early retrieval, Sammy?"

"Yes, I am. And it's no reflection on you, John. There's just so much we can do with what's in front of us. How much more mileage we can get from his wallet remains to be seen. I'd rather get her back in one piece and pay the money."

"She can't wait that long," I say.

"What do you mean—you got something we don't know about?"

I am not going to reveal how tormented I think Elizabeth Hartner is. I know of her in a special way—primarily from the pain she's in. It has mass and darkness. She surely has no knowledge of me, though in the past, some people I've searched for say they've felt my presence. Knowing she's alive has made me realize the feeling of death in the river is not about her at all.

Then, what is it?

"No one can stand such imprisonment for long, Sammy. We need to tease out what they want now, not wait for them to come forward."

"Mrs. Hartner agrees with you. She wants to make a public offering to the kidnappers. The idea was shot down by the new FBI team. We just need to sit tight, work the leads, and pray Elizabeth can hang on. We can't appear desperate."

"Then let's formulate a response," I say. "We can't just sit here."

"We have to. That's part of the reason I'm talking to you two right now. Despite what we think about the progress made and what direction we should go, we have been overruled for the moment. We're not to proceed with any more overt investigations until we receive direct communication from her captives."

"What? Says who?" I ask.

"The new response team in place, headed by the FBI's chief kidnapping and ransom expert. He's successfully negotiated dozens of hostage situations. He's briefing us this evening. He's very liberal when it comes to dealing with desperate, crazy people."

"I don't like the sound of him already," Woods grunts.

"He's also a clinical psychologist and a bestselling author on crisis negotiations. The press loves the guy. He claims there are no real criminals, only innocent people with frantic brain cells."

I know I'm in trouble. What I now want to do will get me sent back to Asheville.

"Ladies and gentlemen, we are not in a crisis with the recent arrival of the Elizabeth Hartner kidnapping tape. We are in the driver's seat."

Lloyd Berkenson, the silver-haired FBI hostage-crisis director, pauses to let that sink in. "As in all negotiations, we seek only to come to a middle ground. In this case, where law enforcement encounters criminal activity, we reach middle ground by changing our attitudes. People do crazy things in life. We have to rise above them and make our mission the following: reach a win-win solution by any means possible."

The conference room at the FBI building is packed with dozens of DC police, FBI agents, agents from the US Secret Service, and guys I have not identified yet. Even Woods is not sure who they are. Sammy is dead quiet. He is telling me, with his big Hawaiian eyes, to stay calm.

"We've learned the hard way, there is an ineffective way to deal with angry people and an effective way," Berkenson says. "My job tonight is to inform you how we will conduct this investigation from now on. Some of you will disagree. But in the end, you will agree when we retrieve Miss Hartner in one piece."

Woods's smile is biting.

"First off, when the kidnapper communicates, we must learn to listen. We must not trivialize any request made of us. We need to stay honest with them at all times, telling them exactly what we plan to do. This softens their responses. They subconsciously move toward "yes" without knowing why. We must never interrupt the hostage taker. He's a desperate, lonely man or woman. Active listening skills are critical on our part. We practice emotional labeling, reflection, and use of open-ended questions. Putting him in a box with demands of our own usually backfires. We meet him in the middle by a process of reflecting on his predicament and empathizing with his despair. Social interaction with him must not cease because of the shame he is in. Critical to the successful dialogue with any kidnapper is the lack of law enforcement decision-making or deadline-setting. We can get to win-win no other way."

"We don't want win-win, Mr. Berkenson. We want Elizabeth Hartner back—and them dead. Period," I say.

Sammy shakes his head and is silent.

"Who said that?" Director Berkenson replies, scanning the crowd.

"I did," I say clearly in the silence.

"Ah, yes, young Detective Wiley. So you are of the old school, are you? And exactly how many hostage cases have you been successful in defusing?"

"None."

"None, is it? Well, I have dozens of successful ones to my record. I believe your intuitive abilities are deemed unconventional, and in some law enforcement circles, even illusionary. I tend to believe you are simply a lucky detective, one lacking real knowledge of psychological profiling of the criminal mind. If you had a better law enforcement background, you would know, when someone dies—as you claim to want—no one really wins."

"Law enforcement's job is the apprehension of those who commit criminal acts. Rehab is not our department. Are you rewriting that premise?"

"Of course I am. Only because, statistically, it will yield a happier and healthier outcome for the senator's daughter."

"Her welfare is foremost for all of us. But our weakness is not."

"From now on," Berkenson says, ignoring me, "we are changing our charter from being an investigative team to being a 'proactive' team. I know the buzzwords make you wince. So here's what I mean. Negotiations are really just business transactions. They want something, in this case, money; and we want something, Elizabeth's safe return. That takes equilibrium. That takes stability. Neither of which this investigation has ever had."

Police Chief Willis Harris's face stays stone cold.

"As the surrender time nears fruition and the perpetrators see we are prepared to submit to their demands, they will come forward and return Elizabeth Hartner. You ask yourself, how we can accomplish this? By backing off on all intrusive investigative techniques. No more illegal wire taps, no more presumptuous surveillance, no more chasing private citizens down the GW parkway."

Berkenson eyes me calmly. "And no more unprofessional public displays of nudity."

A wave of laughter erupts as eyes lock on mine.

"It sounds like weakness, ladies and gentleman, and it is, in a way. But dealing with an 'abnormal' personality, whose only real crime is being a victim of social, political, and chemical pollution, requires compassion. And compassion always trumps power."

"John, it's a bad idea. Stay here with me; you're worked up. I know how you feel, but don't do it. You'll be canned."

Tara's lying beside me on her bed, leaning away from Max's breath. He's not that fond of her, either. I shake my head and walk into her fruity-smelling bathroom with my cell. "Hello, *Washington Post*? Put me through to Gloria Sullivan, please."

Tara angrily moves out of the room. Max takes over the bed.

"Gloria, this is Detective John Wiley. Yes, nice to talk to you again too. I know it's late, but I need to see you tonight. Yes, okay. Sixth floor, the *Washington Post* building. Thanks." I look down at Max with anticipation. "Come on. Let's roll, buddy. We've work to do."

As I pass Tara standing in the hall, I notice fear in her eyes. I also see, for the first time since I've met her, hatred.

Gloria Sullivan is waiting for me in a small, cleanly appointed office, with framed Pulitzers on the wall and African art on the shelves. She takes my hand with her old soft one, offering me a comfortable chair in front of her desk. Her grandmother perfume is, again, killer. Max, by my side, is not content just to sit there. He knows we're going outside soon, and wants to short-circuit the crap humans constantly involve themselves in before action occurs.

"Mr. Wiley, what a surprise. I'm glad you've decided to speak with me finally. Be assured, anything you say will be off the record until you tell me otherwise. I see you've got your assistant along."

She opens her desk drawer and pulls out something. Max moves quickly around to see what's up. She gives the something to him. After happily swallowing, he greets her hand with an earnest lick.

"I make my own homemade beef jerky. My grandma's recipe."

"Nice touch," I say.

"I would never waste such delicacies on the regular people I deal with, Mr. Wiley. This snack is reserved for clients of real merit. As I said to you at the senator's party last month, this town is very interested in you. And now your little friend as well. What's the status of the Hartner investigation this evening?"

"Thanks to the FBI's newly appointed hostage-crisis director, it's nearing cardiac arrest."

"Interesting. What would you like me to do?"

It's dawn when I step out on the towpath of the C&O Canal near Key Bridge. Max, fresh from a nap, is anxiously twirling by my side. A three-man video-camera crew, all smoking cigarettes, has been waiting for me. We chat briefly; then we all move down the path, upriver. Out here, somewhere, is a critical thread to Elizabeth's whereabouts. I've missed it for months. I've been doubting myself. I've been discounting my dreams. I've been told I'm full of it. It's now or never.

Having buried his muzzle in a dirty pair of Elizabeth Hartner's blue jeans, Max is leaping in the air, ready to go. By 10:00 a.m., we have swept the woods between the river and the canal for a mile west. Max has nosed through a lot of trash, clothing, and dead animals. Nothing makes him stand at attention and bark like hell. The TV crew is muddy and frustrated, and not even sure what we're doing. They're here to record the discovery of evidence in the Hartner case. They know this area has been searched many times, by helicopter, bloodhounds, and park police. They've muttered that I'm doing this for celebrity status. "Nothing out here someone hasn't already sifted through a thousand times," says the balding reporter.

"Max hasn't been told that," I say.

"The Hartner girl is a thousand miles away from here."

"I'm not looking for Hartner. I'm looking for the thread that leads me on that thousand-mile journey."

I think about threads a lot in my work. For me now, solving what happened to Elizabeth is not like playing a chess game, as Chief Harris says. It's not a scattered jigsaw puzzle for assembly, like Sammy believes. It's certainly not a business transaction to be conducted, like that freak of nature from the FBI, Lloyd Berkenson, thinks. In my mind, a criminal act is a kind of hellish loom that weaves warp and weft with frightening detail, day by day, until the crime is solved. It must be unraveled.

Viewed from above, the twisted, violent surface of the fabric tells what really happened to the person. What they've knotted together, the felons cannot see. Others, coming after them, get an occasional glimpse of the frightful textile left behind. Many criminal acts remain dormant for months, or even years. But the threads of the original offense are still bound to all involved. Right now, I'm at one end of the strange tapestry called Elizabeth Hartner. I've had no idea so far what design they've made. But today I will.

It's now 7:00 p.m., and the camera crew has had it with me. We've just passed Fletcher's Boat House and are moving slowly back along the canal towpath by the Potomac, just below Chain Bridge. I was told two hours ago that they will be back tomorrow. But still, no one leaves me; they can't stand the fact that something might be found without them.

I'm filthy, hungry, and exhausted. So is Max. Sammy will surely fry me when he hears about this stunt. Small bands of tourists have followed us. Joggers watched us skirting along the riverbanks. I'm feeling foolish and angry.

We walk up onto Chain Bridge, and I thank the crew for a hard day's work. We stand there for a while and watch the river. Waning sunlight is grazing a tranquil beaver pond below. Max is nosing in my backpack. He unzips it with his teeth and paws, then begins ripping something apart. It's one of Raul Gutab's sandals, a scent source that will occupy Max in the coming days.

I pull the sandal away. Max is angry and keyed up, sniffing the guardrail and concrete walkway. He spins, barks, and then yelps harder.

"What?"

He moves back and forth along the rail of the bridge. The film crew follows him. He's more animated now than any time today. He returns to the spot where we stand, sits, and barks brightly. Right where we are standing is a scent match to Raul Gutab's sandal.

"He's got something, Wiley?" the reporter asks.

"Yes." I lean down by Max. "Find more, Max, find more. I wave Gutab's sandal under his nose. He barks instantly and paws the concrete.

"Gutab's scent is right here on the guardrail, yet nowhere else on the bridge," I say. I peer over the rail and look down on the beaver pond below. "Guys, let's go."

We run down the walkway, off the bridge, and through the woods. We start along the bank and work west around the pond's far edge. The crew is nuts now, their sneakers sucking deep into the mud. Max is bounding ahead, his nose tight to moss and mud. We wade through shallows as Max swims beside us. We return to our original spot without success. In the commotion, the beavers have scurried into their muddy burrows and their lodge at the center of the pond.

I know Max wants in there, in that beaver lodge. He's been eyeing it all along. But I've hesitated. Those stick lodges are usually the home of two or three tough males who will hotly defend it. Max's yelping wins me over.

I wade out, hip deep in the pond, and the crew follows. Max is swimming out front, his paws pumping hard. He reaches the branch-covered lodge, climbs up, and starts barking. He finds the roof entrance and shoots down inside. A murderous ruckus echoes as dog and beavers tangle below. Max is barking savagely as two beavers race out the underwater exit in retreat. One spitting, honking beaver remains to fight. The camera crew is focused. The reporter is whispering into his microphone. At last, a big, bloody male crawls out the top, then swims away.

I wade over to the lodge, climb up, and see him panting down below. Max is lacerated across his face and back. He jumps out weakly. Clenched in his jaws is a waterlogged belt with a silver buckle. In my vision, I saw Raul Gutab wearing such a belt that last night with Elizabeth.

I lift Max up, carry him over to the waiting crew, and turn back to the lodge. As the sun dips below the distant, emerald trees, I feel important threads in the case revealing themselves. I sink down underneath and peer at the lodge's cold, murky underwater structure. I surface, take another breath, submerge, and swim around the other side.

Dimly, a form comes into view. Its twisted torso is jammed into place by the beavers' skilled construction efforts. It would surely remain down there forever. I stare at the distorted face of the swollen corpse.

Raul Gutab's body is entombed beneath the lodge.

CHAPTER ELEVEN

Rarely do I attend autopsies in the morgue; it's only when I'm so personally involved, I can't say no. Or I might go out of macabre curiosity. Raul Gutab's body dissection fits the latter category. He's decomposed. His head and neck are violently twisted away from their normal relationship. His eyes are swollen orbs. So, how did I know it was he? My mental image of his face was so strong, his submerged death mask struck me as his alone. Fingerprinting has confirmed, it's him.

Chief Harris, Sammy, Woods, and I have joined a forensic team in the Georgetown University Hospital basement to attend the young man's autopsy. Gloria Sullivan is also there, off the record, cleared by Chief Harris.

So far, I haven't touched Gutab's elastic-looking corpse. But I need to. It would help me to accept the end of a life that I'd found in such an obscure, violent state. Contact with his body could reveal many other hidden things. But I hesitate.

"Initially, he took blunt-force trauma to the back of the skull," announces the doctor. "But it didn't kill him."

"What did?" Woods asks. "Drowning?"

"Yes," he says, "and, possibly, in a most agonizing way. Mr. Gutab had another event happen to him just before he drowned. He sustained a broken neck. Both his top cervical vertebrate are crushed. He may have been conscious, yet so paralyzed, he couldn't raise his head above water."

Sammy nods. "Probably he jumped from the bridge."

"He would have had to dive in, head first," I say.

"He was running from something, maybe, in the midst of a struggle on the bridge. So, he leapt off."

"Sammy," I say. "He was thrown off."

"He was working for them, John. It was an accident. Why would they kill him?"

"I don't know, but I'm willing to speculate."

"Mr. Wiley, go on," says Gloria Sullivan.

"Raul Gutab was enlisted to get to know Elizabeth Hartner. We don't know how yet, but he gained her trust completely. On that last evening, they left the club drunk and drove to the senator's house with intentions of making love. But it didn't go well. Why? Because he knew later that night she was to be kidnapped. He was heartsick about it. He'd fallen in love with his own target."

"Possibly," Sammy agrees. "But not enough to call off the snatch."

"I'll agree, he drove her to the capture spot, but his intention was to convince his associates it was a bad idea. He didn't prevail."

"Why do you say that?"

"Because the strongest scent of Raul Gutab that Max detected in Elizabeth's BMW was in the trunk. Gutab sat in the front seat most of the night, while Elizabeth drove. But on that last deadly trip, he was already in the trunk, stunned from a blow to the head. In there, he sweat enough to make the trunk smell strongly of himself. Micro-smears of his blood should be present, proof he was injured."

Woods nods. "I'll follow up on it."

"So, Gutab was beaten, possibly defending Elizabeth Hartner as she was taken hostage," Gloria Sullivan says.

"I'm certain of it. Then, as her captives were driving her BMW over Chain Bridge with her, they stop, pop the trunk, pitch Gutab in what they think is the deep rapids of the Potomac, and drive off. But it's dark, and they miss the real river by a hundred yards. They don't know they've thrown him into a quiet little beaver pond. That's why his scent was only in one spot on the bridge—precisely where he was shoved, on the rail right above the pond. In the following weeks, his body is never discovered, so his cohorts conclude his murder is concealed. Even the beavers cooperate. Not being carnivorous or particularly hostile, they stash Gutab away where he'll do the least harm to their pond."

"John," Sammy concedes, "I was so wanting to interrogate the little bastard. So many things we could have straightened out, just between him and me. Now,"—he flicks the dead man's toes—"my frustrations will have to simmer once again."

"Sammy, discovering Gutab's body is a big-time corner piece for us. Maybe more can be drawn from his death than anything he begrudgingly would have told you. If he's of the same ilk as those above him, nothing may ever have come from his mouth."

"It would have come readily, just before his accidental rendezvous with a .44 slug."

My eyes lose focus. Tasks stack up in my head. There's a multitude of people to interview around the Chain Bridge area now. The whole crime scene at the pond will need analysis. A deep background search is required on Gutab's family and friends. I need to find Tara and drink a lot of beer. I need to dream about Elizabeth, but can't.

Yet, what I need to do before anything is touch this young man's dead body.

Three hours later, they're done with the autopsy. Two medical techs have cleaned him up and slid him away in one of the honeycombed, cold drawers across from the operating room. I'm drained, still muddy, but hyper, like right before fireworks rip open a dark sky. Only Woods, who knows enough about me to sense my anxiety, has guessed why I didn't leave with the rest of them. She motioned that she'd call me later.

I wait till the room is empty, then cross over, open Gutab's drawer, pull back the sheet, and stare at his swollen figure. I haven't really looked at him closely until now. Even in his pitiful state, he looks determined. Curled around his belly button, his right palm is spread open for inspection. His fingers are long and delicate, his thumb, flat and stubbornly cocked. I study his swollen life, head, and heart lines. I see no close family ties, yet see tremendous concern for tradition. Big-time worrier. Idealistic beyond practicality.

I place my hand across his brow. He's so cold and so densely still; it's as if death had pushed his weight into the tonnage category. I move to his shoulder and keep my hand firm. The soul has gone. I'm standing beside an empty travel bag. The chill of him is receding, and the distant echoes of his life are tingling in my hand. It's not what I had anticipated sensing. Gutab's life was so short, so shallow, yet so hopeful. He feels principled, yet eaten by frustration and envy. There's no doubt for me; he died trying to defend Elizabeth. The last thing I feel, right before I pull my hand away, is his deep regret he couldn't do more at the end. As I slide him back in, I thank him.

I see the next move.

I phone Gloria Sullivan from my truck. It's nearing midnight. Perhaps she can get it done tonight.

"Detective Wiley, you must know your discovery at the pond today made great newspaper and TV news content. Footage is due on our morning TV affiliate. My article will run on our front page. Happy?"

"No."

"Why? You got what you wanted—getting hard, investigative police work back to center stage in the Hartner case. Yours was a perfect example why waiting for terrorists to come forward is a bad idea."

"That was my intention, Ms. Sullivan. But we have an opportunity to move things along further. We are about to communicate to Elizabeth's captors information they don't know. That being, we have one of their own who was involved with her disappearance. That's free information we're giving them. Why reveal that without them paying a price?"

"What I helped you film was for the public domain. That's what good journalism is all about, Mr. Wiley. Tracking down, and in your case, excavating the truth. What else can we do?"

"Lie."

"Detective, you're talking to the wrong person. The gossip rags are in the next building over. I don't intentionally report what I personally know to be false information." She pauses patiently. "Your instincts are good. Too bad we don't have another source."

"You mean another account of the events, other than ours, that might be acceptable for publication?"

"Of course. That kind of investigative reporting is practiced all the time in this town. Who is this other source, Detective?"

"Let's say he's intimately connected with the case. Because of security and proximity concerns he cannot come forward. He wants so much to do more than he's done so far."

"Well, what he knows can be cited as additional source content. Others may brand his views as misinformation concerning Gutab's relationship to the case. But it's a free country."

"Yes, it is," I say. "He's also worried what he says may reveal his identity. Can confidentiality be assured?"

"Mr. Wiley, your source will be fully protected."

"Then we're in business, Ms. Sullivan. What about the morning TV newscast?"

"I'll recommend delay of the Gutab video for a few days. Our friend's methods are going to make him unpopular at the FBI. They may be relieved the Gutab video stays in the can for a while. One lie at a time."

"Can we get the front-page story together for the morning?"

"If you get over here in fifteen minutes, Detective."

Two hours later, the dead Raul Gutab has made his fictitious contribution.

I turn and look at her. Her sleeping face is filled with distress. Tara's hidden concerns about me are something I've picked up on since the first time we kissed deeply. Way down inside her is something I can't figure out. I've learned the closer I am to someone, the less insight I have about them. How nice it would be to pull her close and know what she's feeling. Her skin is so available; yet there's a barrier that blocks us. So, why is it that those whose lives have been harmed or ended are so open to me?

As I sit up in the sheets, she leans on me and closes her eyes. "Don't leave me this morning…stay and play."

"I wish I could. There are too many moving parts in the air. I have an 8:00 a.m. meeting. Something's up."

"I'm not number one this morning, is that it, Wiley?"

I kiss her as if she is, then leave.

An hour later, I'm sitting in a plainly furnished conference room at the Georgetown police precinct. It's too quiet. Sammy and Police Chief Harris are sitting beside me. I've not been told what we're to discuss.

The door opens, and Hostage Crisis Director Berkenson walks in alone, nods dryly, and sits.

"Gentlemen, we have a problem. I cannot manage this operation in the current disrespectful climate. Detective Wiley's stunts last evening are a prime example. Chief, didn't I specifically tell you to clear all new investigative inquiries through me?'

"Yes, Director, you did. I fell behind on this one. Detective Wiley's search by the river was premature. But he's helped us immeasurably with the discovery of Raul Gutab's body."

Berkenson shakes his head. "Wrong, Chief Harris. All Detective Wiley has done is scuttle any attempts we are trying to initiate with these people. We didn't need to know that Gutab's body was there. For all we know, they may have planted his corpse to throw us off. Have you considered that possibility?"

Chief Harris says, "No, sir, I haven't. Detective Wiley's speculation about what happened to his body in the beaver pond makes perfect sense."

"Wiley's speculations are spread all over this investigation. That's why we're still just talking about it, and not moving forward to communicate with Hartner's abductors."

Director Berkenson removes the morning paper from his briefcase and slams it on the conference table.

"Do Detective Wiley's speculations include feeding fabricated stories to the press?" He holds up the front page and points to a big article by Gloria Sullivan, entitled "Secrets of a Kidnapper's Corpse." He reads the text beneath a photo of Gutab's swollen, dead expression: *"Sources close to the investigation indicate Raul Gutab's clothing contained critical information about his role in the kidnapping. A small notebook lodged in his pants pocket contained names, phone numbers, and a timetable related to Elizabeth Hartner's kidnapping last month. Investigators are saying it's a breakthrough in uncovering precisely who masterminded her abduction."*

Berkenson pauses. "What goddamn notebook?"

Sammy pulls the paper over, reads the article, and shakes his head. "I've heard nothing about this."

Chief Harris turns to me. "Detective Wiley, have you seen such a notebook?"

"No, sir."

"Then who is the source of this information?" Berkenson asks.

Chief Harris says, "Gloria Sullivan should know. It's her article."

"I've already spoken with Gloria Sullivan this morning, Chief. She says she cannot reveal her sources at this time. This pain-in-the-ass woman has never once helped me in the thirty years I've had the displeasure of knowing her. I expected nothing less today."

Chief Harris rises. "Sorry we couldn't have been more helpful, Director. I'll see that our detectives clear all their future activities through me."

"Sit down, Chief Harris. I'm not finished."

Willis Harris, former Vietnam vet, Green Beret, and two-decade hard-nosed street cop, pauses. He eyes Berkenson for a long, tense moment, then sits. "Director, what else can I do for you?'

"Because of Detective Wiley's continued unprofessionalism, I'm removing him from this investigation immediately. There's no room for his type on our new hostage-crisis team. We need team players who understand the subtleties of kidnapping negotiations. Not hot shots who have camera crews along when they happen to get lucky."

Sammy rises, furious, but Chief Harris motions him to sit down.

A quiet voice from the doorway says, "Mr. Wiley isn't going anywhere, Director Berkenson. Anywhere but back on the streets where he will continue to do his best work for us."

Senator Hartner, dressed in his usual dark suit and bright tie, stands still and waits. "Any problems with that, Director?"

Berkenson is silent.

As I ponder Max's condition—forty stitches and a week's stay at the vet's—I rewind Elizabeth Hartner's hostage tape and watch it again. I'm missing something in its contents. Tara comes in the bedroom, watches Hartner's slow, tortured movements, shakes her head, and walks out. It's not as though I'm expecting secret messages to come filtering out of her voice if I run it backward. Or that I will see a clue others have missed. But I'm in the business of subtleties. I'm supposed to find things.

Senator Hartner called me an hour ago. He will hold off Director Berkenson as long as possible. Eventually, I will have to break this open or I'll be gone. Politics are second only to power in this town, and the powers at the FBI will eventually see me as an embarrassment. Senator Hartner has power too, but obstructing an investigation will not look good on his resume.

It's enough to get one's juices flowing.

I once again watch Elizabeth's kidnapping tape and wonder how Gutab's sudden publicity will play with her captors. They'll say we're bluffing with the notebook, but they don't know for sure. Gutab is a wild card. He could have held grudges in that tiny fictitious notebook. Their best move is to do nothing.

I'm banking they won't have the patience.

What strikes me most about Elizabeth's videotape is that it's too dramatic. She's wailing, she's terrified, she's moaning. Hollywood couldn't have asked for a better take. It certainly scared her parents. They will now pay any price or do anything to end her torment.

Judging from her condition, she must have been captive for a few weeks prior to the filming. How did they happen to capture her in such a crazy state? My dreams of her had sent me the opposite message. After capture, she quickly entered a state of almost trance-like peacefulness. She escaped to where they couldn't get to her. I'm betting Elizabeth Hartner is a tough, scheming, survivor who would look for any chance to upset their plans.

So, why the theatrics?

Gloria Sullivan rings my cell just as I shut off the videotape machine.

"Mr. Wiley, I'm impressed. Your fishing expedition has landed a nibble."

I'm up, slipping on my loafers and moving toward the door, my stomach knotted. "What have you got?"

"Oh, it's just one of many e-mails I received this afternoon in response to our article on Raul Gutab. Probably nothing. I'm getting hammered by dozens of journalists and law enforcement folk for pushing journalistic bounds. But this one e-mail is different."

"Why?"

"They want to talk to you."

"Really. About what?"

"I'll read it to you. *'Ms. Sullivan, you are close to the detective named John Wiley, I believe. I have something important to tell him about Raul Gutab. I will contact you tonight at 6:00 p.m. by e-mail. See that he's there.'*"

"It's signed with the screen name 'jordanr.'"

"I'm on my way."

It's 6:05 p.m., and I'm pacing in Gloria Sullivan's office, waiting for the e-mail to arrive. She has had the e-mail traced to a web café near Capitol Hill called E-Hits. Woods is there now, at its Pennsylvania and Second Street location, drinking a latte, and watching the young crowd play in cyberspace. She's talking to me via a tiny cell phone headset that's very effective and very hard to spot.

"What you got now, Woods?"

"Some are on Facebook, or in chat rooms," she whispers. "Some are web surfing, some composing documents. It's going to be tough unless I'm right over their shoulders, watching."

"The e-mail's here," Gloria says, clicking on the newly arrived message.

"We got it, Woods. Hang on."

Gloria Sullivan puts on her glasses and reads the message: *"Please follow these instructions exactly. I'll be in the chat room named 'Burly Boys' on Yahoo at exactly 6:20 p.m. Identify yourself as 'jwiley.' I'll instruct you further."*

I tell Woods.

In Ms. Sullivan's office, we log onto Yahoo, enter the chat room, and watch the discussions. "Jordanr" isn't there yet. Burly Boys is a bodybuilding chat room, with big-time discussions about steroid use.

"I'm entering the chat room now as 'little bruiser,'" Woods says.

We see Woods join the discussions.

"Woods, it's 6:20. See anyone logging into a chat room?"

"Hang on."

Exactly thirty seconds later, "jordanr" enters the Yahoo Burly Boys chat room on Gloria Sullivan's monitor and joins the conversation. I enter the room as "Jwiley" and say nothing. A minute later, "jordanr" sends me an instant message: *"Join me for a private discussion?"*

I click on the invitation, and we go to a private chat room where no one else can enter or see our conversation.

"Woods, we're in the chat room together now. See them?"

"Working on it," she whispers.

We start typing to each other.

jordanr: *John Wiley?*

Jwiley: *Yes…who are you…why not use the phone?*

jordanr: *No phone is secure enough.*

Jwiley: *Okay. What can I do for you?*

jordanr: *First, swear you haven't tracked my location down.*

Jwiley: *I haven't had time.*

jordanr: *You've had plenty. Swear you're not watching me.*

Jwiley: *I swear. Now relax. Tell me about your friend, Gutab.*

"Woods?"

"I'm walking to the bathroom," she says, "moving past the folks online by the window. Nothing, yet."

jordanr: *Raul Gutab was used and then murdered.*

Jwiley: *I know.*

jordanr: *How could you know this? You knew him?*

Jwiley: *In a way, yes. Tell me who used him?*

jordanr: *I don't know much about them. He worked for them only this one time. They are layered so well, no one knows exactly who the others are until the time is right.*

Jwiley: *Where's Elizabeth Hartner?*

jordanr: *Hell if I know that.*

Jwiley: *What's your reason for this conversation?*

jordanr: *To tell you Raul Gutab was a good man.*

Jwiley: *Good men don't plan kidnappings.*

jordanr: *The money was unbelievably good.*

Jwiley: *How much ransom they want for Elizabeth Hartner?*

jordanr: *It's not about money.*

Jwiley: *Then what?*

jordanr: *No one knows. Not even Raul knew.*

Jwiley: *I can bring you in right now as a witness. Full protection. What do you think? You won't last long out there talking so freely.*

jordanr: *I've done nothing wrong.*

Jwiley: *You're an accessory, jordanr. We know about you from his notebook. Didn't you help him set things up with Elizabeth?"*

jordanr: *I hooked them up at the metro. He taught her how to race that car. I never realized he had other ideas till the end.*

Jwiley: *Why didn't you tell anyone all this long ago?*

jordanr: *If I did, I'd be dead within the day.*

Jwiley: *Then why tell me?*

jordanr: *When you discovered Raul's body, I felt you were the one I should contact. I read about you. I knew you'd find me sooner or later after reading about Raul's secret notebook. You must know—Raul couldn't go through with it in the end. They killed him for it.*

Jwiley: *Help me vindicate his death. I'll protect you. Okay?*

"John," Woods says, "I've got her. Short black hair, fair skin. Glasses. Early twenties. I saw your screen name on her monitor as I passed. She has her back to me."

"I'm trying to bring her in, Woods. I swore she wasn't being watched. If she detects you, we'll lose her. Don't let her see your face."

jordanr: *It sounds so good, your dream of protection. But you don't know how they are. They are so huge…they'll find me. In a way, I don't care. I'm so depressed about Raul.*

Jwiley: *I can have a friend come right over. She'll take care of everything. Tell me where you are.*

jordanr: *Is she a cop?*

Jwiley: *Yes. She'll take you someplace safe and advise you on all you need to know. I'll join you later tonight, okay?*

Gloria Sullivan whispers to me, "You've almost got her."

jordanr: *Yes, I'll come in. You sure you can do this for me? I'm terrified they are watching me.*

Jwiley: *Don't worry. You're going to be fine. Where are you?*

jordanr: *E-Hits on Capitol Hill. I'm in the corner with dark hair. I'm Raul's sister. My name is Rohini.*

"Woods, we're going to bring her in. Step outside, move across the street, and wait five minutes. Has she seen you?"

"No," Woods says.

"Hang on, and I'll keep her talking. When you reenter, go to her and tell her your real name. She'll be ready."

"Got it," Woods says.

Jwiley: *A short black gal with blond hair will come and sit by you soon. She's an undercover police officer. She'll say to you, "I'm Ginger." Go back to her car with her. Piece of cake.*

jordanr: *It sounds too easy.*

Jwiley: *It will be. Tell me, what's "jordanr" stand for?*

jordanr: *It stands for the Jordan River where Raul and I were born. Our mother was a Palestinian Jew, our father, a Muslim. We were always arguing about everything. But we never forgot where we came from.*

Jwiley: *Your parents, alive?*

jordanr: *No. It's just me left now.*

Jwiley: *Well then, you're extra special.*

jordanr: *Our parents always told us that. We're all the same down deep.*

Woods says, "John, we got something funny happening here."

"What?"

"I think they've spotted her."

"How's that possible?"

"I don't know, but three men just pulled up outside who don't look like the Internet type."

"Woods, don't think about being a hero."

"John, we're so close, I can't let this happen. It's not ethical to sit and watch. I'm going in."

"I'm on my way," I say.

"It's too far away for you. I'll handle it from here."

"Okay, you're right. Just do this for me. When you enter, Woods, bellow, 'Fire!'"

"Detective," she says, wind rushing on her microphone, "that only works in the movies."

"Do it, Woods!"

I turn to Gloria Sullivan. "Call 202-555-3434...tell Detective Sammy Chung to get his units over to the E-Hits location ASAP."

"Fire! Fire! Everyone out, quickly!" I hear Woods shouting in her mic. She's panting, moving into an agitation, chairs slamming, people screaming, voices coming at her loudly.

"Woods, talk to me!"

"Out of the way! Move out of the way!" she screams.

"Woods, draw your weapon. Protect yourself."

"Ain't got time," she yells.

"Where's the girl?"

"I don't know—everyone's running past me. It worked, John! The place is spooked like crazy. Hold on. I see her. She's crouched under the table in a panic. She hasn't seen me."

"Where are the men? Have they entered?"

"They're slamming people out of the way on the far side of the hall. They don't know where she is!"

"Draw your weapon, Woods!"

"If they see my gun, they'll know I'm—" Her mic gets slammed. She's breathing hard. "I'm down under the table…waving to her. She's scared to death! She won't come to me. 'Honey, you want to come with me?'"

"Woods, move her out through the bathroom."

"Come with me. Come on, it's Ginger, it's me."

I hear a cry of relief. "Come on, quickly. Stay low, down in front of me. Don't turn around, it's just a fire drill, okay—that's it, honey, keep going down the hallway—move it, girl!"

"Okay, we're in the bathroom," Woods says. "Got the door locked. Shit, no window. What now, Detective?"

"Pop open the ceiling panel, Woods…stand on the sink…climb up in the ceiling, quick!"

"Yes!" she pants.

"Where are they?" I ask.

"I hear them in the hallway…they're coming this way…looking for her."

"Get her up there, now!"

Woods hisses, "Push it harder out of the way…that's it. Now, pull yourself up in there …yeah, baby, you got muscles!"

"Woods, stay on the top of the wall…Don't move off it…You'll fall down through into another room."

"Roger that. Stay on that partition, girl…yeah, right there. Okay, I'm coming up, too."

Woods grunts as she pulls herself up. "God, that's harder than I thought."

"Woods, push the panel back in place, quick!"

"Man, it won't go…shit, they're trying to open the door! What the fuck…get the panel back in place now, bitch. Christ, do I have to do everything? Okay don't lose it, okay, we'll do it together! Yes, shit yes, okay, that's it…got it!"

"Don't move, Woods," I whisper. "Don't even breathe!"

It's silent on the line.

"Woods, draw your damn weapon!" I plead into my phone.

"Got it drawn, now," she whispers.

"What are they doing?"

"Nothing. The doorknob stopped wiggling. I don't know…"

Gunshots echo in her mic. Woods gasps. "They shot the fucking lock off," she softly whispers. "Oh God, they're in the bathroom. They're going to see we climbed up here."

"Woods, stay cool!"

"I'm breathing too fucking hard," she gasps. "They'll hear me!"

"No, it's noisy in there, they won't hear you."

"Sirens…I hear sirens," Woods whispers.

Another gunshot booms, closer this time.

"Woods, are you okay?"

"Fuck, I don't know! They shot through the ceiling," she moans.

"Are you hit?"

"No, we're okay, there's a bullet hole in the panel a foot away."

"Can you get a shot off?"

"I wish to hell I could…I can't see the bastards!"

"Empty your clip down at them."

"They'll know we're up here for sure and return fire. I'll play opossum till I get a clean shot," she whispers.

"These bloody cowards," I say. "What now?"

"Wait," she says. "The sirens are louder. I hear running…they're running off. They missed finding us. God, they're heading out!"

I hear them begin to exhale in relief.

"Damn, Woods, amazing. One cool cop. How's our witness?"

"Shaking bad, but okay. She's uninjured."

"Woods, listen to me. Sammy's on the other line. He's a block away. Stay in the ceiling till he calls up to you. Don't move out of there yet!"

"Why in the hell would I move out?" she whispers.

It's five minutes later when I look down at Sullivan's computer screen. I see a recent, last entry from "jordanr's" computer.

jordanr: *We know who you are. We'll be in touch.*

CHAPTER TWELVE

"**W**ho authorized Rohini Gutab's status as a friendly witness?" Berkenson asks over the speakerphone in Sammy's office. "Detective Wiley did, sir."

"Oh, yes, Detective Wiley, our resident expert on hostage negotiations. How appropriate. Was I informed?"

"Director, we didn't have time. The situation escalated out of control in minutes. She may not have come in without a deal," Chief Harris replies. "We saved her life. She would have taken anything at that point."

Berkenson pauses. "All right, Chief, process her discreetly. It's imperative to keep her true identity out of the papers. Notify Detective Woods of a job well done."

"I have already."

"Have they come forward with a ransom demand for Elizabeth Hartner, Chief?"

"No. They left a note on the girl's monitor, saying they'd be in touch."

"Good. That's a sign of compliance. They're softening."

"Sir, they tried to kill both women. They vanished into thin air. That's full-blown terrorism."

"Call it what you may; they're on the ropes. Obviously, Rohini Gutab was a loose end they wanted control over. Now that she's in custody, they may be ready to bargain."

"Yes, sir, Director."

"Have her full account on my desk by tomorrow." He hangs up.

"Piece of frigging work, he is," Sammy mutters. "Come on, John Wiley. We have an interview to conduct."

"You know that conspiracy charges are pending against you?"

"Yes," she says quietly.

"And if you cooperate, truthfully detailing all that you know about your brother's activities, you may be given immunity from those charges."

"Yes."

I study Rohini Gutab more closely. She has large, dark eyes, pitch-black hair, and an appeal that seems to grow with her own rising anxiety. We are in the basement of DC police headquarters in deep, well-guarded security. Later, this evening, she will be moved to a safe house at an undisclosed location.

Over the next three hours, Rohini Gutab reveals how her brother met Elizabeth Hartner at the New Carrolton Metro subway stop one early spring night.

He was good looking, confident, and knowledgeable about racing import cars for the street. He was exactly what Elizabeth was looking for. Raul Gutab had just recently joined his sister at the racing site on weekends, but because Rohini rarely communicated with him, his sudden presence in town surprised her. She'd introduced him to Elizabeth Hartner, whom she had known at George Washington University.

Within three weeks of that fateful night, both would vanish.

Raul was secretive, always in trouble, always dreaming. Success of any sort eluded him. He envied his sister's college degree, her citizenship, and her new telecom position in Reston, Virginia. She knew nothing of his lack of a permanent visa or his deportation a year earlier. He had always lied to her about the problems in his life.

"When did he reveal he was seeing Elizabeth Hartner for reasons besides street racing?" Sammy asks.

"Two days before they vanished."

"What did he tell you?"

"That he had been offered a huge sum of money to meet her."

"Why?"

She pauses. "To get to know her, convince her of his sincerity, and then, set her up for abduction."

"How did you react to that?"

"I thought he was insane. I decided he was lying, as usual, crowing about another big, dark fantasy."

"And then?"

"The more he told me, the more I realized it wasn't a lie."

"You tried to convince him it was a bad idea?"

"Of, course. I told him to leave the country immediately, before anything else happened. I would help him out financially. He said it was too late. They watched his every move. He was in too deep to pull out."

"Describe who they were?"

"They were...how did he depict them?" She pauses. "A little United Nations of criminals."

Sammy frowns. "Meaning what?"

"Raul said he met only four of them during his assignment. One of them was South American; one Middle Eastern; one Indian; and one, maybe Swiss. They all spoke English."

"Swiss?" I say in disbelief. "Not all Middle Eastern?"

"Eyewitnesses at E-Hits say the intruders in search of her were mixed nationalities," Sammy says.

"Interesting," I say. "Why so?"

Rohini says, "Raul said they were part of an international group with secret, common goals."

"Goals such as?"

"He wasn't told. They said the longer he worked for them, the more he would learn about their organization."

"Sort of an institute of higher criminal learning," Sammy says.

"Perhaps," she says.

"Did he tell you why they were kidnapping Elizabeth Hartner?"

"He said he thought it was not for ransom money."

"How did he know that?"

"Raul decided they were all too rich to need the cash."

"I doubt that. There's never enough to go around," Sammy says.

"Did Raul ever say he was having misgivings about what he was doing?" I ask.

"Yes, the day he disappeared," she says. "He was going to convince them Hartner wasn't a worthy target for kidnapping. He could find far more influential women in town to undermine. He was confident they would listen to him."

"Was Raul in love with Elizabeth, Rohini?"

"I don't know," she says.

"Rohini, I don't understand. If he was so secretive about the jams he was always in, why tell you any of this?"

"He had panicked. He finally got all he wished for and was immediately in over his head. It shocked him."

"What was he worried about?"

"Vanishing."

"If he didn't follow through with her abduction?"

"Yes. He realized that last day how expendable he was becoming. She believed all the lies of his. He was going to try and get Elizabeth out of their sights anyway."

"Did they know about you?"

"He said no, but I think he was trying to keep me calm. Obviously, they did."

"They were scrutinizing you the whole time?"

"At first, I thought so. But during the weeks after Elizabeth Hartner vanished, I never saw anyone watching me."

"Then how did they know you were at E-Hits last night?"

"Detective Wiley, I was hoping you could answer that."

I smile. "Working on that still. How was your brother recruited—overseas?"

"He wouldn't tell me. Raul said the more I knew, the worse it might be for me."

"Then why tell anything?"

"He was anxious. He had no one else to turn to."

"You two were close?"

"Only when he needed something. In this case, he needed my pity."

"And your introduction to Elizabeth Hartner at the metro stop. How did he know you knew her?"

"I don't know how he knew we were friends."

Her eyes are still. I don't detect lying. "We can't locate where Raul lived," I say. "Have any ideas?"

"He came and went secretly. I think he lived in Arlington, but I have no idea where." She pauses. "Two crimes have been committed, Detective Wiley. Elizabeth Hartner's abduction, and, more important to me, my brother's murder. I will do anything you ask of me to help find these killers. I want revenge."

"I will remember your offer," I reply.

The warm afternoon breeze is soft. I had fallen asleep and awaken now, lying in the grass at Fletcher's Boathouse. What a deep, powerful sleep overcame me. Like a dense cloud enveloping me—I want to return to it, and ask more questions and seek more answers. I lean up and watch the river flowing by, and see that I'm alone out here.

But the dream's gone, like a summer squall with other ports of call. I can't go along, but I can remember. This time I felt Elizabeth—just as one senses the conductor at a symphony. She was there indirectly, her intent to communicate through the content of the dream. She's determined to be found. It won't be difficult to find her, she said. What does that mean?

I meet with Gloria Sullivan a few hours later. She's convinced news of Raul Gutab's phony notebook drew Rohini Gutab out and will soon tease out others. Now that we have Raul's sister as a state's witness, we can apply the weight of new lies to her captors. Sullivan's morning column will report new light has been cast on the investigation since the terrorist attack at E-Hits. It will enrage the FBI, but Gloria Sullivan has the power to pull off one last tweak.

It's dawn. I'm sitting in my truck cab, reading Gloria Sullivan's fresh fabrication. My grande double latte is steaming the windows. In her latest report, entitled "Another Piece of Hartner Puzzle Fits into Place," Sullivan writes: *"Desperate moves by Elizabeth Hartner's kidnappers have blossomed into concrete details about their identities, and possibly, her location. While trying to kill an eyewitness to Hartner's earlier abduction, the perpetrators at E-Hits yesterday were clearly captured on the café's closed-circuit cameras. Arrest warrants may be issued within the week, sources close to the investigation say. Sources also say that, 'As of yet, no communication has come forward from her captors.' They may have scattered due to this increased pressure from law enforcement."*

I spend the morning waiting for Sammy's call that will usher me over to the FBI building, where a seething Director Berkenson will send me packing. He knows I'm working with Gloria Sullivan. He surely knows our source close to the investigation is none other than Raul Gutab, a very dead man. It's one last shot on my part. The payoff will be good if I succeed, not good if I get fired from the investigation. Elizabeth's kidnappers have a different timetable from law enforcement. They want to draw things out to an unbearable length. Knocking them off that timetable is critical. If they succumb to pressure, they show weakness.

I go out to the beaver pond and watch the FBI forensics team photographing, sampling, and analyzing the crime scene. Though the medical examiner has clearly stated Raul Gutab drowned, they do their job, independently examining what took place.

I drive over to E-Hits on the Hill. Fingerprints are being pulled, spent handgun slugs found and bagged, and eyewitnesses interviewed. All very unnecessary, as far as I'm concerned. We're spending too much time in the starting blocks and not enough time speeding around the track toward the finish line.

It's not until late in the afternoon that the call comes on my cell. It's not Sammy on the line; it's Berkenson himself.

"Detective Wiley, have you read Gloria Sullivan's column in the *Post* this morning?"

"Yes sir, I have."

"It appears to be another case of misinformation, fabrication, and sensationalism. All desperately amateurish police work. You're going to tell me you had nothing to do with it?"

"No, sir."

"You don't deny you were involved with these articles."

"No, I don't deny it. Gloria Sullivan and I created them ourselves."

"For what earthly purpose, Detective?"

"To plant doubt in the minds of Elizabeth Hartner's kidnappers, Mr. Berkenson."

"Manipulating actual facts then intentionally publishing them is against what we're trying to accomplish in law enforcement. We're not supposed to lie, Detective Wiley. We have standards to uphold. We both know there were no secret cameras at E-Hits, or arrest warrants in the works. We certainly have no idea where Elizabeth Hartner is. In all my years of police work, I have never seen such a desperate act of orchestration in my life."

"I'm not your normal cop, Director. I push things. I cheat, and I have funny dreams. Detective Chung should have told you."

"He didn't have to, Detective Wiley. You know I'm aware of your reputation. It precedes you, as advertised. You're exactly like they said you were."

"Yes, sir."

"You're exasperating, unmanageable, and not like other, far more seasoned detectives. They are not nearly as creative as you are, Detective."

I can't think what to say.

"Detective, I might as well tell you, as a result of Gloria Sullivan's articles, we have a problem. I'm going to need your help in solving it."

"You want a public apology?"

"Not at all, Detective. I want you in my office, ASAP. We'll need your continued assistance from here on out."

"Why?"

"Because, at exactly 1:00 p.m. this afternoon, a new communication came forth from Elizabeth Hartner's kidnappers. Congratulations, Detective Wiley. They're ready to negotiate."

CHAPTER THIRTEEN

Police Chief Willis Harris is wearing vinyl gloves. He's holding a letter whose envelope is postmarked a week ago, from Karachi, Pakistan. Stapled to it is a photograph of Elizabeth Hartner in front of a recent newspaper.

In Berkenson's office are also an ashen-faced Senator Hartner and his wife. Sammy, Woods, Berkenson's six-man hostage-crisis team, and I complete the group. The chief puts on his glasses and reads the typed letter addressed to the Hartners.

"The return of your daughter will require two tasks. One, the transfer of twenty million US dollars to a specific account number, and two, the release of the five individuals listed below, currently incarcerated in jails throughout the United States. They represent members of the group named Polik. Negotiations are impossible. Elizabeth Hartner will die within seventy-two hours unless all demands are met. More specifics to follow. Prepare."

I stand, move over, and study the letter in the chief's big hands. It's standard font, printed from any desk-jet printer in the world. The Polaroid of Elizabeth shows her muddy, stoic face behind a copy of *The Karachi Times,* dated five days ago. It's a typical proof-of-life document that is demanded from kidnappers, proving their captive is alive.

Berkenson rises from his chair and stands before us.

"Senator, Mrs. Hartner, I know you're relieved that your daughter is still alive. Now, we move to examine in detail what they want. These demands for your daughter's return are quite typical. Remember, kidnapping for ransom is a business transaction. There's some limited give and take. They know we won't release suspected criminals from our jails. They will soon drop those demands when we announce it's not possible. What they really wanted all along was just the money."

"It's always about money," Sammy grunts.

"We'll pay it," the senator says.

Mrs. Hartner's eyes are shut, and she's whispering, "Yes, immediately."

"We can monitor their bank account after the transfer is made," Woods says. "There's no way to hide twenty million these days."

"I don't really care about that," Mrs. Hartner says. "All I care about is getting her back safely. Do you think they'll really do as they say?"

"Statistically, hostages in these episodes usually come home safely. But we must not rock the boat. We must follow their demands coolly but completely. She's apparently in Pakistan, but who knows where. Controlling her release is completely out of our hands."

"They don't say they will release her. They say they will return her. That's different," I say.

Berkenson stares down at the letter now lying on the edge of his table. "Return or release may imply the same thing. They will not go out of their way to bring her all the way back. Perhaps she will simply notice one day her assailants have vanished, and she will walk out a free woman. It depends on the methods of her captors."

"I think they really meant they will return her home," I say. "If she's far away, she will have to be transported now, in time for the seventy-two-hour limit they have set. If she is close by, then they have more flexibility. I believe she's in a nearer location. They apparently mailed this letter before Gloria Sullivan's newspaper articles broke. That means either the postmarks are phony, though I feel they are genuine, or they just happened to send the demand letter at this time."

"Hard to tell which it is, Detective. But she's not around here, I assure you. That would involve more complications. She's more controlled in a remote location."

"What about these men?" Sammy asks. "Who are they?"

Berkenson's head assistant, Nathan Peters, a squat, pale man, replies from his laptop, "Two are in jail in San Diego for smuggling crates of explosives into the country. One's in Florida for the same thing. The other two are here in the Alexandria jail for fleeing after their Mercedes ran over and killed a small boy. Later, they were all charged with other counts after their identities were discovered. Most of them are in this country illegally."

"What are their nationalities?"

Peters says, "They hold citizenship and passports from Lebanon and Egypt. Some have done time for murder, extortion, and kidnapping."

Sammy says, "They're trying to get some of their regulars back on the payroll."

"What's the obstacle with possibly releasing them?" I ask.

Berkenson says, "Big problems, Detective. Uncle Sam doesn't release anyone from anywhere under these kinds of circumstances. It's simply beyond the realm of our judicial system. If we did, everyone would be pulling this crap, trying to get their guys out. Releasing terrorist suspects from jail is just not possible. They dug up these two-bit thugs just to pad their wish list. All they really want is the money."

"Why not just ask for the money straight out?" Mrs. Hartner asks.

"Because, they know we will want to knock down their demands. They don't want it to be the cash, so they offered up a substitute that will make us feel in control. We'll say no, we can't release anyone, and they will bitch and then say, 'Okay, then give us all the funds.'"

"How do we communicate with them to tell them that?" Senator Hartner asks. "How do we know they don't really want these men released?"

"We don't know that at all," I say.

"Confirming their intentions with certainty is not 100 percent possible. They have chosen not to directly communicate with us. It's not unusual," Berkenson says.

"Then we have to assume they want these criminals released until we know for sure," Senator Hartner says. "We have no wiggle room. We need to know all we can about who these men are. Then, we'll be able to assess their real intentions."

"Senator, shortly my team should know a great deal more about this group called Polik. We'll analyze their background with computerized terrorist profiling. In the meantime, I suggest you prepare to raise the ransom money. The electronic-funds transfer they're requiring will override traditional money-tracking methods. We cannot use marked or explosive bills. It may be a total loss of the money for you all. I want you to prepare for that."

"We've been preparing for this eventuality for weeks," Senator Hartner says.

"Then, everyone, be back here in three hours," Berkenson says. "We've got decisions to make and a schedule to meet."

I need prepping for the big fight ahead. From a psychic standpoint, I feel numb. Nothing feels right in my gut about what has just occurred.

I drive to Tara's house, get naughty with her smooth, naked body, tell her how things are going with the Hartner case, shower, dress, then brush my teeth. I shadow-box some quick jabs to their slovenly, kidnapping jaws. She applauds from the sheets. I'm grateful this lady is my pressure valve. It will be a while till I see her again. The next few days will demand all of us pull hard to bring Elizabeth Hartner home. I wish I could tell Elizabeth that she will be coming back soon.

But I'm a receiver, not a broadcaster.

I think about the demands made for Elizabeth's return as I drive back to the FBI building. What's a big group of dangerous men like these killers really want? There is always a hidden motive lurking beneath the surface of any criminal act. Twenty million dollars will soothe a lot of frustrations, and using your 'get out of jail card' to spring your cutthroat friends will be very productive. But these guys are really big, like Rohini Gutab said. Where's the red meat behind all of this? If we don't know, someone will suffer. And it will fall on one person's shoulders.

I'm two blocks from Berkenson's office when Sammy rings my cell. "Change of plans, John. Head over to the Alexandria City jail. Woods will meet you there."

"And?"

"You two are going to ask these Polik guys in the jail over there a few harmless questions."

"Does Berkenson know about this?"

"Not yet. We need insight on them. These two are right in our own backyard. I'll cover your absence with Berkenson. You know how to get under someone's skin without them knowing it. Go for it, Johnny. Call me as soon as you can. I've notified Paul Shank, the Alexandria City Police captain, that you're coming. He thinks you're on a routine investigation. We'll catch him up later."

"Roger, Sammy, big ten-four. You're getting frisky."

"We'll see."

Twenty minutes later, after flying down the GW Parkway, I arrive at the big Alexandria City jail and meet Woods in the parking lot. We move inside, through security, then downstairs and are escorted into a mirrored interview room. Captain Shank steps in for a brief moment.

"Here are their files, Detectives. I've not had time to read them in full. Make yourselves at home. When you're ready to interview these inmates, let us know. They'll be brought down individually from maximum security."

Woods and I sit and read the arrest files before us. The two men are held here without bail because of their auto accident involving the death of a seven-year-old in Old Town, Alexandria, three months ago.

The driver, Josef Mudum, twenty-eight, is an Egyptian citizen. He served three years in a Cairo jail for bombing a seaside resort on the Mediterranean. Soon after release, he was captured at the Canadian border with a tractor trailer full of fertilizer, the crude, truck bomb-making variety. Mudum was bailed out, then vanished into the Canadian pastureland. After the Alexandria car accident, his complete record was pulled, and he was denied bail. Currently, he's charged with vehicular manslaughter.

His lawyer vehemently condemned his incarceration, claiming he was a victim of racial profiling. Says he's a family man with wife and kids. But under current Homeland Security regulations, illegal aliens who have been deported or arrested in the past can be detained indefinitely if they are caught reentering the country.

"Mudum fits the typical MO for the run-of-the-mill terrorist. But this other guy, I'm astonished he's even here," Woods says, pushing me the other file.

The other individual is a man named Gerald Aswan, age forty-five and a Swiss citizen. He travels several times a year to the United States for business. His visa and passport are current, and he has no record of any criminal offense anywhere in the world. He hired the driver, Mudum, for the day while he was doing business in Old Town. He claims the driver ran the red light on King Street but did not see the child in the intersection. The driver was panicked and drove away as Aswan pleaded for him to stop. They were pulled over near Reagan National Airport thirty minutes later, and both were arrested. Mudum has claimed full responsibility for the accident and says Aswan is not guilty of any offense.

Woods is puzzled. "Why is Aswan even being held?"

I study a document in Aswan's green folder. "Gerald Aswan is being held without bail in maximum security because of a memo generated by Homeland Security. Aswan has clients who have been associated with the crime syndicate in Europe. Under new regulations, any persons who are brought up on their new SPD, or Statistical Profiling Database, can be detained indefinitely."

"I know about that program," Woods replies. "It combines all the databases—from the CIA, FBI, NSA, INS, and a half dozen other agencies—to draw conclusions about any individual in the world. It's got glitches, though. Probably, this guy is sitting here because he had one tiny hit on his business profile. It's a combined data snapshot on all the business associations his company has ever had."

"So Aswan is here because he did business with another company who did business with another company who may have been culpable somewhere in the past?"

"Precisely," Woods says. "Even allegations of unscrupulous accounting practices are producing red flags these days."

"Christ, that would mean half the companies in this country might be looked at."

"True. But this program is looking at business associations in the Middle East and Europe, where, traditionally, terrorist plots are funded, planned, and rehearsed. The database is not fully online with US companies yet."

"So, Aswan's company, this Zurich Partners Unlimited, an importer of crystal chandeliers, may have been flagged for no logical reason?"

"It's very possible," Woods says. "There are dozens of cases moving through the courts all over the country, challenging Homeland Security's new profiling activities. Sooner or later, Aswan will probably sue for false arrest as well."

"But why deny him bail?" I ask. "He's no real flee threat."

"Because Homeland Security's new program generated a high quotient about his potential threat to this country, extreme enough for local authorities to keep him jailed indefinitely. It's kind of crazy. Alexandria police don't really have any charges yet to file against Aswan; they're reduced to charging him as an accomplice to the manslaughter charge of the boy."

"What a lame use of law enforcement," I say. "What I don't understand is why Elizabeth's kidnappers want such a man released from jail anyway. He's a nonentity."

"Maybe they threw him on their list to show their disdain for his political limbo."

"Let's bring him in," I say.

Five minutes later, a thin, alert man with dark eyes is escorted into the room in an orange jumpsuit. We request his handcuffs be removed. He is seated in front of us, and the attending guard is asked to step out. There is silence for a moment as Woods prepares what she's going to ask. Gerald Aswan is excited someone has come to see him.

"Tell me about the auto accident on February third of this year?" Woods asks.

Aswan leans forward. "Are you here to help me with my case?" Slight accent, but I can't pin it down.

"Our reason for talking to you today involves clarifying what happened that day the boy was struck. The more we learn, the better it is for you," Woods says. "You don't have to talk with us without your attorney being present. But we will be back and ask you the same questions when he is."

"I'm willing to answer all questions right here and now. Anything to resolve this nightmare. Do you know how long I've been in here?"

"Ninety-three days," Woods replies.

"Precisely," Aswan says. "Please, ask me anything. To hell with my attorney."

"Focus on the auto accident," Woods says. "Start twenty-four hours before it happened."

"Yes, yes, okay. Let's see. I waved good-bye to my wife at the Zurich airport where she drops me off when I fly on business. The flight connected through London, then on to New York as usual. I switched planes after customs and flew on to National—I still call it National. No disrespect to former president Reagan. But I can't seem to…"

"Mr. Aswan, relax. Keep it concise," Woods says.

"Sorry. I'm so astonished someone has come to see me. It has been weeks since anyone has spoken with me other than my attorney and INS marshals. I still can't believe this has happened. I own chandelier stores throughout Europe and the US. I visit them throughout the year. On this trip, I was seeing the Old Town Alexandria unit, which is my newest and, already, one of my most successful. The exotic lighting market has never been more fruitful, even though, since the recent terrorist activity, many hotels and luxury homeowners have curtailed their spending. They're apparently in love with our new line, which combines Old World craftsmanship with the latest in…"

"Stay with the topic, Mr. Aswan," Woods replies.

"Yes. I then traveled from the Reagan National Airport via a car escort service. I prefer not to drive in this crazy traffic when I'm on business. I spent most of the day and early evening at my Alexandria King Street store. Lighting inventories must be better monitored, custom orders often must be expedited, and advertising must be concisely targeted to our clientele. By evening, I decided to forward further instructions to them by e-mail. My flight back to Zurich left New York the following day, and I needed to catch the shuttle back up there that night. It was getting dark when I stepped back into the car. I told the driver to take me back to the airport. He seemed anxious, and when he accelerated down the street, running the red light, I could tell he was not focused on what he was doing. The poor child came out of nowhere, and the driver never even saw him. I felt the impact, saw the boy's body behind us, and, in horror, realized the driver was not going to stop. I've since learned the driver was a wanted man."

"Why fly back to Zurich so soon, Mr. Aswan?" Woods asks.

"My daughter's twelfth birthday was the next day. I've never missed one."

"Where was all of your luggage? Your personal effects don't include much clothing."

"I pack extremely light when I'm traveling overnight. A carry-on bag moves one through the airport much quicker. Have you flown lately? It's a nightmare." Aswan searches our expressions.

"Tell us about your driver, Josef Mudum."

"Like I said, he was my driver for that day. I never saw him prior to that day, nor since. I know he's in trouble for his past, but during the accident he was guilty of nothing but poor judgment."

"Your attorney is quite well known in this town, Mr. Aswan. All your money hasn't bought you even temporary freedom. Are you angry about that?" Woods asks.

Rage fills his expression. "Yes."

"Do you know why you are not being released on bail?"

"I do, indeed. My attorney has told me I'm a victim of a new and very unconstitutional law that can detain anyone for any reason indefinitely under the guise of national security. Your founding fathers would be aghast."

"Your background does suggest unusual business alliances. But you're being charged with fleeing the scene after the boy was killed. That's a felony."

Aswan says, "Detective, I have never compromised myself by associating with anyone unscrupulous. And I have said repeatedly, from the moment I was arrested, I had nothing to do with the boy's death. Help me get these charges dropped."

"Not possible. The state will certainly proceed with prosecuting you. If you are innocent, as you say, then you will be exonerated. That's the way our court system works," Woods say.

"I hope so, Detective Woods." Aswan looks at me. "I welcome any questions you may have, Detective Wiley."

"Have you ever heard of, or are you a member of a terrorist group called Polik, Mr. Aswan?" I ask.

"No, to both questions."

CHAPTER FOURTEEN

Ten minutes later, the other man being held, the driver, Josef Mudum, is brought down and is seated in front of us. He's gaunt and sullen. Woods is smiling at him, and he is not smiling back. "You know you don't have to talk to us without your attorney being present."

"It does not matter," Mudum says. "You will never be able to act on the words I tell you anyway."

"Why is that?" Woods responds.

"Your coming death will stop any inquiries you may make. I have nothing to lose from what you may throw at me. It does not matter. In the end all of you will be defeated, and we shall win."

"Who's 'we'?"

He leans forward. "We are the new rulers of the world. We will destroy all of your society because you are corrupt from the inside."

"Your criminal record indicates you are the corrupt one, Mr. Mudum."

"All of that is your doing," he says.

"We invented your past and are falsely blaming you for it?"

"No. I did what I did in the past because your world needs destroying and rebuilding. I'm part of that reorganization."

"You and who else?" Woods asks.

"Anyone who is living the Western culture will be destroyed. Anyone respectful of the old ways will be part of the New World. It's coming."

"Same old song, Mr. Mudum. Please clarify how running down an innocent child helps make the world a better place?"

"All children are sacred," he says. "There are no exceptions."

"What you did was a criminal act. Perhaps you didn't see him, but you were driving the car. You're responsible for his death, correct?"

He's staring at the ground, his hands clenched across his drawn-up knees. There's a storm raging in him.

Woods says, "You've admitted you were driving the car. Mr. Aswan agrees. That part is a well-known fact, Mr. Mudum."

He raises his head up and looks at me for the first time. His eyes are clear and serene. "I have nothing to say but this—I will not escape punishment. Death is coming now; that is certain. But I am not scared anymore."

"Are you a member of the terrorist group called Polik?" Woods asks.

He is silent and unmoved.

"What have you got?" Sammy asks as Woods and I drive together, back toward DC.

"The Swiss, Gerald Aswan, seems clean," I reply. "I don't know why they want him released. He'll surely be acquitted for the hit-and-run and manslaughter charge. It doesn't really matter. Berkenson said none of them will be released, anyway."

"What about the other guy?"

"Josef Mudum is a terrorist who's got big potential to cause big problems."

"You interviewed both of them?"

"Woods did. I watched."

"Anything revealing about them we should know about?"

"Can't think of it at the moment. Neither inmate seemed to respond to the name Polik. Did agents talk with the other inmates in Florida and California?"

"Already done. The kid in Florida and the two in San Diego were caught smuggling the same kind of explosives. They've all got criminal records in Europe. No passports or visas. They're all three from Lebanon. Arrogant, and uncooperative."

"When were they arrested?"

Sammy says, "Just recently. Two weeks ago."

"So, they're not detained by any additional INS regulations?"

"No. Just good old felony charges. Why?"

"It's strange. Those three guys, apparent members of this Polik group, just recently all got caught. Why kidnap Elizabeth Hartner weeks before these three were even in jail? What was their motive then?"

"The answer's like I've said all along. It's about their greed. They pulled up these guys' names from somewhere, even though they are not remotely connected. Created this phony Polik group to give their idea credibility. Now they think we'll see Polik as a legitimate criminal entity. It's all smoke and mirrors, John."

"Sammy, I agree. I was thinking it was something else."

"Sometimes the obvious answer is the right one. Hang on—I got a call."

He's back in an eternal thirty minutes. "John, an hour ago, Senator Hartner received an e-mail from the kidnappers containing new instructions. We'll all be in Berkenson's conference room. So move."

As we enter the FBI conference room twenty minutes later, there is a heated argument going on.

"That's impossible," Senator Hartner says, "you're telling me you have no way of confirming where this e-mail came from? Aren't you guys the best at covert data acquisition?"

NSA's chief cyber sleuth, George Keith, leans back in his chair nervously. "Senator, the National Security Agency has many tools at its disposal. But the origin of this e-mail is not traceable. It's not that we don't have the capacity, it's that this particular transmission is cyber-sterile. It's a new kind of communication we've just seen recently. It could have hopscotched in from a wireless transmission, so its root server cannot be determined. At the moment, were still on the learning curve with this one."

"That's not good enough. You know this is a critical moment. We must find out their location!"

Woods and I sit and study the printout of the senator's communication.

To: Senator Hartner

Time is running out on your daughter's life, so follow instructions carefully. Today is day one of the three-day deadline. You may respond with one question per day to the electronic address below. The following must occur for her release to move forward. 1) Twenty million US dollars must be wired to a specific overseas account number, which will be supplied to you on day three. 2) All five members, listed below, of the political group named Polik must be released by 2:00 p.m., Eastern Daylight Time, tomorrow. These political prisoners must be in civilian dress, and released on the street directly in front of their individual police stations. Any attempts to impede their progress for twenty-four hours after their release will be detected by us. Such obstructions will void the agreement. A voided agreement will result in Elizabeth Hartner's death. There will be no negotiations of any kind on these demands.

Polik@politicalfreedom.com

"You must be capable of determining their location," Senator Hartner says. "All Internet traffic leaves tracks. Who the hell is this politicalfreedom.com, anyway?"

"Sir, we traced out this communication an hour ago," Keith says, "and found no specific domain associated with that website. All communications sent back to them will certainly become just as lost. The NSA cannot guarantee we will have luck tracking your responses to them, Senator."

Berkenson says, "Senator, I'm sure Mr. Keith and his agency will do all that they can in the short time they have. But counting on the NSA to track down these people quickly is a long shot. These kidnappers have sophisticated means of communications. We may have no choice but to comply."

"Impossible!" Hartner cries out. "There are no constitutional means to release criminals such as these, short of a Supreme Court decision. This country has never succumbed to political blackmail or extortion to such a massive degree. It's not a possibility."

"We may have no choice, Senator," says Police Chief Willis Harris. "They have made it clear what they want. Thinking this kidnapping was solely about financial gain was wishful thinking. Though it's clear all of these Polik members are seemingly unrelated, there is a method to their madness. We cannot see why they want these men yet. In the short time left us, we may not determine it. So, we must seek a solution based on their release. Are you and your wife prepared financially for the funds transfer?"

"Yes, we are. We will be bankrupt, essentially. But it doesn't matter. The money is meaningless. It's all about our daughter."

"Then that part of this wretched deal is secure," Berkenson says. "Now, we have to pursue two new goals quickly. One, explore their possible release. Senator, because you are head of the Senate Judicial Committee, you have enormous influence with the US Justice Department. I don't think there is any doubt they targeted you and your daughter because of your power in Congress. The kidnappers felt that threats to your daughter could pressure you and create possibilities of releasing these men."

"You're correct, Director Berkenson. I began to fear that the moment we received the videotape of Elizabeth last week. They seem to forget this is America. The Congress and its members must operate by rules, just like all other citizens of the country. Even if I could apply pressure on the courts to release all of these men, the whole country would learn about it, and conclude it was done outside of the normal court procedures. There would be public outrage if it were known this country had succumbed to terrorists' blackmail."

"By that time, the deal would already have gone down and your daughter would have been returned," Sammy replies.

"And I would have to resign from the Senate the next day," Senator Hartner says. "I'm not ready to throw all my money and my career away just yet, Sammy. What's your second goal, Director?"

"We must decide which single response gives us the most benefit," I say. Berkenson nods in agreement. "They say it can only be one question a day. Tomorrow we must release all the Polik members at 2:00 p.m. So, we had better make it a useful one."

"Exactly, Detective. We must assume we will not determine their location in time to stop them, even though we will pursue that action. And the senator says releasing known criminals under duress is not something the courts will likely do without just cause. Amassing enough evidence to convince a judge to drop the charges or even just release these men on bail may take days."

"So, our single response to them should not be a question, but an offer," I say. "We must test their determination. Make them a counteroffer and see what they say. They must expect us to knock some of their demands down. We need to find out where the real rubber meets the road."

"What do you have in mind?" Senator Hartner says.

"Force them to say what they really want. Formulate our response to them with complications, so they must respond back to us. We can then respond back again. We need to open the dialogue. We need to break this one question rule."

Berkenson says, "Detective Wiley, for someone who claims never to have worked on a hostage case, your instincts are good. Go on with that thought."

"We have other leverage points we can use. One is the press. We don't want the public knowing the real details of their demands. They would instantly gather outside the jails, watching for the Polik members to walk free. But we may want to pressure the kidnappers with more misinformation."

"We must be careful," the senator says. "We must do nothing to further endanger Elizabeth."

"I agree," says Berkenson. "Detective Wiley, newspaper misinformation is your specialty as of late. Your assignment is to formulate a phony press release through Gloria Sullivan that can run in tomorrow morning's paper. Then, draft a disruptive response to the kidnappers that we can send them."

"Yes, sir," I say.

He turns to Woods. "Find out if there's a possibility any of the Polik group could legally be released from jail. Detective Woods, work with these gentlemen, my assistant, Nathan Peters, and Mr. Keith from the NSA to analyze each Polik member. Assign a difficulty factor for each one of them for, say, a simple bail hearing. You have three hours."

All of them nod and move together in discussion.

Senator Hartner says, "Quickly, now. I may be able to use two of those profiles with the local district court judges. An initial release, starting with that Swiss National right here in Alexandria, might fly. From what I've learned, he's the cleanest of the group."

"He may be the one we should review right away," Berkenson says. "His background appears straightforward. He would be an appeasing initial candidate if they would have him. But they may not care, which would indicate they didn't really want him all along."

My gut begins to churn. I feel sick. I take a few deep breaths, sit down at the table, and ponder what I must do in the next few hours. I've lost my bearing. I need to sense a solution, something to give me insight. But I haven't time to let a solution evolve. I have to do it the old-fashioned way: think.

CHAPTER FIFTEEN

Inside Berkenson's conference room, solutions are being formed, then dashed. A dozen laptops blaze as printers spit out solutions, only to be discarded. I'm in my second hour on the phone with Gloria Sullivan. She's giddy the endgame is upon us.

At first, Woods and her group are hopelessly lost in too much data, courtesy of the FBI and NSA data banks. There is no computer program designed to do what they must accomplish. Another new, three-man FBI team is also with us, their sole task—to uncover what Polik really is. Are there valid reasons for these five men to belong to this group, and, if so, what is their mission?

The world is full of such politically diverse and dangerous groups. Their agendas are usually self-centered, extreme, and doomed to eventual failure. If Polik's undersides can be revealed, that information can be very useful in our communications with them.

It's 2:00 a.m.

Woods smiles for the first time in days. She's done it. She moves to Berkenson and Chief Harris and confers with them for a long moment. She smiles coolly at the senator, Mrs. Hartner, and two aides who are seated nearby. Shortly, the fifteen people in the room gather around the big conference table. Berkenson says, "Detective Woods, present to us what you all have uncovered so far."

Woods replies, "We compared the five Polik men's current criminal charges against previous convicted felons with similar charges. We compared the Polik members with this control group for the following: possibility of grand jury hearings, formal charges being filed, the possibility of plea-bargaining, and, finally, jury trial and eventual conviction. The results are as follows: there is a 96 percent probability that four of the Polik members will be convicted if they are not released through bail. If released, all will be a near100 percent flight risk, with a near 0 percent probability of their capture, in this case. By releasing these four men through the terms demanded by the kidnappers, the government could actually be held culpable."

"And the fifth man?" I ask.

"Gerald Aswan, the Swiss businessman, despite being labeled a high security threat by the new Homeland Security program, has no criminal activity in his background whatsoever. He's the odd man out, as we said. He likely will be acquitted of the local manslaughter and hit-and-run charges. Unless more damning connections can be made to his business practices, his detainment by Homeland Security agents will not stand up in court. He may not know it now, but he will never go to jail in this county for any of the charges they filed against him. If released on bail, he will be a near 0 percent flight risk. He's the only one who has even a remote chance of being legally released on bail tomorrow at 2:00 p.m."

"Detective Wiley, what have you got for us?"

"What Detective Woods described," I say, "is what we all feared we might discover. We are in a legal bind with no way out. We have four very bad guys whom we are reluctant to let go, even if we could. So, I propose we send a communication to the kidnappers immediately. We understand why they want the four felons out, but not why they want Gerald Aswan out. We need to know the connection between him and the others. It's critical, I believe, in understanding their motivations."

"John, with all due respect," Sammy replies, "we all know why they put Aswan on the list. He's the runt in the litter. They'll toss him out in the end when the bargaining gets tough. He's there to pad the list."

"Sammy, I first thought that too, but I don't think so now. I think it's worth a shot to find out more."

"Specifically what do you have in mind, Detective?" Senator Hartner asks.

"Tell them we are in a position to release the entire Polik group, except Gerald Aswan. Twist the whole thing around. Explain to them that Aswan cannot post bail at this time, due to complicated legal technicalities. His case is more involved constitutionally. Tell them we will meet all of their demands, including the money transfer—except his release. Because of his apparent innocence, he will be out legally in a few months, anyway."

"They will jump on that immediately," Sammy says.

"I'm willing to bet they won't," I say.

"Why?" Chief Harris asks.

"I believe they're hiding something they don't want us to know."

"And if they do take that offer?" Berkenson asks.

"Then we will be in the same boat we're in already. We'll quickly reply back, stating we've encountered sudden complications, and it will delay the group's release for a while."

"What will we have accomplished, besides wasting precious time?" Sammy asks.

"We will have shown immediate concern for their demands. Shown that we are on top of it."

"It's risky," Berkenson says. "If we say we're going to release them, we better well be prepared to do it. Senator, where do we stand on your side of the aisle?"

Senator Hartner has been staring at the paisley carpet. He looks at his wife sadly and says, "I've been on the phone for the last hour with the most powerful man in this city, a certain gentleman at 1600 Pennsylvania Avenue. Nothing but the deepest sympathy came my way. I was turned down across the board. Even if we could find legal means for these men politically, releasing them would be suicide. The current feeling in this country toward any terrorist group is total hatred. No judge will touch this."

"And, what about Gerald Aswan? If push comes to shove, could we get him out tomorrow?" Berkenson asks.

Senator Hartner nods darkly. "Aswan's case is not in the same category as the other four. I could arrange his release. But I don't think he will be a satisfactory reward for them. So, Detective Wiley's possible response to them, suggesting we will release them all but Gerald Aswan, has some merit. He could be a bargaining chip." He pauses and rubs his exhausted face. "It's all looking like such a long shot. Somehow, we must stall them. Anything but reveal to them that we cannot release the other four."

Berkenson turns to the Polik research team. "What have you gentlemen got for us? Anything on this Polik group?"

"Nothing, Mr. Berkenson. In the brief amount of time that we've been looking at them, all we have found is that this group is either super secretive, obscure, or nonexistent."

Sammy says, "I agree with the latter theory. They made this group up to give credibility to a bunch of murderers they need to help them pull off their next job. All politically subversive groups like to advertise themselves—not hide in the shadows. The fact that the most powerful and secretive unit of the FBI can't determine who they are speaks volumes about their existence."

"Or they could be a cover for a larger organization," Chief Harris says. "Organized criminal networks are well organized throughout the world. Every country has its own mafia. This Polik may be nothing more than that."

Berkenson says, "We need insight on them but are lacking it. And time is running out. I propose we send correspondence to them. And I think Detective Wiley's suggestion has possibilities. Detective, what about your newspaper article. Is it prepared?"

"I think we should hold back on that just now. Use one tool at a time."

"Then let's send that response to the kidnappers," Berkenson says, "and pray to God we're all on the right track."

It's 6:00 a.m., and we're all waiting for their reply. The scheduled release of the Polik group is only eight hours away. Somehow, we must wrestle away their demands and make them our own. A response may never come forward from them, and that possibility is now an agonizing threat to the Hartners' peace of mind. Their daughter's fate now seems to be slipping away. I'm beginning to wonder if my theory was correct. But we have no other course to follow. The Polik four will stay in jail until their trials begins.

Senator Hartner is continuously monitoring his office e-mail, where the original demand was sent. But that's not how the kidnappers' reply comes in.

Instead, at 7:15 a.m., a call comes from the senator's office announcing the arrival of a Federal Express overnight envelope, addressed to him. He instructs it to be rushed over to the FBI building. We gather around the table, and the senator opens it. Inside the jacket is another smaller envelope containing a handwritten letter. It startles the Hartners. They recognize the handwriting as their daughter's. The senator reads it aloud to us:

"Mom and Dad—

Your one valuable response to these men was a sad waste of resources. As you read this, you have only a few hours remaining to arrange the release of the five Polik members. None of my kidnappers' conditions are negotiable. A partial release of the Polik group is unacceptable. All members must be released together. If you cannot use your influence to make this happen, you are a compassionless father. Do it now, for my sake.—Elizabeth."

"She would never write such trash," Mrs. Hartner exclaims. "She would never submit to such a ruse. She is certainly scared, but also very principled."

"Then how in the hell was this letter written?" the senator asks us all.

Woods examines the letter carefully, holding it up to the overhead light.

"This was created on a laser printer. There are no writing depressions on the back. It's some kind of forgery."

NSA's George Keith responds, "Actually, its creation is probably similar to a technology employed on Capitol Hill when politicians send out personal correspondence. It's signed in their own hand, apparently. But its font is based on a computer program built around that person's personal handwriting. They must have gotten hold of some of Elizabeth's writing. Nicely done. It has punch."

Berkenson takes the note and reads it again. "It certainly does. But for what reason? Why not just make the reply by e-mail? Why all the different communication modes?"

"Because they want to show power," I say. "Each time they communicate, they use a different form. That's meant to confuse us and make us think they are everywhere and in total control. It really means desperation. A few hours ago we offered them twenty million dollars and four of the worst scumbags on the planet, and they said no. Why? Not because they are stubborn and want all the marbles. No group making demands would ever turn this one down, unless the real reason was they basically want Gerald Aswan!"

"But, why?" Mrs. Hartner cries. "Why is he so damned important to them? Who is this man, anyway?"

"He's nobody," Sammy replies. "He means nothing to them, I guarantee it. They're bluffing, John, and you just can't see it. They only want the money. At the last moment, they will give in and take the cash. Trust me."

"Can we risk taking such a chance, Sammy?" I say. "No way. We have only two choices left. Either plead with the powers that be in this town to take another look at releasing the other four, or..."

"Or what?" Mrs. Hartner says.

"Or switch gears and offer them only Aswan and all the money," Berkenson says. "There's no other choice."

"But if Aswan is so critical to them, Mr. Wiley, why is his background completely clean?" Senator Hartner asks.

"The man is far more than a chandelier salesman," I reply. "We need to dig deeper and uncover who that is."

An hour later I am sitting by myself in the basement of the Alexandria City jail, staring at Josef Mudum, Gerald Aswan's driver. His eyes are bloodshot.

"I'm here to talk to you again. Are you willing?" I ask.

"Yes."

"You don't look well. Did you sleep?"

"No. I will not sleep much from here on. But that doesn't matter. I have fulfilled my destiny in life," he replies.

"I see. Well, okay then."

I rise and hold out my hand and offer it for him to shake. He hesitates, then shakes, thinking I'm leaving. But I'm not. I am scanning his body for deception. It occasionally works for me. His hand feels damp and complicated. Filled with torment. Most liars, even the best, have to work with an extra effort to lie. They are juggling two balls in their minds, the real truth, and the lie. That task takes more attention and energy. The real truth comes out without strings attached. He's hiding something.

I sit back down. "Actually, I want to ask a few more questions. It now occurs to me you might want to tell me who was really driving the car that struck the boy. The final piece of your car accident can now be revealed."

Josef Mudum exhales and stares at the floor. "I have already told you what happened."

"So, it wasn't decided that you would take the rap for Aswan?"

"Certainly not."

"No?" I say. "Then, tell me this: why is Gerald Aswan such an important man?"

Mudum laughs in a burst of absurdity.

"What's funny?"

"You don't even know that?"

"I know some. Help me out."

"Why should I tell you any more? I have cleared my mind. Betraying him would not get me to heaven any quicker."

"Well, I think he betrayed you, Josef. He will happily allow you to rot in jail for the rest of your life while he continues enjoying his freedom. What's fair about that?"

"Aswan is the lifeblood of the New World order. He must be free to continue that role. I am expendable. I have done my best to disrupt the Western world and its values. Each man has a role to play. Mine is small. His is much bigger."

"So, your Lord will excuse you for ruthlessly killing a child, just to accommodate Aswan's own busy schedule?"

"The child is a martyr. He's in heaven, awaiting us," Mudum says forcefully.

"I see. You have children, Josef?"

"Yes, I have five."

"So, if Aswan asked you to run them down, it would be all right with you?"

He leans forward. "Mr. Aswan would never do that."

"Yes, he would. He's a busy man. He's too important to be concerned about the little ones. So, there's one problem with Aswan. Real warriors kill the enemy soldiers, not the enemy's children."

"You are trying to trick me. It will not work."

"Then you are a coward," I reply. "Your own children might be next. Aswan doesn't care!"

He rises in his chains and stares at me in confusion. I let him tower above me. The guard is moving past the window, starting to come in. I wave him off.

Mudum finally sits, flustered.

"You must miss your family," I ask. "You will probably never see your children again. Is that what you want?"

"No."

"Then stop betraying them. Give them the possibility of being with their father again. Tell me all about Aswan. We can make a deal. Your testimony against him might buy you immunity."

"I have told you all you need to know," he says.

"Then I say to you, he is not the real leader of the New World order. He is just a criminal whose life is devoted to personal power, not principle."

"You have no idea whom you are dealing with. I pity you."

"Where is Elizabeth Hartner?"

"I don't know anything about her."

I rise and take his hand. It's trembling.

CHAPTER SIXTEEN

"They want you to interview Aswan, ASAP," Sammy tells me on my cell. "Senator Hartner has gotten authorization for a bail review in one hour for Aswan, which will certainly be approved. He could be on the street soon after that if we decide to go that route. We've got a dozen agents running background on Aswan from child-birth on. We're drafting a new response based on offering just Aswan and the money. But we all need to know what you think, John. If you feel he really was driving the car that killed the kid, then he is a mur-derer. If you think he is bigger than he seems, we need to know that. Releasing him might be a bigger mistake than releasing the other four combined."

"He's coming down now, Sammy. I'll call you in a half hour."

"Make it quick. Time's running out."

I see Aswan pass by the window. He is escorted into the interview room and seated in front of me. He eyes me carefully, expecting me to have his chains released. Not this time.

The guard leaves, and I reach out and shake Aswan's handcuffed hand. It's not at all what I felt last time, which was really nothing at all. This time I feel a supreme confidence radiating from him. He smiles.

"Detective Wiley, have you good news for me?"

"Perhaps, Mr. Aswan," I say. "There is a lot of recent interest in your case. Are you aware of the nature of it?"

"Yes."

"Tell me what you know. It will help me."

"My attorney says there has been a petition for a bail hearing. I will be released today, with luck."

"That's true. We are working to make it happen." His eyes are dilated, and his upper lip slick with sweat. He seems a caged animal, having nearly pried open the bars enough to slip through. There is no sign of defeat in his posture. I wonder who in the hell he is.

"Do you know why we are considering releasing you on bail, Mr. Aswan?"

He smiles, and just for an instant, I see a devious flash of arrogance. I see a demon.

"The reason you are releasing me is because I am innocent," he says.

"That's not entirely the reason, Mr. Aswan. You see, I believe that your driver, Mr. Mudum, wasn't driving the car when the boy was struck."

"No?"

"You were. Isn't that true?"

"Before I answer that, Mr. Wiley, answer me one question."

"Go ahead."

"Wasn't it your cousin, Duncan Wiley, who was killed in that hunting accident when you were twelve?"

It seems he has grown larger by the mere nature of his question. His smile is unrelenting. How he knows such a fact is beyond me. My family history is quite obscure. But he has shown he has the resources to delve into me. I've opened him up. Let's see what he's got.

"Yes, he was shot accidentally."

"By his own father, if I'm not mistaken."

"Your sympathy is appreciated. Why the inquiry?"

"Well, I just thought you'd like to know, I know it was no accident."

"What?"

"Your Uncle Phil, rest his soul, was never the same after that, was he? How could one blame him? Drunk as a skunk when he pulled the trigger. Thought he saw the white tail of a big buck, but it was really his own son's blond ponytail, blowing in the fall breeze. Even after all those years in the asylum, poor man never recovered. Of course, you knew your uncle was an alcoholic, right, Mr. Wiley?"

"My father explained all of it to me. It was just an accident."

"Psychiatric records tell a different story, Detective. I can see why the family would hush it up. Shameful, Mr. Wiley. Very shameful."

"Explain your intentions by asking such questions," I say.

"I wanted to show how easily one could obtain information on someone if they wanted to. If those in law enforcement had done a fraction of the research I've done on you, they would have uncovered the facts about me. My business connections are clean. Apparently, your local police force has decided that as well. But ninety days late, Detective Wiley."

"Actually, your background is still under consideration. We have not concluded anything yet. You have considerable investigative resources for a man who's been in jail so long. How did you find out about my uncle?"

"My attorney made some inquiries," he replies.

"Why?"

"I had a lot of time on my hands, Detective."

"Why not dig up trash on your arresting officer?"

"Because you are the man who has come to see me. I like you, Detective. I was struck by your approach to criminal investigation. Your reputation is colorful for such a young man. I believe you are a psychic?"

"Hardly."

"Ah, a modest one."

"When you ran over that boy, Mr. Aswan, was it purely out of impatience?"

"Detective, you're reaching. The boy's death was merely an accident."

"But you admit you were driving?"

"I admit nothing. You wish I would confess to that? Then my upcoming bail would be denied, wouldn't it?"

"I'm not in charge of that aspect of your case," I say. "I'm here to clarify what really happened. So far, you have been evasive, and sadly melodramatic. Resorting to such inquiries about my family is not going to buy you any leverage with me. Those details about my alcoholic uncle made all the front pages years ago. It's no secret what he did."

Aswan pauses. He's not sure whether to believe my lie.

"Where's Elizabeth Hartner, Aswan?"

"Mr. Wiley, surely you don't think I know that?"

"I thought, with all your inquiries, you might have run across her whereabouts."

"Not her, but other females in your world."

"Such as?"

"A certain young lady who keeps your company while in town. Ms. Tara Chin, I believe."

I feel a growing sense that I'm not really here, that I'm watching all this from behind a director's lens. It happened in my earliest crime-scene days. "What do you know about her?"

"Everything, Mr. Wiley."

"Share some of your secrets with me."

"She's innocent, intelligent, passionate, and very vulnerable. Don't break her heart by leaving her high and dry when you return to Asheville."

"What's her eye color, Aswan? Surely your attorney didn't miss that."

"Her eyes are the color of amethyst and cobalt, all rolled into one," he replies. "Correct?"

I want to smash his face.

A text message vibrates on my cell phone screen. It's from Woods. I glance at it without his detection. It reads: *"Aswan's a scholar on the ancient civilization of Sumeria, which is now modern-day Iraq. He was born near its old city of Lagash. Maybe there's a link between Sumerian history and his role in Polik. Polik is the modern translation for a mythological Sumerian god named Enlil, whose role was often destruction and misfortune! Good hunting, W."*

I begin to rise. Aswan seems mystified that I no longer want to talk. I pause, sit back down, check my cell phone for messages. I need time to think. He grows impatient. I open his file and flip through its pages. I sign my name off on areas that seem important. He's sure he's free.

I rise and start to leave. He hesitates. "Am I going to be released?"

"I cannot approve it, Mr. Aswan. Our interview together was your final hurdle. I detect nothing but deception in your responses. You'll have to wait out your time before trial here in jail."

"What?"

"Sorry."

He leans in close to me. "Do you have any idea whom you are talking to?"

"I believe you are an ordinary businessman who was in a hurry, did something awful while driving a car, and can't admit to it. You are like so many rich folks in the world who think they can buy their way out of trouble. Running over that little boy is not an inconsequential matter."

"You are more incompetent than I thought, Detective. My life is far more involved than merely selling chandeliers. Are you clueless?"

I say, "We all know you had nothing to do with Elizabeth Hartner's kidnapping, if that's what you mean."

"Yes, yes, that's correct."

"And we know from your background you are probably innocent on charges that may come from indictments by Homeland Security."

"That's true."

"Then what's left, Mr. Aswan? What else should I know about you?"

"It really doesn't matter now, Mr. Wiley. I will be getting out this afternoon regardless."

"Why is that?"

"My attorney says my release is related to Elizabeth Hartner's hostage agreement."

"You know about that?" I ask.

"He informed me earlier today."

"Who notified him of that action?"

No one in this town could possibly know his release was part of the hostage agreement. He's slipping.

"My attorney is well connected."

"Why do you think they want you out?"

"I have no idea," he says.

"I agree. I can't understand what her kidnappers would want with you!"

He says nothing.

I stare at the ceiling and laugh. "Certainly you couldn't be connected with these fools who actually think they are Sumerian gods? Man, did all the cops howl when we heard that one."

Aswan is ice cold. "You are aware of the kidnappers' philosophical background, are you, Detective?"

"Yes. Are you?" I ask.

"Certainly, I am knowledgeable about the most ancient of world civilizations. The Sumerians were the original culture from which all other modern civilizations arose. Their brilliance cannot be overlooked. I myself was born right where their culture flourished, five thousand years ago."

"Then, tell me, who was this Enlil?"

"In Sumerian mythology, Enlil was their air god, Detective. He made the world the way it was. He gave them their early technology, like picks and hoes. When needed, he was also a ruthless destroyer."

"What god was above him?" I ask.

He pauses. "The god above him was named An, the Sumerian's heaven god. He was the supreme one. The big man."

"Which one are you, Mr. Aswan?"

He laughs. "You cannot bait me, Detective. I need freedom."

"So does Elizabeth Hartner."

He rises, and refuses one last handshake.

CHAPTER SEVENTEEN

I call Tara as I'm moving out to my car. She's not there. I'm in a semi panic about her safety. I tell myself that Aswan's knowledge of her was only used to intimidate me.

Sammy rings me as soon as I turn up Independence Avenue toward the FBI building. "What's your gut feeling about Aswan, John?"

"He's definitely connected to the kidnappers. He's even aware of details about Tara Chin, a woman I see in town. Sammy, he even knows about Uncle Phil."

"Fine. He's resourceful. Did he admit being connected to the Polik group?"

"No."

"Then what do we have on him?"

"He's an arrogant, dangerous egomaniac. He's in deep, Sammy. Letting him go may have been their goal all along. Did the kidnappers respond back to our last offer?"

"Yes, John. That's why we all wanted to know what you felt about Aswan. They've agreed to release Elizabeth if we pay the twenty million and release only Aswan."

"Then that's the magic combination they've been after."

"It's unbelievable, but true. We studied the three Polik group arrest docs in detail. All of them were caught, blatantly trying to smuggle explosives across the border with little or no concealment. All arrested two months after Aswan was, just to throw us off. The scheme worked, John. They've got us."

"So, this whole thing was planned after Aswan was refused bail?"

"Looks that way. Aswan may have grown furious when he couldn't be released on bail. Probably thought his background, whatever it is, would eventually come to light. He panicked, not realizing he would have walked free if he'd just waited."

I say, "He was the one driving the car that killed the boy, Sammy. I feel that for sure. Mudum, his driver, has kids of his own. Though he's certainly a terrorist, I can't see him carelessly running down that child, but I can see Aswan doing so. There's something bizarre in that man's eyes. Kidnapping Elizabeth was all about putting pressure on Senator Hartner to get himself released."

"Bingo, "Sammy says. "Aswan may have orchestrated this whole thing right from his jail cell. We believe his attorney is the primary conduit to his organization."

"And that group is huge. But they have no common connecting thread. So many different nationalities are involved."

"They're big, John. And Aswan is their man."

"Then the release is on for this afternoon?"

"Yes. The kidnappers want Aswan's release and the money transfer to occur simultaneously, at 2:00 p.m. Elizabeth will be released twenty-four hours later, presumably from Pakistan, where we think she's being held."

I say, "It's all completely insane. Can we afford to let him go now, Sammy?"

"What choice do we have? We have nothing to hold Aswan on but a bunch of conjecture. He's only been denied bail due to analysis of his business partnerships by agents at Homeland Security. Even the American Civil Liberties are whining about unconstitutionality. If we had more concrete details, it would be different."

"Give me another two hours, Sammy. Let us work it a little deeper."

"John, we've had a change in plans. Now we don't want to find out any more on him. Senator Hartner is pleading with us. He just wants his daughter back. Let it go. Elizabeth will be freed tomorrow. That's what we were all working for. It's a loss for us, but a victory for the Hartner family. I can live with that."

"I can't."

I hang up and look at my watch. It's 11:00 a.m. I've got three hours.

I finally reach Tara on her cell phone. "Where are you?" I ask.

"I'm in the campus library. You okay? You sound funny."

"Stressed. Wanted to know if you were okay?"

"I'm good. What's up with the Hartner case? Making progress?"

"Elizabeth is about to be released," I reply.

"Amazing. I'm proud of you, John Wiley. You made it happen."

"Not sure about that. But I need a break now. Why not go up to the mountains for a few days? I'll meet you there soon."

"I have a thesis review next week," Tara says. "I need to stay in town."

"Don't go back to your townhouse. I'll reserve a room for us at the Four Seasons in Georgetown to celebrate. Check in today as soon as you can. Stay there until I join you…"

"I can do that. Are you really okay?"

"Will be, soon. I have something important to tell you. Ciao."

I call Sammy back and tell him what I've been worrying about. "I think we have a bug in our group," I say.

"You mean a mole?"

"Yes."

"What makes you think that?"

"Since I first arrived in town, I've felt it. But they always seem to know what we're up to. They watched me early on, but I never caught them in the act. They vanished when we got near, like after the attack on E-Hits. They always seem to know our next move."

"I felt that too, John. I even went so far as to run background checks on our whole investigative group."

"Everybody check out?"

"Generally. Who's your suspect?"

I hesitate. Who am I really thinking about? The idea that someone infiltrated our group has often occupied my thoughts. I've been close to many people in this investigation, and I'm a pretty good judge of a person's honesty—though not good at judging those close to me. Maybe that's why I have no insight now. "I'm thinking about Raul Gutab's sister, Rohini."

"What made you suspicious?" Sammy asks.

"She was lying at one point when we were taking her statement."

"Do you recall the question?"

"When we asked if Raul had received any up-front money from Elizabeth's kidnappers, she said no. I knew she was lying, but I couldn't prove it. She's been in seclusion via witness protection since she was brought in. If she's working with them, she's not inside enough to buy them any information. Who are you looking at?"

"Woods."

"What? She's our top gun, Sammy. What was the problem in her background?"

"She didn't receive the police academy commendations indicated. She's not even a college graduate. Only has a two-year degree, from a local community college there in Louisiana."

"Anything else?"

"No. After this investigation concludes and we get Elizabeth back, Woods will be investigated. But she's a hell of a rookie detective, John."

"When did you first suspect her?" I ask.

"I knew about her lies from day one."

"Why didn't you tell me?"

"I wanted to see if she was leaking data. I fed her false docs just for a test."

"Did she pass?"

"Yes. The kidnappers always seem to know far more than she did."

"As far as her working for Aswan, that's just impossible."

"I'm glad you said that, John. She's too good a cop for betrayal. Where you going?"

"To see Rohini Gutab at her safe house."

"Whatever you find out, Aswan's still walking out of jail at 2:00 p.m."

Rohini Gutab looks stressed, and even thinner than the last time I saw her. Maybe even more beautiful. The furnishings in her three-bed-room prison in Arlington are old and nasty. "When will I get to return to my old life again?" she asks me, her plea worn thin with the other agents seated nearby.

"Never," I say. "Your life will never be the same. But you'll be alive."

"Staying alive is not enough. I want my job back, and my house back."

"That's not happening soon, Ms. Gutab. Elizabeth Hartner's kidnappers are around every corner. Their people will detect you in this town even a year from now. You will have to relocate far away, assume a new identity, and a new life. Why ask me now?"

"I can't take this sitting around. My life is an endless series of Styrofoam meals and restless nights. If my brother's murderers are so good, how certain are you they don't know where I am right now?"

"Witness protection has its risks. Most of the time, it works well. The fact that you're talking to me now means something. Isn't part of your fear simple worry about all that money?"

"What money?"

"The cash your brother received early on from the kidnappers. I know he received it. And I know he gave it to you for safekeeping in case something happened to him. How much was it, ten, twenty thousand?"

She's caught off guard.

"If you don't tell me the truth, Rohini, I'll recommend you be released on the street within the hour. Tell me the truth about the money."

"Why are you asking me this now? I've only tried to help you."

"Answer the question. How much did he receive?"

Her eyes fill with shame.

"Fifty thousand."

"Where is it now?"

"Hidden in my apartment."

"Why didn't you tell me when I asked you before?"

"I was afraid if you knew I had his blood money, you would think I was my brother's accomplice. I hid it the day before he disappeared, and I haven't touched it since."

"I'm not convinced."

"I could easily have spent it if I had wanted to. That money represents all the pain and suffering my brother went through. Take it. I wanted only to burn it when I had the chance."

I ring Woods on my cell. "Are you available?"

She says, "I've got one hour till I'm due back at the Alexandria City jail to oversee Aswan's release."

"Get over to Rohini Gutab's condo in Rosslyn and confirm the existence of fifty thousand dollars hidden there."

"How did you dig that one out of her?'

"I'll tell you later."

"I have to move quickly. Where is it hidden, John?"

I ask Rohini.

"Woods, it's taped up inside the vanity in the guest bedroom. Call me ASAP when you find it. Have forensics remove it after you call me."

"Don't think I was about to come traipsing out with her fifty g's." Woods hang up.

When I turn back to Rohini Gutab, I see relief on her face.

"What else haven't you told me about your brother?" I ask her.

"I said we weren't close. That was a lie. Raul and I were very tight. That's why he confided in me about what was happening to him and Elizabeth. He was sick about the whole thing. He didn't know what to do with the money, so he gave it to me."

"Why keep your real relationship with your brother secret?"

"I thought if I appeared distant from him, I could be safe from prosecution. What good did it do?"

"It helped. Elizabeth Hartner will probably be released in the next day or so. Your knowledge put pressure on her kidnappers to come forward before they wanted to."

"I'm happy for her. But will my brother's death be avenged?"

"Tell me something that will help keep Gerald Aswan in jail. He's the one they wanted all along. Do you know who he is?"

"Raul was never told about anyone. They only wanted him to set her up for the snatch."

"Were Raul and Elizabeth actually in love? Last time, you said you didn't know."

"They met secretly a lot there at the end. Talked about the future, even played silly games. Like lovers do."

"Games?" I ask.

"He said he knew she loved him because she showed him all her childhood games her father taught her. Middle Eastern people don't know these. He was so proud of them."

"Show me."

She locks her fingers together. "Elizabeth's childhood favorite one went like this: *'Here's the church, here's the steeple, open the door, and where's the people?'*"

I watch her hand movement patiently, think a moment, then rise to leave. "Thanks for that insight, Rohini."

Rohini Gutab is unnerved. "How did you know about Raul's money, Detective?"

"I didn't."

I drive over to the Four Seasons Hotel on M Street, book a room for Tara and me, and leave a note on the bed for her. Now is not the time to write such things, but I write them anyway. I feel a big hefty hammer swinging my way. I need to find out what's in Tara Chin's mind right now.

I know that I have reached the end of my rope with Aswan, that no amount of data about him will stall his bail. But it's not really Aswan's release that's eating me; it's that I don't know how all the pieces fit. There is something else bothering me. Rohini Gutab was telling the truth this time. I saw it in her eyes, and I felt it in her hands.

I need to get over to the jail and join the Aswan release group. But I find myself driving though Georgetown, out Canal Road, the opposite way from the Alexandria City jail. If I hurry I can make it back there by 2:00 p.m. I need to go to the Potomac River one more time.

I park beside the beaver pond's still waters. Right here, a man died, and a woman was kidnapped. Max knew there were answers here. If he weren't still in recovery, I'd set him loose right now.

I study the Chain Bridge span and wonder again why Elizabeth's kidnappers would go that way to get out of town. The obvious choice would be to stay west on Canal Road, then up the GW parkway to the Capital Beltway. Why take this old bridge up into the rich Virginia neighborhoods over there?

I feel the tapestry of what really happened reveal itself briefly. Could it be they really didn't take Elizabeth overseas—could she be nearby instead? Another thread pulls tight. I think about the Elizabeth Hartner hostage tape, where she was so visibly animated. What was she trying to tell us?

I dial Sammy on my cell. He says, "John, we need you over here. Pronto."

"Sammy, I'll be there. Are you still in the FBI building...do you have access to Elizabeth's hostage video tape?"

"Yes, but I'm leaving the lab right now. What's up?"

"Run it one more time. Help me confirm something."

"John, this better be good. Whatever you hope to find won't count for squat now."

"Just do it, Sammy. Run the tape one more time."

A distant blue heron flies to the pond and begins rooting.

Sammy comes back. "I've got it rolling, John. What am I supposed to see?"

"Look at Elizabeth's hands. Are they ever clenched together?"

"They are briefly, but then they separate again."

"Rewind it. Study the index fingers. Do they come together to form a peak?"

"For a moment, yes."

"Keep watching her hands. Do they come together again, later?"

"Right at the end. She opens her palms with her finger still locked. It's all meaningless. Her hands are making other gestures as well."

"Sammy, I think that's only to disguise what she was signaling."

"You're telling me she was communicating to us the whole time?"

"Yes, yes. I believe she's using a simple childhood game to communicate. Rohini told me Elizabeth taught it to Raul Gutab for fun, and in doing so, realized her captors wouldn't be familiar with it. *'Here's the church, here's the steeple, open the door, and where's the people?'* She's signaling she's in a church, Sammy. A church, with no people!"

"I can buy it if you look at it that way. But what good does it do us now? There are a million frigging churches on this planet. Which one is she in?"

My cell phone battery dies, and Sammy's gone.

I put it away, and exhale deeply for the first time in weeks. He's right. Even if we could delay Aswan's release, how to find that single church, now?

The river tells me a moment later.

I look across its white churning water, then up the cliffs, to the big homes above. Upriver, I see it. It makes me shiver that I never saw it before. A portion of its peeling white steeple is rising above the trees. An abandoned church.

I feel like I should go for it, right now, and confirm this notion. I should call Sammy and let him know what I've seen. What would he say? *"So she's right up there on the cliff, in the old church? Nice convenient location. Have you been up there, John? Have you been inside? Have you seen her? You only have a bunch of theory. Verify, John, verify."*

Okay.

I speed across Chain Bridge into Virginia, turn right onto Chain Bridge Road, then drive up the hill past the million-dollar homes. Am I crazy to think they'd keep Elizabeth Hartner captive right here in this neighborhood? When I come upon the old church I stop and study the scene. The church is undergoing renovation, and is sealed off at the street by a chain-link fence. Bulldozers are grading the grounds. Carpenters are fitting on new oak siding. They look over at me momentarily and resume talking. I turn around in a big driveway and head back. As I pass by one more time, the workers are walking toward the church.

There's that gait again. That stride I've seen before. This time, dressed in overalls and with a nail bag around his waist. It's my man. It's

Chameleon. The guy who photographed me weeks ago, in a jumpsuit. The same guy at the Mid-East Market at dawn the next day, dressed in a suit.

Should I call Sammy and reveal this? What if I'm wrong? I'm going to stop Gerald Aswan's release from jail for a last-minute police raid on an old renovated church? I'll jeopardize Elizabeth's welfare based on a gut call. I hesitate. How to access this church?

The river.

I drive back across the river, down toward the beaver pond. It begins to sprinkle outside. I park, walk out to the water, and look upstream. The church is a quarter mile upriver. I walk along the bank till I'm directly across, looking up at the old white building. A tall chain-link fence guards the rear grounds at the cliff. The rain is starting to pound now, and the men are moving inside.

There is no way to get over there but across the water in front of me. The weather is bad, and the visibility is getting worse. If only I could swim across, I could reach the other rocky bank and climb up. But the current is moving fast, and I'll be swept downstream before I can get halfway across. I trek farther upstream a hundred yards and look across the river to the church grounds. The workers are all inside. Now.

I plunge into the river and swim hard.

The current is moving me so fast, I know I'll miss the other side. I see a fallen sycamore ahead and swim for its huge, half-sunken trunk. I slam into it, then spin past, grabbing for limbs, but they slip from my hands. I feel myself rushing along again until my pants yank me to a halt and pull me under. I'm trapped in the current, caught by a deep branch. I gasp, take a big breath, go under, and release my pants.

The river spins me loose and drives me into a crotch of slimy, fallen branches. I hang on for a few seconds, my arms anchored on its slick bark. I climb up and steady myself and shimmy down its main trunk. Rain is pounding so hard I can't see the other side I just swam from.

My clothes weigh me down, and my arms burn. A minute later, I wearily crawl up on the bank of the rocky Virginia shore.

I look up to the steep cliff above me. There is no way up these slick rocks but a path I must make myself.

I feel blinding pain now, as my right pinky finger throbs. It feels like a razor cut; I look down but see no blood at all. Then I hear it come echoing through the rain—a young woman's scream.

I have no idea whose voice that is, but it doesn't matter. The rocks are huge slippery slabs, mossy, lacking handholds. I get ten feet up and see it's useless. I hear distant sobbing now. I start another route with more urgency and get up the cliff a dozen yards, then reach an end. This route cannot get me there either. I climb down, slip at the last moment, and fall down to the shore's rocky soil.

This time, I scan the whole cliff for a route that can get me up there. I see it downstream. The only way to get to it is to swim down there.

I slip back in the water, speed past the sycamore, and stroke hard for the shore, finding myself flying downriver faster than before. I see my landing spot ahead and swim frantically for it, feeling lost and cold. The riverbank greets me hard as I slam into the steep rocks. Here, there is no shore at all, only big, slick slabs. I haul myself onto a crevice and look up. It looks impossible.

This is my lonely beach, my Normandy invasion. There is no other way but straight up. One handhold at a time, I tell myself. I don't look up; I don't look down. I grab, pull, rest, and do it again. Soon, I'm halfway up, but an ancient fear stirs in me—heights. I push that fear away, but not before I look down. A fall here would shatter my skull.

The rain is pouring so hard—how can it pour like this without a pause? Where is God now, when I need him? I huddle there and wait a moment. I cannot climb any more until the rain slows. My watch reads 2:14 p.m. Aswan must be on his way out to freedom.

Then, as quick as it started, the rain passes. I move up the rocks a bit, and curse my body for its lack of strength.

I see an opening in the cliff above me. Ten more feet, and I can reach it. But there are no natural grips to get to it. Nor is there any way around it. I look down, and realize I'm in trouble. I cannot climb back down, and I don't think I can climb up anymore.

I hear sobs coming from the opening above. I grab hold of a flat rock and try to pull myself up. I lie spread out on the face of the wet cliff, and as the pitch lessens, I move up, inch by inch.

I can see the lip of the cave; it's slick and jagged. I pull harder and rise up to peer into the opening. A tunnel more than a cave, it's no place for a real refuge. My body would barely fit into it. I hear sobs again, softer now.

I pull myself up, almost onto the ledge, but my hand slips and I crash against the rock. I pant and recoup. If I slip again, I'll fall. A lucky handhold saves me, and I pull up into the narrow tunnel, my legs dangling out in space. I rest a moment and study the interior. It recedes back ten feet and then dead-ends. The light is dim, and no one is here.

Where is the voice coming from?

I crawl farther into the tunnel, and another childhood fear strikes me, one more powerful than the fear of heights: being buried. I look back out to the light and tell myself I can work my way back out later. The tunnel looks solid, even ancient. It's lasted this long without caving in. It will hold a few minutes longer.

There's crying, now. I hear it from within the tunnel, and realize the opening doesn't dead-end; it runs off to the right.

With every inch that I move deeper in comes a rising dread of entrapment. The light's growing dimmer. The air's growing thicker, and I feel like I can't breathe. I have no idea what's around that corner. As I reach the turn in the tunnel, steel bars greet me a foot away. I pull myself closer to the bars.

On the other side it's dark, and I see nothing. But I hear breathing; I hear moaning. My eyes adjust to the big, cavernous room below. This tiny barred window sits at its top. Down at the bottom I see it, a filthy bed and trash everywhere. I look around the room, but see no one.

Then, there's a movement. A figure in the far corner rises and stands motionless, cradling their hand to their chest. A woman.

144

CHAPTER EIGHTEEN

She's staring straight ahead and whispering to herself.

I scan the room, looking for her captors. No one's there. I see a steel door on the side wall, solidly closed. She hasn't seen me up here.

"If you're Elizabeth Hartner," I whisper down to her, "nod your head. Don't speak. I'm here to help you."

She looks around slowly, saying nothing. She grows still again.

"Are you injured?"

She sits down against the floor and buries her head. She sobs lightly.

"Nod your head, Elizabeth. I'm really here."

She looks around in disbelief. She wants to nod her head, but waits.

"I'll help you. Don't say a word. I'm up here, at the window. Look at me."

She slowly looks up. I see her muddy, desperate face. The soul whom I've searched for for so long is down there. She looks like she did in my dreams.

After a long moment she nods her head.

I give a thumbs up. I want to scream. "Can they hear us talking?"

"I think they've gone…who are you?" she whispers.

"I'm John Wiley. I'm a police detective."

She stares up at me. She can only see my silhouette. "You're lying…"

"Believe me. I'm not here to torment you."

"This can't be real," she says quietly. "I've come to believe I'll never see home again."

"Yes, you will. We'll make that happen. What have they done to you?"

She says darkly, "They've just cut half my finger off."

I lean back in the rock tunnel and stare up at the sandstone. I look at my own hand and know that, somehow, I felt her finger being severed earlier. I fight back tears. I curse my lack of detective skills for not unraveling her clue sooner. "How's your wound?"

"I wrapped it with a sock. It's bleeding less."

"Don't let go of your courage, Elizabeth. Hang on. This will end soon. I know you've been strong. I know you've gone away in your mind so much of the time. You've survived that way. You're one tough girl."

"How'd you know about that?"

"I've been working on your case for months. I was brought in by your father and DC police to help find you. I've sensed your torment. I'm good at that sort of thing."

She sits quietly.

"Why did they cut you, Elizabeth?"

She whispers, "Something didn't happen on time! So, they held me down and sliced my fingertip off and put it in a plastic bag and sealed it shut. They photographed my bloody hand. They said they're going to send a little piece of me to my father because he missed a deadline. Help me, please."

Glitches must have surfaced with Aswan's release. But what? Her captors retaliated forcefully.

"I'll help you," I say. "Keep your bandage tight. Stay still. We'll need to move quickly. When do they come to see you?"

"Every few hours. But you can't beat them. They have my whole world under their control."

"Wrong. We'll punish them all. They missed the clue you sent us in the videotape. They're vulnerable."

She looks up at me. "You understood?"

"Yes, I did."

I see her face brighten. "I can't see you," she says. "What do you look like?"

"I'm tall, and kind of skinny. I'm twenty-seven."

"Do you have short blond hair and dark brown eyes?"

"Yes," I say.

She's quiet for a long time. Then, she says, "I've sensed you too."

146

"I'm glad."

"How's that possible?" she says.

"Many things are possible, including the most important one, getting you out of here."

"How can you do that? There are so many of them."

"Tell me everything you know about them. I need to know their weaknesses. We don't have much time."

She looks up at me with dark, swollen eyes, searching my image.

"Three guards come to check on me every few hours. They open the door, come in, say nothing, and just look at me. They always study the room. They think I'm going to dig my way out of here. They give me something to eat only once a day. I'm always famished, so I eat it all. Rice, and rotten-smelling fish, and warm water. The meal will arrive just as the darkness comes to my window up there, where you are. Where does that window go?"

"It's a tunnel, high up in the cliff overlooking the river. It's an old structure. Perhaps part of slave quarters from a plantation."

"Yes," she says. "When they dragged me down here, months ago, I remember the halls walled with old planks, and the floor was dirt. It was like a maze getting here."

"Have they ever let you out?"

"Never."

"They brought you down here through that old abandoned church above?"

"Yes. Late at night, with all the lights out. Through the main sanctuary, then down a flight of stairs to a small room. Many were waiting for me. They beat me badly, then dragged me in here."

"So, the way you came in is a no-go?"

She says, "Too many men that way."

"They're all over up top at the church too. The bastards are pretending to renovate the place. They're a very well-organized group of criminals."

"Can't you call for help now?"

"I have no phone," I say. "I could climb back down, but it would be hours till I could return with a police force. I can't abandon you now, so we'll have to do it together. Can you help me?"

"Yes," she says.

At that moment the door to her cell swings open, and men move in quickly, surrounding her. I duck back out of the way and gaze down into her cell. They stand above her in the dim light. One is lean, the others bigger. "Who are you talking to, bitch?"

Elizabeth looks up at them. "Leave me alone…haven't you done enough? I'm talking to myself."

"You do that all day long. We know that tone. You sounded hopeful just now. Why?"

"I'm praying I will be released soon. I'm praying you'll get what you want."

"You're lying." He turns to the others. "Search everything again!"

They pull her away from the wall and sift through the trash scattered across the dirt floor. I see, out in the hallway, others.

The men stand over her slumped form, now crouched in the corner. The lean one says, "Better pray hard that your father has more fucking influence with his government. Or tomorrow we'll send a more intimate part of you back to him."

He turns and looks up at the window, saying nothing. He studies where I'm hiding, back in the darkness against the corner. He walks from the room with the others.

We wait a long time before talking again. They were near her door before. We cannot afford to let them uncover me, hidden in a hole on the side of this cliff with no weapon. I left my Glock in my truck. It's not the first time I've done that. For some reason, a handgun blocks me from seeing clearly. It's a dumb habit I should have broken long ago.

"I'm getting you out of here tonight," I whisper.

"How?"

"Through this window. I'm going to loosen the bars. It will take time, so be patient. There will be moments when I'll ask you to weep. I need a loud distraction to pull them free. When that's done, you'll throw me up your bed sheet. I'll strip it and tie it together. I'll form a harness and pull you out through this window. Got it?"

She stares up at me and whispers, "Thanks for helping me. Please, tell me one thing. Do you know a man named Raul Gutab?"

"I'm sorry, Elizabeth. He didn't make it."

She stares at the floor for a long time.

The five cast-iron window poles are more solidly in place than I thought. With a sharp rock, I chip away at the base of the first one for forty minutes before I finally see it jiggle. She cries out, and I grip its length, twist hard, and pull it free, splattering mortar chips down to the floor. I replace it in its hole and begin working on the next. She is more thrilled at this than anything that has happened in months.

"Quickly," I say, "scatter the chips around the room—out of the way. They cannot find them."

She moves weakly, her injured hand against her belly, finishing just as her door swings open. They're coming back now. She's lying on the bed facing the wall.

"What are you doing?" one demands.

Elizabeth stares up at them, saying nothing.

They move around the room, giving it a quick sweep. One plunks down her grimy dinner bowl. As they leave her dungeon, the slim one takes one last look around. He doesn't study my window.

We wait a few minutes, then she turns and looks to me. I start digging again. By the time the second pole pulls loose, I am bleeding from a cut on my palm. I pull out my shirt, tear off the front shirttail, and wrap it around my hand. Pink quickly appears in the white.

She's eating her food like a starving extra in a Hollywood movie. I can smell its stench up here. I swear her next meal will be at her father's home. Orange, then blue light, then darkness, comes down my tunnel. Bats are screeching outside the hole. My back is aching.

The third pole is not like the other two. It has been re-cemented recently. New mortar encases it on top and bottom. I change tools from the small, smoky quartz dagger I have been using to a bigger one.

Little by little the new cement gives way. I soon see moonlight bathing the entrance of the shaft.

They have not come for hours. She has her candle lit, her only light source. It's enough illumination that we can look at each other from time to time. I know they will surprise us soon, so I am very slow, very methodical. She has been scattering all my mortar chips. They do not come.

The third pole is spinning in my hands. It's slick with my blood as I pull it free, then reset it again.

"Which way will we go once we crawl out from the tunnel?" she whispers in the amber room.

"Whichever way looks the easiest."

"Is one way easier than the other?"

"No."

The sound of a rope slapping the stone outside the tunnel reaches my ears.

I back out slightly and see a thick climbing rope dangling past the opening. It wiggles as the man on it begins to rappel down. They're coming to check the tunnel. I'm trapped. I shinny back in and look down into her cell.

"They are coming down from outside," I say.

She stares at me. "Then you must come inside here!"

I look back and see the rope swaying back and forth. In seconds there will be a man with a flashlight and a gun, looking in on me. Not a good way to die.

I crawl over to the bars and pry free the three loosened ones, revealing a one-by-two-foot opening. I can't fit. I don't have time to loosen the next pole.

"You can make it," she says.

"I can't."

"You said you were skinny. Prove it!"

I hand her the poles, then push my head through into her cell. My shoulders catch on the opening. I back out, then push my arms through, then try again. "Push," she whispers. "Push!"

I wriggle hard, scraping my arms and ribs as my body passes painfully through the hole. She comes over and says, "Hold onto my back. I will keep you from falling."

I reach down and place my arms on her shoulders. She feels weak, like old porcelain china, close to fracturing. I lower down and finally touch the ground. I pull her bed over to the wall, stand on the iron headboard, and reseat all the steel bars back in place. We peer up and see, seconds later, a bright flashlight beam illuminating the tunnel. Then, voices in the hall.

"Under my bed," she says.

"What?"

"They'll never look underneath it."

I drag her bed back across the room, crawl under it, and ball up tight. She throws her filthy sheet over the front and sides, then lies down. I hear her scared breath against the wall.

Her cell door opens, and boots walk past, stopping in front of her bed.

"What do you want now?" Elizabeth spits out.

The boots move close. A slap rings out. "Bitch, shut your face!"

He yells up to the tunnel man. "No one?"

A distant voice says, "No, nothing. It's clear."

"Then get back up top and maintain your post. Next time, get down that cliff faster. Any fool could have seen you coming."

Another slap echoes. Elizabeth cries out.

"Don't ever talk to me that way again, slut, or I'll cut you open, top to bottom."

On the mattress above me, I see her body leaning against the wall. I hear her tears.

The boots move away toward the door, then they stop. He could be looking at the window bars. From a distance they look okay, but walk close and he'll see they are loosened.

A hellish thirty seconds pass. They say nothing, and Elizabeth turns to the wall. She does not want them to see her face; perhaps it will give it all away. When the door slams shut, I think they're tricking me. I cannot move for many minutes. I barely breathe, and Elizabeth does not utter a sound.

Now, her good hand comes down from the bed.

I roll out and stand up. She's shivering, and in a panic. Her black hair is matted, and her eyes are sunken and haunted. I sit down next to her and take her bandaged hand in mine. Her body sends me a most intense sensation, as if all the feelings I've had about her were only weak carbon copies of the real agony she's in. There's such despair in her heart, and there's only pockets of sanity left. She's nearing a breakdown. Yet beneath all of it is a distant but clear, good thing. Anger. "They have brutalized you?"

"Yes," she whispers.

"Have they raped you?"

"Not physically, but in every other way."

"They're animals," I say.

"Yes."

"Then keep that fury close to you. Don't let it go. We'll need all your rage."

"Why?"

"To make your body do what it may not be capable of doing, to escape with me. If you're too slow, or too weak, we'll be caught, and all of this will be for nothing. If you're strong and we get out of here, then your revenge will be very sweet. We'll slip right out from under their noses, proving how stupid and weak they are. They have guns, but we've got brains. We've got them outfoxed so far. We've won the first round, but there are many more rounds to fight. Ready?"

She sits up. "I can't do it. I'm scared they'll catch us and cut me again. And they'll kill you."

"You weren't meant to go through all that you have only to give up now. And I'm far too stubborn to let you slip through my fingers."

I hoist her up; she pulls the bars away, and she crawls up into fresh air of the tunnel. I grab the fixed bars and pull myself up, realizing I cannot insert myself into the opening on my own. I will need to get down, pull the bed over, and stand on the headboard. But I hear voices in the hall, and she looks back at me. "Grab my feet. I'll pull you up."

I reach in and grab her ankle. She begins pulling me up with a power I didn't feel she could bring forth. Little by little, I twist and turn up into the opening.

"Keep crawling toward the outside," I whisper.

"It looks wonderful out there. I can smell the river."

"Don't get too excited."

She reaches the outside of the tunnel and stands up weakly on the ledge. "It's raining…it feels so good."

"Stay down. There's a guard up top, watching the river."

I crawl out, stand up, and we lean against the rock. I look up the cliff and see no one. Hard rain is moving in now, and the wind is picking up. Down below, the river looks dark and swift.

Angry voices echo out from the cell tunnel. "Where the fuck is she?"

I untie her bed sheet, wrap it around her waist, and quickly lower her down to the next boulder. Her face recedes in the dark, like a ghost, and I wonder if all this is only a dream, if I'm only wishing I could do all this. But the furious voices behind me are all too real. A face at the other end of the tunnel is staring at me.

"My gun!" he screams.

The man vanishes. A handgun emerges from the hole, and a boom erupts. I look down at myself, searching for blood. Another shot wails. He's shooting without aiming. I jump to the edge and look down at her. "Hurry!" she screams.

I pull up the sheet, slip it in a crack, lean over the cliff, and race down, knowing the guard in her cell cannot get through the narrow opening. Two more shots ricochet past me as I move down to Elizabeth.

Searchlights whip all around us, but we are below the abutment, and their beams don't reveal us. I point to the rock slabs below. She slips over the edge, and I see her bandaged hand is wet with blood. Her eyes are lost, all of this another dream for her. She has gone away again, like she has all these months. I lower her down again, and she touches down on a slippery boulder tip.

I slide my chest down on the slick surface, but my grip is shaky in the pounding rain. I fall, slamming into stone without knowing what's coming. The breath is crushed from my lungs. A long red gash opens up on my thigh. I try and catch my breath, but it only comes in gasps.

We must move sideways to reach the shore, but it will mean being more visible from above. We creep over the boulder tips, then down along a thin ledge. We are twenty feet from the shore. I lower her once more, and she reaches the sand and stands up, astonished. I lean over, yet feel no footholds. I will have to jump.

The light above suddenly finds me, illuminating my face. Climbing ropes are flying down the cliff, one landing near me. I grab it and slide down its length toward Elizabeth, but I feel a man on it, its tension rocking me against stone. Bursts of gunfire spray around me. Rock shards pierce my face, and my skin is splattered with blood. I reach the shore, grab her, and look up. Another rope is spiraling down, a second man coming.

"In the water now, and I'll follow you!" I command.

She's panicked. "You didn't tell me about this; I can't swim."

"Too bad. It's the river or them…"

We look up and see men rappelling down past our tunnel.

"Go," she pleads. "Leave me, I can't make it any farther."

"Wrong answer," I say, pulling her over to the rapids.

"I'll drown!"

I drag her down to a splintered log, lash her to its length with the sheet, and yank her to the edge. She won't look at the churning river. "No!"

"Follow instructions," I say, shoving her into the tossing, dark river. She shoots away in the current, clinging fearfully to the log.

The first blow to my head feels like a fist, and I turn and see the man preparing another strike. He's smiling. "We will kill you both."

He steps in for the punch but slips on the rocks, falling against me. He claws to regain his footing, pulls out a flashing blade, and spears at my leg. I step aside and crash my fist into his jaw. I strike again, slamming his temple, and he slumps down, motionless.

As I leap into the river, another man is on me, clutching me as I dive. His fingers claw my face, as the cold water spins us around like a tornado. I surface, catch a breath, and try to push him away. He's not surfaced, and will not let go of my waist.

We churn through the tossing rapids, approaching the bridge, its iron span brooding darkly above us. This crazy river is mad with fresh rain, bigger, faster—possessed. Now I feel hot, piercing pain as his blade chops in the waves, and I stroke hard and yank free of him. He surfaces and swims at me in a rage. Waiting for him to grow near, I kick underwater, catching him in the groin, and he vanishes.

Flying downstream in the dark, I pitch high in the waves. Dim lights on the shore give me no bearing; this is no river—it's an ocean of freezing swells. I see a brief glimpse of Elizabeth, twenty yards ahead. Her log is bobbing high, her dark hair standing out against the white bark. As I approach, I see a swimmer moving toward her. A glint of his blade flashes in the waves.

I swim harder, yet I grow no closer. How did he reach her so quickly? His form grows close to her, and I feel sick that I am so far away. She screams out. I take a dozen powerful strokes and submerge, swimming hard in the darkness till I see his legs. I come around him, surface, and slam a headlock against his throat.

We spin around underwater, his blade swiping in violent jabs. I surface and swim back toward Elizabeth, her body twisted around the trunk so powerfully, she's gasping. I rotate the log and loosen the sheet from around her waist.

"Look!" she gasps.

I turn just as he surfaces from below, his knife spearing down on us, slamming into the log's midsection. He tries to pry it loose, but it has sunk too deep, and he dives away, down into the darkness.

"I can't hold on any more...I swallowed too much water!"

"Hang on, we're almost there."

"He's down there. He's coming back, the one who cut my finger!"

"We're swimming for the shallows. Okay?"

I roll her on top of the log, and she floats high, her face free of the waves. She stops gasping and closes her eyes for an instant.

"He's got me...!"

Her body sucks below, down in the river, vanishing. Only her lashings keep her from going all the way under. I dive down and see his murderous face beside her. He spears his hand at me, catching me in the throat. I surface, gag, spit water, then dive back down. Elizabeth's face is wailing under the water. He's jabbing, keeping me away a few moments more, drowning her with his other hand. But he's unaware of something.

I've un-lodged his blade from the log, and whip its edge from behind my back, piercing him in one powerful thrust. I plunge harder, driving it all the way to the brass pommel. He releases his grip from her leg. Blood swirls around us in rich plumes, and his eyes begin to grow still. It's him. The Chameleon.

He floats away in the currents now, in weightless death.

We paddle toward Fletcher's Boathouse landing, where the thick, cold sand greets our numb feet. The mad river has reluctantly lets us go, for now. I pull her up on shore, untie her from the log, and carry her up on the coarse, wet grass. Her bandages are gone from her hand. I see what they have done to her.

She weeps deeply now, for the first time, without any fear.

CHAPTER NINETEEN

"I got her. I got Elizabeth!"

"John, where the hell you been?"

"Did you hear me?"

"I don't understand. You've got Elizabeth where?"

"Sammy, she's standing beside me here at the old boathouse, upriver. She's in bad shape. But she's alive. Cancel Aswan's bail. Don't release Aswan!"

"How the hell …where was she?"

"Underneath an old church atop the river cliffs—captive in the underground caves. She's free."

"John—it's really her?"

"Yes, yes. We're at the pay phone. I lost my truck keys in the river."

I hand the receiver to her. "Tell Detective Sammy Chung it's you."

She cradles the phone in her shaking hands. "I don't know how he did it but he got me out of there," she utters. "It's me, Uncle Sammy, it's Lizzy." A warm, relieved conversation passes between them, then she hands me back the receiver.

Sammy's ecstatic. "John, amazing job, young man. We're on our way. Are you in any danger?"

"I see no pursuit, but others may be on their way. Surround the Old Riverside Church up on Chain Bridge Road. They're up there, Sammy. Aswan's whole group."

"We will, John. But we have little hope right now. I'm sure they're all gone."

"Sammy, we just busted out of there!"

"John, Gerald Aswan was released a few hours ago."

"What happened?"

"Aswan's bail release at 2:00 p.m. earlier today was temporarily blocked. Homeland Security revealed that his identity is linked with major terrorist groups around the world. Two hours after his delay, Elizabeth's severed fingertip and photo were delivered to the senator's home. Hartner immediately pleaded with a circuit court magistrate to re-review just Aswan's traffic case and had Aswan released on bail."

"Was the money wired to Aswan's account?"

"Yes, unfortunately."

"Where's Aswan location now?"

"Aswan's group had a dozen men, including two body doubles, waiting outside the Alexandria city jail. When he walked out, they all mixed together, then got into different cars and sped off in different directions. All airports and major highways were monitored. We think he was driven from the city, then flown by helicopter to a waiting ship off the coast.

"Basically, John, we lost Gerald Aswan."

In the big library of Senator Hartner's home are a dozen people. I'm sitting in the middle of a big sofa, with Elizabeth and Senator Hartner on either side of me. Mrs. Hartner is in a velvet chair, eyeing me like a long-lost son. Director Berkenson, Police Chief Harris, Sammy, Woods, and others in law enforcement are eating fragrant hors d'oeuvres on fancy china. Outside, swat teams are guarding the premises. I'm stitched up, with knife wounds on my shin and thigh. Elizabeth's pinky finger spent four hours in surgery and was sewn back together by the best surgical team on the East Coast. Gloria Sullivan's front page article on her portrayed Elizabeth as a tough, creative survivor.

A sense of closure is permeating the city. The smiles in the room are genuine. There is a new bond that formed between the senator and Elizabeth the moment they hugged a week ago, a bond that may not have existed before. Happy people celebrating the outcome of a criminal investigation is a rare sight for me. At this stage of a case,

I'm usually leaving the morgue or walking from a courtroom as a convicted murderer is taken away.

There is something wrong with this picture. There is a man still out there who got away with too much criminal mayhem. He's the source of a nationwide manhunt, soon to be international. I feel he will never be found.

Homeland Security has been vague about the exact nature of Gerald Aswan's identity. They are not happy he was released on bail. His relationship with organized world terrorism is certain, but his exact role is not being divulged. His primary domestic crime is suspicion in orchestrating the Elizabeth Hartner kidnapping and ransom demands. That is enough to raise him to the top of the FBI most-wanted list, a notoriety that doesn't come easily.

My role now is unclear as I sit here. Chief Harris has offered me a permanent post as a senior homicide detective here in the city. It's tempting, but I really don't feel comfortable in DC, though I certainly know the Potomac River pretty well. If I do stay bureaucratic layers that I skirted during Elizabeth Hartner's disappearance would soon become an ongoing obstacle.

In Asheville, they tolerated me; they know my dad. In DC, I'm popular for the moment, but the grins will soon vanish when I begin to disappear off on my own again. Woods knows this about me better than anyone. She was not reprimanded for her doctored resume, as threatened. Sammy pushed it under the carpet and, instead, hired her.

I need to go home. But there is the problem of Tara Chin.

Her image was always in the back of my mind during Elizabeth's rescue. When I saw Elizabeth's face, I also saw hers. Tara floated around as I entered the high tunnel, and pulled at the bars, and got shot at. The deadly fight in the sweeping waves of the river seemed to bring her along. She was shadowy, not always readable, obscure—phony sometimes. But also, caring. I seem only to remember that aspect. I say "remember" because she hasn't returned my calls. She came to the Four Seasons, to the room I booked for us. She took the note I left, then vanished.

I've been so hammered with interviews and briefings, I haven't had time to go by Tara's. I want to see in her eyes the respect she must have for me. After leaving the Hartners' dinner celebration, I find myself driving to Agnes Sloan's Georgetown townhouse. I have reservations about the relationship I had with Tara.

I walk up the old brick steps of the townhouse. I ring the bell and wait, feeling foolish, feeling like it's a first date. Mrs. Sloan answers the door with a bright smile. She takes my hands.

"Congratulations, Mr. Wiley, on your super police work. The whole town is thrilled."

"Not really, Mrs. Sloan. But I know you are. Where is your young boarder this evening?"

"Tara left last week. Said she was doing more thesis research in the mountains. You didn't know?"

"No."

"She wanted to be with you but said she had to leave town. You called her cell phone?"

"No answer, Mrs. Sloan. Where did she say she was going?"

"Little Washington…out near the valley."

"Thank you, have a good evening."

I step down to my truck, then move around the side of her home and into her small backyard. I step over to the French doors, peer in, and study Tara's darkened room. Nothing exceptional but one thing: the bed is made. I always had to pull her covers up before I lay down.

I drive out Route 211 toward Little Washington, Virginia, where the pastures swell like green tidal waves, frozen on their way somewhere. Last month we spent one weekend out here at The Inn, as it is called, a very comfortable establishment. Now, as I return to this tiny mountain town, I sense Tara is not here.

They remember me, and have one room vacant. Its tiny fireplace is blazing when I step in. I sit back, watch the sun go down, and order dinner. Squab and wine and a rich dessert all flow into my mouth without pleasure. The sheets feel too cold and too starched. I sleep.

I'm up at dawn, back on the solitary roads of this Virginia mountain county named Rappahannock. In search of that valley that I saw in my dream. I move up windy Route 522 toward Front Royal, then turn back and move south again. The sun rises into deep western clouds, then rain moves in, sweeping across the pastures. My wipers cannot keep up with the torrents. By lunch, I head back to DC, alone.

"The man you called 'Chameleon' has been identified," Sammy says.

We're at the Tombs for our weekly half-pound burger. "He's a Lebanese national. His body was recovered, tangled in mooring lines in the Old Town boat harbor yesterday."

Sammy pauses. "Besides Raul Gutab, he is the only other member of the Aswan team to be positively identified."

"Any criminal record?" I ask.

"Has a history of criminal activity going back thirty years. Two prison terms for robbery and assault in Spain. His name is Phillipe Ottoman."

"Does Homeland Security have anything on him?"

"We're having trouble with them. Since their charter, they have been worse than the CIA about revealing info. Their composition is the seasoned best and brightest of the other agencies. They're used to doing everything in secret. Old-fashioned spooks who prefer good intelligence work to fancy satellite data. They'll dig something up on this Chameleon of yours. But it will take time."

"Why are you telling me this?" I ask.

"Because we need you—Asheville doesn't."

"To do what?"

"Bring in Aswan."

"He's gone, Sammy. Finding him will require time and energy from law enforcement around the world. I do the East Coast only."

"I know that. But there's a new task force forming under the direction of the NSA. All their raw intelligence data concerning any of Aswan's electronic activities will be available to this new team."

"For what purpose?"

"Revenge, John. The project's just been okayed by the Senate Select Committee on Intelligence. The senator wants Aswan's head for what he did to Elizabeth. He wants his money back, too. The team will be composed of a few from Elizabeth's kidnapping task force, but also personnel from the NSA. Time and money are no object."

"All those resources spent for revenge?"

"Technically, Aswan has now been labeled a terrorist. That gives us plenty of latitude to pursue him outside the normal realms of police work."

"Sammy, I'm a detective, not an intelligence analyst."

"We'll stretch you a bit."

"No travel?"

"Not unless you want to."

"All of our activities will be outside of Homeland Security."

"They'll know about us," Sammy says, "but they will pretend they don't. Their jurisdiction encompasses all terrorism within the US. But this one is ours."

"I'll need Woods."

"We know."

I sense I'm going to stay. I want revenge too. Not just because of what Aswan did to Elizabeth's mind and body, but because of what's left unresolved. Hollowed out inside that strange shell is the mystery of Gerald Aswan—not the Sumerian god he wishes he was.

CHAPTER TWENTY

Tiny Francis Scott Key Park in Georgetown is deserted, except for Woods and me. "We're starting over, aren't we?" she wonders.

"Yes and no. Elizabeth's kidnapping is solved. But all the elements need to be sifted again. We're looking at an even bigger crime scene than before."

"Why?"

"Because it's all part of the same transgression. Gerald Aswan's existence is the real crime. Elizabeth Hartner just happened to get in the way. Her abduction was never about money. Aswan gladly took it, but the real issue was about his inconvenience. He was on his way out of town, killed a boy, then grew furious when he was detained. That's where we need to start. His massive, criminal ego."

"That's our weak spot," Woods says. "We have no data on him. Homeland Security has findings, but we're not going to see them."

"NSA may give us his electronic activities, but we need his history up to the point when he called for Elizabeth's abduction."

"Where do we start?"

"The morgue," I say.

We drive over to the campus, then move down into the basement of the GWU hospital where "Chameleon's" body is being held. We speak with the attending doctor, who presents us with the autopsy.

Woods reads it, then hands it to me.

"I know already," I say. "He bled to death from a deep knife wound to the abdomen."

"You had no choice, John."

"I have never killed a man before, Woods. At the time, it was all reflex. Do you think there will be other deaths on my hands before my career ends?"

"The world we inhabit is ruthless. We have to defend ourselves. It's part of our job."

We move over to the wall where a dozen corpses are stored. I pull open the drawer, slide it out, and pull the plastic back from Phillipe Ottoman's body. He is small, muscular, and fair-skinned, with black, thinning hair and a goatee. His belly wound is not as nasty as I imagined. A thin, clean slit is all there is. When I see dead folks, I always think they will suddenly rise up and wink in amusement. But this man is dead. I put my hand on him and hold it there for a long time. Distant horrors rise up from his flesh into me, for he is a killer of great accomplishment.

I put my hand on his belly and sense the defeat he felt when I knifed him in the river. He is a man with a complicated history, most of it cold-blooded and murderous. There is a driving compulsive nature to him that must have served him well in his profession. He was without much of a conscience, except for his godlike admiration for one particular person. The release of Gerald Aswan was so very important for him!

I see in him a familiar face. His chin, nose, and brow are sharply wrought, as if a plaster mold were employed in the creation of this death mask. I study him for a long time, then ask Woods, "Have you seen this man before?"

She nods. "The mouth is like Gerald Aswan's."

"Actually," I say, "the entire face bears a very close resemblance. Perhaps he's a relative. We'll need clarification on his criminal activities. Like a typical background check we do on any suspect."

"True," Woods says, "but Aswan's men are international criminals whose backgrounds are not accessible from our databases. Middle-Eastern connections are extensive, yet very vague and unwritten. What paper trail there is on them is so obscure that only deep undercover work will reveal it. We don't have people on the ground there."

"Well, short of flying to Yemen, what are our alternatives?"

"We'll have to suck it up and attend the NSA briefings and work with them."

I say, "We need an edge on Aswan. We need to know what Aswan thinks we cannot uncover about him."

"How can we do that?"

"We'll have to work outside the system."

"John…"

"Woods, you're going to come with me?"

"Where?"

"I know someone. He may help us."

"What's his name?" Woods asks.

"Sinclair Johnson."

"Where is he?"

"In maximum security, in North Carolina."

"For?"

"He hacked into the Pentagon's big mainframe a few years ago and planted a nasty virus in those big servers that knocked them out for two weeks. He's world class."

"I'll be glad to join you, John. But only unofficially. I can't jeopardize my new post with the DC police."

"You won't have to, Woods. All you have to do is talk to him."

"Why me?"

"He's a big, cocky black man who hates white folks. He'll talk to you…"

"Is he dangerous?"

"If he saw me, he might become so."

"Did you put him away?"

"No, I kept him out of the electric chair."

"Then why the hatred?"

"I'll tell you on the way down."

I relay the strange story of Sinclair Johnson to Woods as we drive south toward Raleigh, North Carolina.

"I first heard about him when I was in high school," I say. "Johnson was the star fullback on a Durham, North Carolina, high school football team whose record was always ten-zero at the end of the season. They beat every team in the state, and it was always because of his physical skills. Johnson was big, fast, and agile as a cat. On top of that, he was a brilliant student who had a free ride to any college in the country. At Florida State, he set rushing football records all four years. Afterward, Johnson returned home, got picked up by a Research Triangle telecom firm, got married, and began living happily ever after. Then, trouble started."

Woods muses, "It's either gambling or drugs."

"The latter. Johnson developed a nasty steroid addiction in college. It soon bloomed into cocaine, then, finally, methamphetamine addiction. Toss in a weakness for bourbon, and within a few years, he was divorced, unemployed, and saddled with multiple DWIs. All those brains couldn't help him."

"Men are so predictable," Woods decides.

"The story's not over, Detective," I say. "For a local boy to fall so fast from grace was big-time news down there. To escape the notoriety, he moved from Raleigh up into the mountains near where I lived. He rented a shack and got toasted day and night. He made money working for a company in Silicon Valley, all of it done remotely from his home. Johnson was a genius in designing security systems and firewalls for corporate LANs that were more effective than anything on the market."

"All while drunk?"

"He claimed it helped him to be creative," I say. "Sinclair Johnson was badly addicted and alcoholic, but he was never a criminal. His drug supplier, a big-time meth and cocaine dealer named Archer, definitely was. A pistol fight one snowy night on an abandoned mountain road left Archer dead and lots of incriminating evidence pointing toward Sinclair Johnson."

"Were you in on the original investigation?"

"I was working another case, but I followed it. The county's prosecuting attorney felt the evidence was overwhelming and charged Johnson with murder one. There were fingerprints and personal items in Archer's car that belonged to Johnson. The motive was revenge. Johnson had been seen numerous times arguing with Archer in a local bar."

"Johnson had no alibi?"

166

"He claimed he was alone at home the night of Archer's murder. But no one could back him up."

"Was there really a motive on Johnson's part?"

"Sure. Archer stuck it to Johnson, charging him double for the drugs, knowing he had money. Archer was a good old boy from the Smokey Mountains, and he enjoyed the fact that the famous Sinclair Johnson was so dependent on his wares. He taunted him a lot."

"Sure he didn't really kill him?"

"At first I wasn't sure. But later, after I got involved, it was apparent Sinclair Johnson couldn't have killed Archer."

"Why did you get involved?"

"In my dreams I saw Johnson being set up for a crime he didn't do. I studied the case, then uncovered evidence proving his innocence. I kinda stepped on a bunch of toes. But, hell, I was right."

"What happened?"

"Johnson's DNA was all over Archer's car—hair, spit, cigarette butts, the works. The two of them hung out sometimes and did lots of drugs in the vehicle. The bullet in Archer's head was a .38, a slug from a handgun similar to a weapon later found in Johnson's shack. Ballistics didn't match, but the State argued Johnson owned many guns and had thrown the real murder weapon away that night. Banking records revealed numerous checks Johnson had written to Archer for drugs. Witnesses lined up against him, testifying that resentment was the motive for this famous young black man's murder of a local white kid. It looked bad for Johnson."

"Then, you stepped in…"

"Well, I had to. The State's case was all circumstantial. I spoke at length with Johnson's attorney, who finally let me interview Johnson. He distrusted me, thinking I was secretly working for the prosecution. I don't think he's aware I was the one who came up with the answer."

"What answer?"

"Johnson's alibi was that he was home, alone, working that night. But there were no witnesses. There was one form of verification, however, that everyone overlooked. An electronic witness. Sinclair Johnson's drinking problems were so bad he suffered from memory blackouts. Yet, somehow, he could still function, working on the computer late into the night. Part of the security protocol for his job was password log-on. But that occurred only once earlier in the evening, giving Johnson plenty of time to go kill Archer and return. Only when I reviewed Johnson's computer activities for that night did I uncover an additional iris scan he had to employ for password ID. He'd used it throughout the evening, but because of his condition he couldn't remember. Iris scan is the ultimate proof of identity. It verified his alibi, proving he was home all night the evening of the murder. The jury agreed and acquitted him."

"Then who killed Archer?"

"Archer was murdered by a Jamaican drug runner whom Archer had ripped off weeks before. The man's now serving life."

"Then what's Johnson doing in jail?"

"After the trial was over, Johnson was bitter. He grew more and more isolated, and his drinking got worse. Finally, one night, he lost it and began invading highly secure government databases, which was effortless for him. Within a few weeks the FBI had arrested him for hacking into some of the most secure computer systems in the country. At his trial he admitted that his reasons were personal. The prosecuting attorney at the Archer murder trial was a former Pentagon JAG. Johnson hated the man, and he felt the US government was to blame for falsely accusing him of murder. He was merely inflicting the needed retribution on his own country."

"Didn't he know he would be caught for such blatant intrusions?'

"No, he was very careful. But someone who recently had become intimate with Johnson's computer skills and activities informed the FBI. They tapped his phone and quickly caught him."

"Who was the informant?"

"Me."

I'm sitting on the other side of a mirrored window, watching Woods talk with Sinclair Johnson in a secure interview room. He's big and ripped, obviously, from hitting the weights in all of his spare time.

His face looks more serene than the last time I saw him, two years ago. Drugs in this highly secure prison on the outskirts of Raleigh are probably available, even here. But he appears clean and sober.

Johnson leans back and closes his eyes. "I'm touched by your concern for my welfare, Detective Woods. There must be more to your visit. Why are you really here?"

"Because your expertise is needed."

"Which skills are you referring to?"

"Aren't you in here for breaching and then destroying government security databases?"

"Yes."

"That's the skill we're looking for."

"Woods," I whisper to myself, "I hope you know what you're doing."

Johnson stares at her for a moment, then laughs hard. "You're here to get me to break the law again?"

"No, not break the law, Sinclair. Use your talent for law-enforcement purposes. Interested?"

"Hardly. I'm banned from any computer use while I'm in here, then for another year after I'm released. That's in two years if I keep the parole board happy. What's in it for me?"

"Nothing, probably. Nothing but tracking down a very secretive, notorious criminal."

"Not interested at that price."

"What would it take?"

"More than you can pull off." Woods watches him move toward the door. He pauses. "Exactly which kingpin are we talking about?"

"Can't reveal that, Mr. Johnson."

"Then how can I help you?"

"You have to agree to help us. That's the first step. There will be many hurdles after that, but we may both benefit from the relationship."

Johnson walks back over and says, "Who's us?"

"Detective John Wiley and me. There may be others as well."

Johnson eyes her coldly. "That fucking bastard sent you in here, didn't he?"

"Yes."

"You know what he did to me?"

"He helped you."

"He put me in here!"

"You put yourself in here, Mr. Johnson."

"Nonsense. He purposely accessed my computer files, then used that information to finger me."

"Weren't you guilty of the crime?"

"Yes."

"Then Detective Wiley did what he was trained to do—apprehend law breakers. Did you expect him to look the other way while you zipped around the Internet, invading top-secret databases?"

"He set me up! He used my murder trial as an excuse to spy on my computer activities at my company. Then he turned me in two months later."

"John Wiley saved you from death row, Mr. Johnson. Aren't you aware of that?"

"Bullshit. How?"

"He was the one who discovered your forgotten use of iris scanning the night of Archer's murder. Had he not delved into your activities you may have been found guilty of a crime you never committed."

Johnson eyes Woods. "I was told by my attorney that he uncovered it. Not John Wiley."

"That's not true."

"How do you know all this?"

"I'm an associate of Detective Wiley."

"An accomplice is more like it."

Woods leans close. "Mr. Johnson, what I'm offering you is an opportunity to help yourself. If you can help us, your actions may go a long way with that parole board. They may look favorably on such cooperation."

"So it's blackmail?"

"No, just a chance to dig yourself out of your current hole. This kind of offer is seldom extended to a prison inmate."

"How do you know it will fly, Detective?"

"Leave that part to us."

Johnson says, "Sounds like the same old manipulation I've always heard. 'Sinclair, gimme just one more touchdown, one more championship, one more newspaper interview, one more patent agreement.' My whole life's been wasted helping other people get what they want."

"And you've been well rewarded. Most people would die for your skills, intelligence, and success. All of your life is in front of you, Sinclair. You can turn it all around, starting now. You still drinking?"

"Not today."

"Then blessings are already upon you. Don't let it stop now. What do you think?"

"Are you telling the truth about John Wiley uncovering that evidence in my trial?"

"Yes, I am."

Sinclair Johnson sits back and stares at Woods. For a long while there's nothing but silence. Eventually, he exhales. "All right. I'll help you."

From behind the glass I raise my fist and salute Woods's remarkable persuasion. Now, how can I make good on her offer? I lift my cell phone and call the only man who can help us, Senator Jack Hartner.

CHAPTER TWENTY-ONE

"Was any of this cleared with Sammy?" the senator asks.
"No."

"Where are you, now?"

"Watching Woods and Johnson through the one-way glass."

"You're down there already? Is he really the man who can help us, or is this a long shot?"

"He's the man," I say. "Off the record, many consider him the best hacker in the country. Not because he wants to destroy anything. He's just super-intelligent, creative, and, now, sober. That's a good combination. The problem is, he's in jail, Senator."

"Detective, I believe you. I think he would be an asset in tracking down Gerald Aswan. But there are limitations to even my influence."

"You managed to have Aswan released. Why not Johnson?"

"I knew that was coming. There's one big difference. Aswan wasn't convicted of anything. Johnson's doing time for treason. That's a much bigger fish to fry."

"Senator, I want this man released under my care. I will transfer him up to DC, and see that he's taken care of and very securely watched. If he runs, I'll take the responsibility."

"That could backfire if he vanishes, Detective. You could lose your badge."

"It's a chance I'm willing to take. Gerald Aswan's world is best viewed through the skilled mind of a man like Sinclair Johnson. He'll uncover all the hidden data on this criminal. He's our best way of finding him."

"If this gets out, I could be in a lot of hot water."

"Senator," I say, "you know, we never talked about the reward money you were going to pay me for finding Elizabeth."

"That's very true, Detective. I've been remiss in discussing it with you. You earned every penny of it. The reason I haven't come to you is—"

"Senator, I know. After that twenty-million-dollar funds transfer to Aswan, you are broke."

"I'm sorry. I'll pay you as soon as possible. I never forget a debt, especially one like this."

"Senator, I'm not about to try and collect on it. I told you some time ago I'm not in this business for the money."

"Detective, I remember well. But a deal's a deal. I owe you."

"Then return it in another form."

"And that is?'

"Have Sinclair Johnson temporarily transferred to my custody. In doing so, the debt will be cleared."

"Detective Wiley," Senator Hartner says after a long pause, "one day I would like you to come work for me."

"Why?"

"You would go far on Capitol Hill. Let me work on it."

It took exactly eighteen hours for the North Carolina penal authorities to release Sinclair Johnson to our custody. The official explanation in transferring him up to DC was termed "National Security—Sensitive."

His temporary relocation would fulfill an obligation for a routine interrogation about his Pentagon computer intrusion. No other details were given. North Carolina penal authorities complied.

Now, the following day, Woods, Johnson, and I are sitting in a sparse, three-bedroom apartment in the Watergate apartment complex, overlooking a gusty, wave-tossed Potomac. It's a spare Senate flat that Hartner has access to. I'm sure it's bugged to the hilt. Down in the lobby, a nondescript-looking agent waits patiently, preparing to shadow us wherever we go. On the sofa in our apartment is another agent, who says nothing. Both men's instructions are to kill Sinclair Johnson if he attempts to make one move out of the ordinary. I've learned his existence is far more significant than I thought. What he can do in cyberspace is feared by the US government.

Johnson is hesitantly facing a slew of bright computer terminals. He's in shock. Two years behind bars drained him of simple joys that he desperately wants to re-experience. As he sits there, I see him staring out at the river.

Tracking down Gerald Aswan is not really the first order of business for me—Vishava is, the mysterious company that possessed Elizabeth Hartner's diamond earrings six months before Gerald Aswan's men used them to bait her.

Though Johnson's top security clearance used to buy him access to many sources, his default instructions are to only use legal means in his Internet searches. Sooner or later, deeper penetration will be required. Then, it's my call to instruct him to breach the security of certain databases. The temporary use of this man will either get me in big trouble or get me closer to Aswan than the NSA group will ever get.

Taking Elizabeth Hartner for a ride in the country is not easily accomplished, but she needs it badly. Her father won't allow her the freedom of her old lifestyle until Aswan is behind bars. Few believe the man is content to leave them alone. Why not go back to the Hartner money well once again, some day in the future?

Security at the Hartner residence is tight. I walk in and find Elizabeth in the library—she's ashen faced and staring at her wounded finger. Her mood instantly brightens when she sees me. After five phone calls and two hours, Senator Hartner allows her to come along, but armed security will follow us.

Soon, we are far to the west, moving south on the Blue Ridge Parkway, with glimpses of lonely farms filtering through the trees. My Toyota slows through the hairpin turns as we rise and fall along the two-lane road. I've left Detective Woods to tend to Sinclair Johnson, further building on the chemistry they seem to have established.

"Elizabeth, are you feeling okay today?"

"I am since I'm with you. Still lots of nightmares."

"When you feel safe, they will pass."

"Then I will always have them."

"Not true. Taking control of your life will help; that's one reason I brought you out here."

"You're always on task, aren't you?"

"True, and for today, you're my special assistant. I need your help. I'm worried about a friend of mine. She disappeared days before you were rescued. She hasn't been seen since."

"Is she connected to Aswan?'

"No. But somehow, I can't move on with his investigation until I know she's okay."

"What can I do?"

"Just as I dreamed of you being held captive nearby, I'm now dreaming about my friend, Tara. In my most recent dream, you call me up to the mountaintop to see more clearly. Have you dreamed that?"

"I would be happy to have that dream instead of my nightmares. This may be a waste of time," she says. "I'm not the psychic type."

"All folks are the psychic type. My special muscles are simply in better shape than most. Tell me about your nightmares."

Elizabeth closes her eyes. "I'm somewhere dark and cold. I'm hiding, staying still, because in my dreams, I'm still running from them. They're around every corner, steps away from finding me. I run every night. When I awake in the morning, I'm exhausted."

"Do they catch you?"

"No, but they're on the verge."

"Then do something about that nightmare."

"What?"

"Break the illusion it has over you."

"How?"

"When you have that dream again, don't resist. Let them catch you. Prove to yourself that they can't hurt you."

"I can't do anything heroic in my dreams but run in a panic."

"I'm not suggesting for you to be strong in your dreams, Elizabeth. I'm suggesting you surrender in them. You never allowed yourself to do that when they held you captive. Your courage got you through the real nightmare. You don't have to be strong in your dreams now. You just have to break the dream's grip. Giving in will help. And it will help me, as well."

"How will it help you find her?"

"I don't know yet."

After riding the Virginia Skyline Drive for a few hours, we book a mountaintop cottage for the night. Security around us has been beefed up, and additional men are positioned in the woods and cottage driveway. Senator Hartner agrees to the overnight stay if Elizabeth's home tomorrow.

"You're not just doing this out of the goodness of your heart, are you, Detective?"

"No. Your daughter has more to offer the new investigation than she thinks. I will protect her with my life."

"I hope so, Mr. Wiley."

We order room service from the nearby lodge, light the gas fireplace, and turn on the air conditioning. She showers, comes out in jeans and a tee shirt, then joins me for dinner. Her eyes don't meet mine until we begin to talk about what we went through during her rescue. After her tears, we end up lampooning her kidnappers. When she walks off to her bedroom and clicks the door shut, I don't remind her about her dreams. Ordering them up on demand is impossible.

Early in the morning I make coffee and wait for her to come out. Two hours later she emerges and says it was her best sleep in a long time. She can't remember even dreaming.

My cell rings. It's Sammy. "You're under surveillance, John. Are you aware?"

"Sammy, I'm in the mountains with Elizabeth with lots of backup. What makes you say that?"

"Your security detail has been updating me at the senator's request. They've seen two teams of men in the woods a few hundred yards away from your cottage. The dirt road in either direction is blocked with auto accidents. Something's going down, John. Can you get out of there right now?"

I look over at Elizabeth. "Go for a ride?"

Monroe, the detail chief just outside the cabin, rings me. "Detective Wiley, these men are moving up slowly. Far enough away not to be obvious. How do you want to handle it?"

"Rush two agents out of here at high speed in my old Toyota, as if Elizabeth and I are leaving in a panic. She and I will leave the other way. You have another four-wheeler?"

"My black Suburban is out back. Which way will you head?"

"I'll take that nearby old fire trail down the mountain. Are you going to engage them?"

"If necessary, yes."

"Good luck," I say.

Two agents run to my truck, back down the driveway, then race out onto the dirt road. Elizabeth pulls her hair in a bun, and slips on a ball cap and my spare police jacket and sunglasses. We walk out to the Suburban and ease through the woods till we encounter the fire trail. We head down the mountain along the rutted road, jostling over the potholes. As I make the turn, I see two men step out in the road, fifty yards below.

I pull my Glock from my pack, release the safety, slip it between us, and look at Elizabeth. She's wide-eyed. "Why did I ever agree to come with you? Is it them?"

"I don't know. Let's see."

"What?" She starts panting, pulling at her blue jeans, scratching her calf nervously.

I move down the fire trail deliberately, without hurry. Our big vehicle cants back and forth as we approach them. They're wearing camouflage gear, packing walkie-talkies and face paint. Their weapons are drawn but at their sides.

"Don't stop, John. Please, speed past them!" She's scratching her leg madly.

"I can't go any faster. Besides, those are paintball guns."

"What?"

I pull up beside them and stop. "What's up, fellas?"

A lanky, pimply-faced kid walks up. "You guys know where the Appalachian Trail is? We're lost."

"It's running over that ridge there, near the top," I say. "It's marked with blue paint."

The kid looks briefly at Elizabeth. "Thanks, folks." He motions the other three standing nearby to move back through the woods. I study them as they fade back into the brush, talking on their radios.

"How did you know?" she asks.

"I shot paintball as a kid. I know all the gear."

We move farther into the wooded hollow, winding down in elevation, crossing streams and abandoned orchards. We meet a hard-packed road. I stop when Officer Monroe calls. "Where are you, Detective Wiley?"

"On the west side of the ridge," I say. "We're okay. Any trouble?"

"No, the car accidents blocking the road were real. And the guys in the woods, just kids playing paintball. We were off target. Is the senator's daughter okay?'

"She's fine. We're heading back now. We'll meet you in Sperryville for your escort home."

On the ride back over the mountain pass, then through the county of Rappahannock, we relax again. I don't tell Elizabeth that paintball is illegal in national forests. No one ever shoots there. Nor do I reveal that their paintball guns didn't look typical. Maybe they let us pass because they didn't recognize the vehicle. Maybe I'm just growing as paranoid as Elizabeth.

As we grow closer to Warrenton, I see, to the south, a distant valley. Just like in my dream. I will return to it later.

The moment I step into the Watergate apartment back in Washington, I know they've hit pay dirt. Woods is smiling. Johnson Sinclair is looking like a man who's done an end run. Woods hands me a fifty-page printout entitled "A Political and Financial Profile of Gerald Aswan."

CHAPTER TWENTY-TWO

After an hour of reading Gerald Aswan's bio, I stare out the windows of the Watergate, down at the glassy Potomac. I'm impressed. Sinclair Johnson and Woods have dug up a lot of details about this very obscure man.

Aswan was indeed born in Iraq, as he boasted, but his family soon moved to Switzerland for his education. His parents were not Muslim, but Iraqi Christians who were heckled enough to finally call it quits and head to Europe. His father was a banker, his mother a historian. From those two careers came his influences. In his teens Aswan returned to Iraq to live with the family clans. One favorite family pastime was the Chinese game of Go.

He was very taken with one uncle who was tragically shot in a family squabble over land ownership. Aswan saw the incident as a brutal injustice over a very simple but confusing notion—property ownership in the Middle East. That concept would captivate him from then on, gaining personal security through amassing commodities. He majored in finance and economics in Zurich. He continued to travel to the Middle East, cementing connections that would later reap big power.

Gerald Aswan married at twenty-five, then rose swiftly in the Swiss banking world. He formed his first business at thirty, a textile import firm. Within twenty-five years, his empire would grow worldwide, with over a hundred diverse concerns. He built banks, novelty stores, and textiles and exotic-home-furnishing businesses. He avoided the oil world entrenchment, and instead moved gold and jewelry, his salons featuring the best pieces in the world. But his biggest holding of all is real estate. He owns whole blocks of downtown property in the biggest cities around the world.

Perhaps, to avenge his uncle.

According to Woods's and Johnson's calculations, Gerald Aswan has money in thousands of bank accounts all over the world. His estimated wealth is in the billions of dollars. Why are his funds spread so thin?

I'm sitting at an intensive NSA briefing on Gerald Aswan on the second floor of the FBI building. Woods is still with Sinclair Johnson at the Watergate, working on uncovering Vishava—a task that so far has yielded nothing. I told them to return to it again, using Sumerian history as a guideline to uncover the term and its significance.

I haven't told the men and women in this room about Sinclair Johnson. The NSA would surely want his skills for themselves, so I'll make my investigative sources known to them when I have a full portrait of Aswan.

Into the second hour I get a text message:

It's crazy—but I want to go clubbing tonight. It's been so long! You're the only one Daddy will agree to. Come by soon. Regrets only, Elizabeth.

I listen to their briefing, detailing Aswan's Swiss bank connections, his Gibraltar connections, and his Grand Caymans connections. Then aspects of his personal background. The NSA has managed to uncover in one week about 10 percent of what Sinclair Johnson did in two days. I keep my mouth shut and leave when it's over.

I know it will be trouble. But I head over to Senator Hartner's anyway.

"Where are you thinking about going?" I ask, sitting in the Hartners' brightly lit kitchen. Elizabeth is outfitted in tight clothing and shining hair. I see a carefree young lady.

"Anywhere, Detective. Just get me out of here. There are new clubs all over town. I'm ready to see the world again."

"Weren't you scared in the mountains?"

"There was no real threat. Fear has to be confronted. After you explained about those paintball guys, I realized my kidnappers are gone. My finger's screwed up, but I'm free."

"Not necessarily, Elizabeth. Aswan's reach in the world is enormous."

"He got his money, didn't he?"

"True."

"And he got his freedom, right?"

"Yes."

"Then he has more important things to worry about than a nutty girl with a stitched-up finger."

Perhaps so. Aswan's incarceration is over. He'll make it a point never to be so careless again. That would mean not returning to the scene of the crime. He and his network will fade into history, as far as Elizabeth Hartner is concerned.

"Take the BMW," Mrs. Hartner whispers, standing in the doorway.

We eat dinner in DC's little Chinatown, below an Oriental grocery.

"You never explained how your earring got trapped down in the engine of your car," I ask.

"It was?"

"Tell me what happened?"

"As you know, Raul and I left my parents' house really late. We decided to drive down Canal Road and park. The night was cold, so after we parked by the river, we left the engine running. Raul wasn't touching me anymore. They were coming."

"You mean your kidnappers?'

"Yes. He got out and popped the engine hood. He looked around. I guess that was their signal, because a minute later, they came flying up and jumped out. Raul argued with them in the headlights in front of the car. They pulled me out and shoved me around. Raul lost it and began swinging at them. One slapped me so hard my earring flew off. I never knew it fell in the engine."

"Detective Woods and I discovered it our first day on the case. It was good evidence. It got things rolling. Then what happened?"

Elizabeth says, "They ganged up on Raul and beat him unconscious. They threw him in the trunk, and me in the backseat. When they got to the top of the bridge, they stopped and threw him into the river."

"Did they say anything when they were driving?'

"They were whispering. The driver kept looking back at me as we sped toward the church, saying something under his breath."

"What?"

"A strange word. Sounded like 'Shiva.'"

"Vishava?" I say.

"Maybe. What's it mean?"

"It's the company that owned your earrings before you. Perhaps one of Aswan's jewelry businesses."

She puts her hand up. "Let's not go into it tonight. I need down-time." I see her scratch her leg, revealing that nervous tick left over from her kidnapping experience. I want to put my hand where it is bothering her and feel what she's feeling. But I don't.

She leaves me by the bar and spends the evening dancing with young men she's never met. The club is dark, loud, and smoky. I nurse a gin and tonic and study the room. She's enjoying herself, dancing close, the pink shooters fueling her brazenness. Part of me wants to yank her home.

All nationalities are in here, all of them drunk and wild. As men stare at her, I grow concerned. At midnight, she's back, sweaty, and tugging me to the dance floor. I reluctantly go.

My feet are out of sync with my arms. She moves closer, her breasts slick, her hair spinning. I push her away, but she presses against me. She's so hungry for escape, hungry to get away from her concerns.

"Why don't you want to touch me?"

"I'm still on duty."

"You're afraid of me?"

"Probably."

"Don't you want me against you?"

She jams into me and shakes with the pounding music. She goes lower till I tower over her, then she's back up again. I find my arms reaching for her, feeling for her lean hip bones. She pulls my arms around her, against her firm tummy. I want to put my mouth against her soft neck.

It happens so fast, I don't know how I catch it. Maybe it's the look in his eyes; maybe the way he moves. I recognize him.

One of the paintball guys.

I spin her away from his view. He's scanning the room. This cannot be a coincidence.

Elizabeth looks up at me, then pulls me down to her mouth. Her tongue spins me away into a dream with a deep kiss. I want a different life. I don't want to be in charge now. I smile at her, and see two more men beside him. They're smoking and talking. They're focused. Not here to dance.

"Let's get a drink," I pull her off the dance floor.

"No, dance!"

"We'll do a shooter, then come back."

We wedge through the bodies. She's hanging tight as we move toward the dance floor on the other side.

"A melon-ball shot, right?" she yells.

"I want to show you something!"

We slip through the crowd over to the window glass. The men are watching us through the bottles in the bar, waiting for a sign we've seen them. Beyond the windows is an exit door.

I pull her toward it.

"Where we going?"

"Let's get some fresh air."

I scoot us down the hall, then down two flights of darkness. Elizabeth is too drunk to detect my concern. We hit the warm air of the street, then walk fast, turning the corner into the alley.

"Detective? What are you up to?"

"Nothing."

Down at the streetlight, a figure emerges and peers into the darkness at us. We're hidden behind a row of Dumpsters, yet he looks as if he can see us. She slips her arms around my waist. "Did I ever tell you how much I appreciate you saving me?"

"Yes," I whisper. "Many times."

The man's studying something, like an electronic devise.

"I mean how much I really appreciated you!" She leans on my chest. "I have never been with a man like you, John."

"Really?"

He's looking right at us. Another one arrives, and they point this way. There's no way they could have seen us, no way they could have heard us.

She looks at the men. "Who are they?"

"No one. I'm just being protective."

She's swaying now. "That's what I like about you, Detective. You're so caring. Kiss me again."

In the name of her silence, I kiss her once more. It's not passionate, but practical. They're charging this way.

"Let's go," I say.

"Who's after us?" she slurs.

"Police looking for DUIs. Back to the car."

We circle the block, then dash down the pavement into the underground parking. I screech her car around, passing us through the pay booth, then out to the street. They're running right toward us.

I fly the other way, rip down the street, then make a series of turns. Within a minute, a car quickly approaches us. It's them. I cut the headlights and move down through side streets, and soon we are speeding down K Street, alone.

Elizabeth is crooked against me, fast asleep. In the flashing streetlights I see her bare calf, rubbed raw from her constant scratching. Centered in the redness, is a tiny, silver thread, gleaming in the light. I see it for the first time now. There's something in there, something under her skin, like a foreign object.

CHAPTER TWENTY-THREE

"How was it possible no one found this?" Senator Hartner bellows.

The family physician flushes. "Senator, it's not something we looked for. This thing is almost microscopic. It may be just a metal shard."

"Wrong, Doctor. This thing is a device intentionally planted in my daughter's leg by her kidnappers. Correct, Detective?"

The law enforcement officers in the senator's library stare at me. "Yes, it is. But don't blame the doctor, Senator. I saw it by accident. Only after wondering how these men kept track of us did I conclude it was a planted bug."

"How is that possible?"

"I don't know. But I'm sure it's a device that is used to determine Elizabeth's location."

"For what purpose?" Mrs. Hartner demands.

I look to Woods. "Detective, what have you got?"

She addresses us with urgency. "According to an international kidnapping forum held this year, repeat abductions are up 50 percent in the last five years. Worldwide kidnapping is a huge problem because of its high profitability. Apparently, once a big ransom is secured, it tends to highlight the financial capabilities of the family who paid the money."

"But isn't the family nearly bankrupt after paying such money to kidnappers?"

"True," Woods says. "But it also indicates the resourcefulness of the parties to do whatever is necessary to get their family member back. If they will pay ransom once, the kidnappers believe they will find a way to pay it again. There is a tendency on the part of the kidnapping victim and their family to believe that it will never happen to them again. That's not true."

"So Aswan's team is attempting to kidnap Elizabeth again?"

I look at Elizabeth's worried expression. "Yes. And by means that I have never heard of. Detective, any data on these implants?"

"Actually, there is," Woods says. "What was just pulled from her leg has been seen in Asia for a few years. It's not always discovered because, physically, the device is nearly nonexistent. There may be former kidnapping victims walking around with this tiny beacon still in their skin, thinking all is well. Then, one day, they are suddenly abducted again. It goes in the skin, without detection or anesthesia, so the victim doesn't ever realize it has been planted. Because it is so tiny, no one sees it. It transmits a clear signal under most conditions, though it can be shielded, which will temporarily block its transmission."

I nod. "That's why the paintball guys in the mountain didn't know it was us. The vehicle we were in was loaded with telecom gear that blocked her signal at that moment."

Chief Harris says, "Then Aswan's abduction of Elizabeth was typical of operations he conducts. He had the teams already fully functional, as well as the unique technology for it. This man is a master planner of abductions. He kept us in the dark for months. He would have picked her up again had this discovery not been made."

"Where do we go from here?" Sammy says.

Elizabeth's hand is clutching mine. Now she pulls it free. "Does this sensor you pulled from my leg still work?"

"Yes," says the attending NSA officer, staring down at the sliver in the Pyrex dish. "Its casing is not ruptured. It still appears to be emitting a steady frequency. It draws power from the body's own weak voltage to accomplish its task. It's a frightening technology."

"Then they don't know we've discovered it." She studies our faces. "I'm enraged even more, now that I know this thing's been violating my body all this time. I don't want to forget about it—I want to get this man. If we can grab his kidnapping team, we are that much closer to Aswan, and luring them to me is the best way."

She says, "I want to be kidnapped again."

It's early evening, two weeks later. We've spent many hours out here by the river. As we walk the C&O Canal towpath, the sun is lingering, allowing us a fine view of the Potomac. Elizabeth is at ease tonight, talking about everything but the nightmare that changed her life.

We turn around and head back toward Georgetown, preparing to walk the streets like two carefree people. I reflect on how, a few weeks ago, she seemed a broken woman.

She recounts what has happened in her dreams.

She saw her kidnappers and fled, then realized they could be banished if she stood her ground. She looked them in the eye and announced, "You cannot hurt me anymore…you are wasting my time. Blow away!" They began fighting each other until there was nothing left but dark ashes lying in front of her. Soon a breeze blew the ashes away.

She awoke.

The pain in her stomach was gone. No more heaviness in her temple and shoulders and arms. She was back in charge, full of sudden determination.

I get a comment from Woods in my hidden earpiece. "John, how's Elizabeth?"

"Happy."

"I think we have something," Woods says. "Not like the other nights. This one looks like the formation of the final team. Same players as the previous nights, but in different combinations. Two of the team are a hundred yards up the path from you, on a bench, talking. One by the river, pulling up their canoe. Four downstream from you, strolling your way."

"What makes you sure?" I say into my collar mic.

Woods says, "They're the same people we've seen other evenings near you, but tonight they've switched partners. Last night, the Scandinavian woman by the canoe was with the Asian guy. Now she's paired with the skinny black guy. It's a subtle error on their part. I must commend them on their racial diversity, though. Aswan is certainly an equal-opportunity employer. Sammy says they've been marking time, observing you two. They may have been concerned about a trap. Tonight they've concluded it's safe to attempt Elizabeth's abduction again."

She pauses. "John, they're moving in."

"Roger that," I say.

I look down the path and see the four whom Woods mentioned coming our way in the distance. We will cross their paths in a couple of minutes. They look like tourists.

"Woods, you and your guys are ready?"

"Roger that."

Elizabeth keeps talking, oblivious to the significance of the discussion. We have rehearsed this scenario over the previous evenings. She thinks we are merely doing it again.

I head right for them, unconcerned. They are talking among themselves. I see nothing to suggest they are about to attempt a blatant abduction. I see no sign of our own law enforcement backup that is supposed to be poised nearby.

As we draw near, I look at their eyes. One man is studying us calmly, as a casual tourist would. Three others are talking with animation about a humorous event. We pass without occurrence.

A minute later Woods says, "They've turned around and are following you. We think they've decided the path is too visible. They will probably go for an alley in town."

"Total coincidence, Woods. You're mistaken on your surveillance. They looked innocent."

"John, I don't think so. Are you going to take the footbridge, up by the Ukrainian Embassy?"

"Yep, just like last night."

Elizabeth looks me over. "You're all right?"

"Hungry."

We soon cross over the canal on the footbridge at Thirty-Fourth, then move down on the sandy towpath into Georgetown.

"John," Woods says, "the four tourists have moved up quickly. They will catch up with you before you can leave that isolated stretch. There is no escape route on the path. They will take you there."

Old brick buildings line the canal ahead, blocking views, blocking witnesses. The path ahead is empty, but then I see three men turn the corner and walk the sandy path toward us.

"Woods, I agree—more coming. Is your team ready?"

"In the alcove, twenty yards ahead—waiting for you."

We walk along the path till we reach a vestibule in the brick wall. I pull Elizabeth in, and we enter the darkness near an exit door.

A man and a girl who look just like us, right down to the clothing, await us. I rip the bandage off Elizabeth's arm containing Aswan's skin sensor. I slap it on the new girl.

"Go!" I whisper. From the dim corner, Elizabeth and I watch the two decoys step back onto the path. Their movements are remarkably similar to our own.

"Is this real tonight?" she whispers.

"Yep."

The group of four that was following us walks quickly past the opening in pursuit of our decoys.

"Woods, what's happening?"

"North and south groups are converging on your doubles, John. The one group has stopped to ask your doubles a question. Looks innocent. But coming up from behind are the other four. We're moving in!"

We creep to the end in the alcove and look fifty yards down the path. Our doubles are engaged in conversation with all seven kidnappers. There appears to be nothing happening other than discussion. But then, I see one man rudely grab Elizabeth's double and start walking her this way. The others take my double the opposite direction.

"Woods, you're late!"

Sammy says in my ear wire, "Stay cool, John. We want them separated before we take them."

Then, moments later, a group of police rushes past us, gravel crushing beneath running feet. A single gunshot ricochets off the brick walls, then, more shots echo around the canal. Elizabeth pulls free and runs out and around the corner.

I yell, "No!"

She races down the path toward them. Pistol shots are raging as two groups battle, one twenty yards away, another farther up the path. A deadly encounter ensues as all of the abductors are cornered. They don't surrender, but instead return fire, oblivious to the dozens of officers who have converged on them.

Within moments, it's over. Three kidnappers are motionless, down on the ground. Elizabeth's decoy has killed one, while others have gunned down two more. My double has shot another.

I pull Elizabeth back away.

Woods runs up. "John, Sammy wants Elizabeth out of here, ASAP."

A deadly silence lingers over the canal as a pink dusk ripples peacefully on the waters. Ambulances race up, and their EMTs work the scene. I escort Elizabeth away and down the path to the waiting police cruiser. I look back one more time. Six men and women are lying by the canal, shot to death in the gun battle. Only one of Aswan's kidnappers has survived, and he looks critically wounded. It worked—perhaps too well.

In the hospital room, the cadence of the abductor's respirator sounds like a death bell. This rarely ends with anyone walking out recovered and well. Two cops are by his bedside, another two outside the door. No one will get to him without a fight to the death. This remaining kidnapper is fair skinned, tall, and noble featured.

"How long has he been in a coma?"

Woods says, "All day. If he recovers, he may be of little use to us, John. His heart and breath stopped for two minutes there by the canal. His brain may have permanent damage."

I lay my hand on his temple and feel the clammy skin of a man lost in a blank, empty, white world. He is neither dead nor alive, just on pause. Coma patients have so little soul activity; their diminished brain waves block me from seeing into them. Oddly, a dead body is more open for images.

My cell rings. "Detective," says Sinclair Johnson. "I need to see you."

"What is it?"

"I'd rather show you. I know you're busy. Detective Woods told me what happened today at the canal with Aswan's men. But this is important."

"I'll be right over."

Woods frowns. "Need me?"

"Stay with our man. Call me if he comes around."

A half hour later, I am seated with Sinclair Johnson in front of his terminals. He's unshaven, surrounded by a sea of pizza boxes, and looks exhausted, as if he's trying to do everything at once.

"I have unraveled Vishava for you," he says.

"I'm all eyes and ears," I reply.

He displays a screen awash in figures. "Aswan's worldwide bank accounts gave me my first indication of how to analyze him. Data on his companies is scattered all over the place, so there is no central database server for his holdings, no central bank. That's unusual for someone who is running a legitimate business. He's decentralized for a reason. I breached his individual accounts one at a time, then analyzed his day-to-day banking activities for the last year."

"What does that have to do with Vishava?"

"You helped me understand where to look. The term 'vishava' is indeed a Sumerian word. It means 'to exchange.' Vishava in the days of that culture also implied 'to barter.' The vishava was the man whom you would trade goods with."

"So he makes trades?"

"Exactly."

"What kind?"

"It's not clear. His cash flows from his business fronts to bank accounts in completely different countries, instead of going to local banks where he has accounts. He's taking the long way around the world just to deposit his money."

"What kind of sales is he doing?"

"They're listed as general merchandise: custom furnishings, jewelry, antiques—a hundred different headings."

"How much is the average deposit?"

"Anywhere from fifty thousand to ten million dollars."

"That's a lot of home furnishings."

"Yet the word 'vishava' is never written in any of his financial communications. It's understood to all involved, but never mentioned. It helped me understand how he operates. How he arranges his money. As if he were bartering with a thousand different customers at the same time. For instance, if the sale of a rare painting for thirteen million dollars occurs in this account, then those funds are transferred around the world a dozen times before finally settling in offshore accounts in Grand Cayman. By then, it has split into thirteen individual one-million-dollar accounts."

"How long did the funds stay put?"

"Twenty hours. Then the accounts were all drained and closed."

"By Aswan?"

"No. Individuals representing thirteen different companies."

"Have any data on them?"

"Not yet."

"Find some. Everything you can. Is that transaction typical of Aswan?"

"He moves money like that hundreds of times a day."

"Excellent, Sinclair. Get some sleep."

I rise to leave.

"One other thing, Detective. It's critical you understand something. Aswan's watching what I'm doing in cyberspace."

"How can you tell?"

"After accessing one of his servers, I found his spyware attached to the data I downloaded."

"He's aware that we're aware?"

"Yes. But I temporarily took care of that. I designed the program to eavesdrop on his activities without his knowing who the real source is."

"Who does he think you are?"

"My intrusions past his firewalls look like visits from Visa, MasterCard, the FBI, and the IRS. And the AARP, just for grins. He will be confused. But he will determine our identity very soon. Then, it will become hazardous to stay here, Detective. This man's very adept technically. Within a few days he will determine this location."

"Skip the sleep," I warn him. "Get me data on those thirteen companies."

I have no time to do this.

Yet I drive into Georgetown to Agnes Sloan's townhouse anyway. This time I'm not intruding; I'm responsibly inquiring about a girl named Tara Chin—who's definitely not around. I ring the bell and peer in through the foyer windows. No one comes. I look to the upper-story bedroom window and see that the whole place is unlit. I move around, back to the basement window. Tara's bed looks the same.

My American Express card fits in the gap of the French door's lockset. As I enter, the air smells musty. The light switch doesn't work. The AC is not running, and the house reeks. I move up the basement stairs in the dark. The house is too quiet. The hair on my arms rises. Up in the kitchen, the dishes are dirty; the fridge is dark and full of rotting food. I move to the study and open the curtains and illuminate the room with streetlight. Bills on the desk lie unopened.

I lift the phone and hear no dial tone. I raise my cell and call the electric company. The power was cut off days ago for nonpayment.

I don't want to go upstairs. I just want to leave. If Tara is here, I don't want to see how she must be. Mrs. Sloan never raised my suspicions, but then, some people can fool me. I move to the front door, planning to walk out and leave the place. But I walk back to the kitchen, open a drawer, and, after a nervous hunt, find candle and matches.

As I approach the steps to the upstairs, I smell the same odor the fridge is giving off. The upper story of the townhouse reeks. A single loud chime from the clock in the hallway shatters my concentration. I shouldn't be here.

The Touch

Three large bedrooms are upstairs, and the first two check out fine. The last one's obviously Mrs. Sloan's room, its rich maroon drapes and thick carpet well-coordinated.

The odor is agonizing, and I want to run. I raise the candle and pray I can sweep the area quickly and not find Tara. But her image sharpens in my mind. I hear her laugh, and I feel the softness of her cheek.

She's here.

I see a bare foot on the tile floor, its sheen luring me into the darkness of the bathroom. My candlelight illuminates a calf, then a knee, then a naked thigh. Then buttocks, then bare breasts. The dried, bloody hole in her ashen forehead is perfectly round, making her look like an extra in the wax museum. Her body's been here for some time. Why didn't I come over and search here before? I had concerns.

I reach out and touch her stiff flesh with my shaking hand, making contact with her dead body for a long time. Never have I gathered so many sensations from a murder victim, and yet, I feel nothing but innocence in her. My relief feels morbid in a way.

Whoever killed old Mrs. Sloan caught her just as she was stepping from the shower.

CHAPTER TWENTY-FOUR

"Agnes Sloan was a longtime resident of Georgetown, John. Rich, widowed—hubby, a former State Department big shot. Both their backgrounds are clean. That part of town hasn't had a homicide in years. There goes the neighborhood."

Sammy sighs as we drive toward the hospital where the remaining kidnapper is still struggling for life.

"What did your forensic guys conclude about her?" I ask.

"They're calling Sloan's murder a robbery-homicide."

"What was robbed?"

"Sloan's wall safe was open and very empty. You notice that?"

"No. Where was it?"

"In her study behind an ornate screen."

"Any fingerprints?"

"They pulled a bunch. We'll know more in a few days." He pauses. "What were you doing there again?"

"Trying to locate Tara Chin. I went by to talk to Mrs. Sloan. I was afraid I might find Tara…"

"John, I know you're upset about the young woman. I'll initiate an investigation about her disappearance. But I need you on Aswan, full time. You gotta back off, okay?" Sammy's expression holds deep layers of stress.

"Sammy, what I do in my off hours is my business, right?"

"In your off hours, you are ordered to sleep."

His cell rings. "Excellent, Detective Woods. We're on our way."

He grins. "The kidnapper awoke from his coma."

As we walk up the hall toward his hospital room, Woods is waiting by the door.

"What have you got?" Sammy asks.

"He's alert, and pretty lucid. A real tough one."

"You got anything out of him?" I ask.

"The man's uncooperative to the point of nastiness. Couldn't even get his name, so we ran his fingerprints. He's an Irishman named Jack Green. Has a hefty criminal background—including IRA connections."

I peek in the window and see the big man sitting up in bed, his legs and arms shackled, his face stubbornly set, an IV in his arm. His temple and neck wounds are wrapped tightly.

"We need to know what's in his brain, John. Do you want to go in and pick it?"

"Not yet. We have a tiny window of vulnerability with him. Go back in and start playing good cop, Woods. Pretend you're changing tactics. Talk nice and turn on the TV. Keep it on ESPN—no news channels. I don't want him to see anything about his capture."

I walk the other way, down the hall.

"John, what's up?" Sammy says.

"I need to see an elderly newspaper reporter."

I'm sitting across from a very annoyed Gloria Sullivan. "You're using me again, aren't you, Mr. Wiley?"

"If I answer yes, will you help me?"

"Regardless of your answer—you are guilty, Detective. Just because I'm a famous journalist in this town doesn't mean I can be summoned any time for more of your shenanigans. That's what you're here for, isn't it?"

"Yes."

"You have completely shut me out of your activities lately. And it was because you didn't need me, true?"

"Yes."

Her face, though lined, still echoes remarkable beauty. I refrain from telling her that, knowing she'll nail me on it. What I need of her will require a lot of work in a short amount of time, and she has the connections to produce it.

"Mr. Wiley, what's in it for me?"

"What do you want?"

"I want to know details of your daily activities. I want to know what's happening in the Aswan investigation. Everyone's dead quiet."

"It's still ongoing," I reply.

"That much I can conclude. How hard is the government going after him?"

"A lot of muscle is being flexed. Lots of law enforcement is involved."

"The senator's driving this?"

"Yes."

"Share the book and movies rights with me, and I'll do it," she decides.

"Gloria, this is a criminal investigation, not a Hollywood screenplay."

"You're totally wrong, Detective. This is certainly about justice, but it's also about entertainment. This story's got feet and plenty of red meat. You have continued to stay at the center of it ever since you rescued Elizabeth. When it's over, you will tell me the whole story, right?"

"Doing that will compromise the government's methods and means, which would send me to jail, Gloria. You really want that?"

"I will decide if it will send you to jail, Detective. I'm an expert at blurring that line. In the end, everybody knows everything in this town anyway. Why not tell it accurately and entertainingly?"

"I'll try my best, Gloria."

"Not good enough." She rises.

"All right, I give you my word. You got the story—but only if I can successfully bring in Aswan—only after his trial is over."

"That's better."

She smiles warmly, an expression I suspect she's produced a thousand times over the years after she's won. "Now, what do you want me to do, Detective?"

A day later, I walk back down the secure hospital hallway toward the room where the remaining kidnapper still resides. I pass the videotape in my hand to a waiting officer. He disappears into the bowels of the hospital to begin running the tape Gloria Sullivan has fabricated. Many hours were needed to accomplish its details.

Woods and Sammy are waiting there to play their parts.

Woods and I enter the kidnapper's room and stand in the corner for a discussion. Jack Green lies there, staring at his covers, darting his eyes at us. CNN is running on his TV now, instead of ESPN. He's waiting to hear anything about the attempt to re-kidnap Elizabeth Hartner.

A commercial runs. That's our cue.

Woods grows more guarded in her conversation, and we move out of the room for privacy. Green is there alone, without guards—only his body straps holding him in place. Our discussion grows louder outside his door, but not loud enough to distract him from seeing a newscast that begins running on his TV. It runs forty-eight seconds, expertly slipped in the broadcast on the tail end of the hour.

It shows Gerald Aswan's haggard face, as he is led away in handcuffs. A young reporter is giving details of the mastermind's abrupt, thrilling recapture. The FBI is pleased at this unexpected breakthrough in the Elizabeth Hartner kidnapping case…

We don't look in the room.

Moments later, I move back into Green's room. I cut the TV off, as if worried he was alone with the CNN broadcast. I pick up his medical paperwork, and two guards come in. I point to Green, and explain he's been discharged, and needs to be prepped for transport to "maximum security."

Jack Green says, "Detective Wiley, what are you doing?"

He hasn't ventured any other comment since he was arrested.

I keep talking with the uniformed officers.

Green interrupts. "Where are you taking me?"

"Out of here."

"Not till I get my phone call."

I tower over his face. "The only call you will be making is to the main operator in hell."

He snarls, ripping at his restraints.

I grow closer. "Green, you're a dead man, and dead men don't make calls. As far as the world's concerned, you died in this room two days ago. You refused to cooperate, so now you don't exist. You have been an idiotic soldier in a doomed cause. Now you'll spend the rest of your life in the worst possible conditions.

"Why? Because, occasionally, we get to take advantage of certain circumstances. All of your fellow kidnappers died in the shootout. Only we know you are the last one alive. Senator Hartner is homicidal about Aswan's renewed threat on his daughter's life. He's taking it out on you."

Green's eyes glint anxiously.

I start talking with the cops again. They move to the closet and pull out a bright orange prison suit. One officer pulls out his revolver. They begin their task.

"I want to talk with the black detective," Green whispers.

"Forget it. You had all the face with her you'll ever get," I say.

The police remove Green's bedcovers, cuff his feet and hands, then remove the bed restraints. I walk from the room, then turn and say, "Enjoy your stay in hell, Mr. Green."

"Wait, Wiley. Wait!"

I do and he hesitates.

"What?"

"I want to make a deal."

"Too late." I open the door.

"Let me talk to that detective, now!"

I grab a roll of duct tape from the table. I rip a piece off and move toward him. "Too late, scumbag. You are about to disappear forever. We don't need your help now. We've already got Aswan!"

"I can help you!" he screams.

I plaster tape over his mouth.

Sammy walks in. "What's up, Detective?"

"Nothing."

"What did he say?"

I look at the cops. "He's just mouthing off. Right, guys?"

They nod.

"I heard him say something about a deal. What was that?"

"Nothing."

Sammy says, "Remove the tape from his mouth."

"You'll only hear bullshit," I say. "Don't waste your time. He knows it's over. We haven't got time for his lies. Get him out of here, guys."

Green's screaming through his tape, his eyes wide.

Sammy pauses. "If he's got nothing to say, out he goes."

We walk outside as the cops prep Green. As he is dragged into the hallway, Woods, Sammy, and I are talking to ourselves.

Green yanks on his handcuffs and stares anxiously at Woods. His face is beet red.

"Take him down the freight elevator, guys," Sammy says. "Remove the tape so he can breathe."

We stroll away. They lead Green off in the opposite direction. Right before the elevator opens, they pull the tape off his mouth.

"I'm ready to talk!" he bellows to us.

We keep walking.

"I know Aswan's entire network. Now that you've got him, I can help you put him away for good!"

Woods looks down the hallway at Green, then pulls us aside.

As the elevator doors close on the prisoner's trip downstairs, a hand moves in to prevent its closure. Woods steps in, places the elevator on hold, and lets the door shut. Two minutes later, she emerges with a shaken man. They place him back inside his room and secure him back in his bed. Woods comes back out.

"He's scared to death," she says.

"We've got to move fast," I say. "He may reconsider if he has too much time to think. He may give us phony data, so we need to verify his statement as we go along."

Sammy says, "John, this will never be used in court. These kinds of tactics are totally illegal."

"What he tells us is only for our eyes and ears, Sammy."

"Good. Now get in there before he smells something phony."

Woods moves into Green's room. She dismisses the guards, places a tape recorder by the prisoner's side, and starts her interrogation. I wait ten minutes, then move into the room. What Jack Green blurts out about Gerald Aswan takes just an hour for Sinclair Johnson to confirm.

Gerald Aswan doesn't just use banks around the world to hide his illegal transactions.

He's begun buying them all.

CHAPTER TWENTY-FIVE

The Watergate apartment we're using in Washington is littered with fast food. A balding Treasury agent named Logan is working with Sinclair to help him untangle Aswan's connections with international banking systems.

"Will Green's confession give you Aswan's location?" I say.

"Perhaps," Sinclair says.

"When?"

"A few days."

"We have that much time before he uncovers this location?"

"No."

"Then how will you do it?" I ask.

"Wireless Internet access," Sinclair says. "Aswan will have to intercept cellular phone activity to find us. He may not have that resource. We need to get out of this apartment now, Detective."

I say, "We have your new location set up in Winchester, Virginia. Woods will escort you all out there in an hour."

"What about all these computers?"

Logan says, "We'll continue using them in order to lure Aswan's men in."

Sinclair says, "I'm glad I won't be sitting in that chair. With this man's capabilities, no one is safe."

"What makes you think Aswan can't intercept your wireless Internet activity?" I ask.

"I will disguise all my future inquiries. It will buy me time."

"What disguise will prevent Aswan from recognizing you?"

Sinclair says, "The guise will look like an Internet site with millions of hits a day. All that activity will swamp him."

"What business would that be?" I ask.

"Porn," Sinclair announces.

Logan says, "Mr. Johnson must go to these lengths so we can delve into Aswan's own bank records without him realizing it."

"What bank are we talking about?"

"Gibraltar Funds International Bank."

"Can you overcome it?" I ask.

"Perhaps," Logan says. "But his funds also move back and forth, using untraceable commodities like diamonds and gold. That kills the connection we need. Mr. Green's confessions will help us, but we need a few more days. When this is over, the Treasury Department will likely want to hire Mr. Johnson. Possible?"

"No."

My cell vibrates, but I can't get it. I'm on the way to an Aswan task-force update in the FBI building. I finally pull it out and read a text message:

John I need to see you. Life is crazy for me. Check your e-mail!—Tara.

Well, well.

I sit through the FBI task-force meeting on reacquiring Aswan. They know now about Sinclair Johnson, but skirt the issue. Two different inquiries are going on: One, the formal, slow methodical one by the FBI. The other, my own covert one. Jack Green is mentioned only in connection with Elizabeth's attempted kidnapping. They don't know of his confession, and Sammy reveals nothing. They want Aswan as much as I do, so, looking the other way, they proceed in the only way they can, with institutional slowness. They're waiting for me to break it open, then they'll claim ignorance as well as victory.

I move from the concluded meeting to an empty office. I retrieve Tara's e-mail, dated three hours ago:

John, meet me at Kent Island on the bay at 11:00 p.m. Baybreaker Lodge. Room twelve. Miss you. T.

I call her cell. No answer.

A half hour later, I'm driving around the beltway toward the Chesapeake Bay to see a woman whom I truly feared was dead. I cross the Bay Bridge and study the dark, slate-colored water glistening below. A slivered moon reveals Kent Island's faint, overgrown features.

I take the deserted highway south, through darkened farmland, till I reach a brightly lit, lonely motel. As I step up to the motel door at room twelve, I pause.

I have not seen this woman since the day before Elizabeth's rescue. My last communication to her was in a note left at the Four Seasons Hotel room. Some of its contents were true feelings, others, a test for her. She was the only woman I'd met where all aspects of our personalities seemed to fully mesh. And that was the problem; I know of no such woman on earth.

I knock on the door, but no one answers. I enter and see her on the other side of the room on the phone. She turns and smiles, dressed now in a linen summer suit and pumps, and with different hair. There's sadness in her smile. She whispers, "Okay, Mama," then hangs up.

We stand in silence for a while. I want to say how relieved I am to see her, but she's in another world.

"Where have you been?" I ask.

"California."

"You're okay?"

She moves toward me with that mysterious expression that I missed so much. Yet she's different in this light, in these clothes. She's quickly in my arms with an urgent, powerful kiss. I easily fall into the feel of her body again, her unsupported breasts firm through her dress. Her face is against my chest, and her eyes grow wet. "So much has happened," she says.

"Tell me."

"My father died in a car accident in San Francisco." A sob comes, and I feel her grow weak. We move to the bed. "We buried him two days ago."

"Tara, I'm sorry."

She pulls me close and she cries. I feel an emotional drain pouring out from her. I ask, "Have you been back to Mrs. Sloan's?"

"No."

"She is..."

"What?"

"You've not talked to her?" I ask.

"I tried to call her, but no one answers. I wanted to say good-bye."

That she knows nothing of Mrs. Sloan is fortunate. Now is not the time to tell her. "Why are you out here all by yourself?"

"I've suspended my studies, and am flying out from BWI tonight, back to live with my mother. I loved the bay and I wanted to see you here. I got your note at the hotel, but I had to leave that night for California. I'm proud of you, John. I missed you."

There is a moment during our lovemaking—or maybe I should call it just good sex—that is pure pleasure, yet pure pain. She loves me differently this time, yet more freely than ever. More crudely, too, revealing hidden tendencies I'd not sensed before. Perhaps a young woman, like a young man, never grows up till she loses her dad. The girl in my arms is clearly a woman.

And now, oddly, I'm in pain. I feel it as my body releases from her damp skin, her dark hair and our hot breath all mixed together.

I sleep deeply for the first time in weeks, maybe for an hour. As I lean up in bed and feel a dull spike of pain run up my back, I realize Tara has already left for the airport.

I shower and study her sink. Makeup dust lingers, as does her perfume. I am grateful she is alive, but sad she is gone. She said she will call in a few weeks. As much as my senses can reveal someone's intention, I could not read hers. But I do know this much—she won't call. And I am blinded by our encounter.

"John, we've uncovered some very deep complexities about Gerald Aswan—"

"Slow down, Sinclair. Give me the simple version."

It's a humid Washington morning. I'm in my truck on my way into town from Sammy's. "Where are you?" I ask.

Sinclair says, "At the hidden location in Winchester."

"Who's with you?"

"Logan, and three agents. It keeps coming up the same."

"And that is…?"

"Gerald Aswan's banking maneuvers are more involved than we thought. We've linked him directly to terrorists in the Middle East and South America, as well as Asia. The funds come from low-level criminal activity, then filter up to organized crime syndicates, then up to the major state-sponsored terrorist groups such as those in Yemen and Syria. Then—farther."

"Give me an example."

Sinclair puts them on speakerphone. Logan says, "Detective Wiley, you are acquainted with conflict diamonds?"

"No."

"The process goes like this. In West Africa, crime syndicates kidnap helpless villagers and use them as slave labor to mine diamond ore illegally, which they then sell for cash or gold. The buyers take the raw stones to Belgium and have them cut and polished. Then they sell them legally on the world diamond market. There's no way to follow the funds trail since the end sale is legit."

"Okay."

"Aswan performs that same kind of activity, using hundreds of other commodities. His business networks take in illegal goods such as stolen jewels, property, drugs, or other kinds of contraband. Then, he directs a fencing operation that resells those goods for profit. Finally, he deposits the cash in his own banks, perhaps part of it ransom money from his huge kidnapping operations. All of it is disguised as profit from his storefronts. I secretly dug out all these details from Aswan's buried database files."

"Then the real fun begins," Sinclair says. "The funds are shot around the world from bank to bank, finally ending up in new, electronically laundered bank accounts."

"You told me that before," I say.

"And you told me to find out who accessed those accounts. For the most part it's not the original criminal organizations, and not Aswan."

"Then who?"

"Corporations with world-class reputations."

"What?"

"I know it's insane, but it's true. We're looking at dozens of successful companies—some of them recent start-ups, some were well-established. Even Fortune 500 big shots are accessing these accounts."

"Where's the bank?"

"Gibraltar."

"Sinclair, why would anybody risk associating themselves with Aswan if they were running a legitimate business?"

"We asked ourselves the same question."

"What have you concluded?" I ask.

"Two possible scenarios. One, the clients don't know where the funds originally came from and think they are utilizing their own accounts. But that's unlikely. Two, they are in trouble financially and are leaning on Aswan to temporarily prop them up."

"Sort of a global electronic loan shark?"

"Exactly. If you look at the financial statements from the companies that access these accounts, they were in the red the quarter before. Then, magically, the next quarter they are profitable again. Perhaps after the infusion from the Gibraltar accounts."

"Why would any company risk doing that?"

Logan says, "To keep the board of directors happy, or to keep the stock prices up. And, of course, to secure the quarterly bonuses the top officers will receive if they achieve their financial projections. It's all about the money. It's easier than having to cook their own books."

"Gentlemen, you are throwing down a major indictment about business practices in this country. I hope you know what you're implying. But, suppose you're right. If these companies are borrowing funds from this man to boost their bottom line, they surely have to pay it back. How does that occur?"

There is silence on the phone.

"Well, guys?"

"We see no trace of repayment."

"There must be some payback," I say. "Have you profiled them to see a common business practice? What do these companies do?"

Logan says, "They are in Telecom, fiber optics, data storage, and security systems."

"Any big government contractors?"

"Yes, a few in Orlando that work in information systems."

"Logan, before this investigation began, had you ever heard of Gerald Aswan?"

"Never. He's been unknown as far as international bank fraud is concerned."

"How is that possible? He's running a huge empire. He's tied to so many criminal networks. So much technology. How could he have stayed unknown?"

"Maybe," Sinclair says, "he uses technology to conceal himself. Meaning he's been able to, by the use of his information manipulation, delete anything stored anywhere in the world about himself. He's quietly been playing good-guy banker and businessman all this time. If you look at the distressed companies he's working with, they all have one thing in common: they have access to vast amounts of information. The clients who access his accounts might be paying him back in the only currency they have at that moment—information."

"When I first met Aswan," I say, "he startled me with facts about my family and about events that occurred in my early life. I wondered how he had found out such specific info. You think he's actually buying data on people from these distressed companies?"

"It would make sense," Sinclair says. "From there, he could target anyone in the world for extortion, blackmail, robbery, and of course, kidnapping. If he had access to all the details in the average guy's life, just think what he could do."

"And," I add, "because his profile seems so clean, he may present himself as a typical data miner for Internet commerce. He shows up at the right time with cash to help out an ailing company, and in return receives data on anyone in the world. But this doesn't tell me his location. Where is he, gentlemen?"

Logan says, "He has residences all over the world. He's not been seen at any of them. NSA reports no cellular activity by him, nor any visual sightings of him anywhere since his escape."

I feel a wave of disappointment, and sudden fatigue. Something about this case becomes, at this moment, overbearing. My enthusiasm had been red hot the whole time. Now I feel it slip away. This man is so big, and so connected, and so out of the country, it makes little sense for me to keep banging my head against the wall. I have accomplished what I came into town to do, find Elizabeth Hartner. Nothing else matters. She is safe.

Aswan may be out there running around forever. What other cases will I put on hold just to stay connected to this one? If he's not found soon, the FBI task force will be disbanded. I'm discouraged, and, for the first time in months, exhausted.

I go Sammy's house, pull the shades, and sleep for fourteen hours. When I awake, I search my mind for dreams. For details about Aswan, or Mrs. Sloan, or Tara. Nothing. I sit on the edge of the bed and realize I cannot sense anything. I feel the absence in my forehead. The empty freedom I prayed for for so many years is upon me now. I cannot sense the unknown world in my gut. Most of all, I think I cannot dream anymore.

CHAPTER TWENTY-SIX

I wearily look up at Agnes Sloan's townhouse, as bright sunshine shoots across the roofline. I know what happened to my attitude was that I was pushing too hard. The twenties are more stressful than my dad ever let on.

The last time I was here, I found a dead woman. When I leaned down to touch her, I felt in her such fear and confusion, and ultimately, rage. She was furious that she had been murdered. That's the last clear image I have of her. I had no sense at that time of the proximity of the killer, or their identity, or their intentions. Sammy claims it was a robbery. But there's a problem with the investigation, and he wants me in there now. As I walk up the steps, I feel an alien sensation—lack of confidence.

Inside, Sammy and two forensics guys are waiting.

"Johnny, you look rested. Help us a bit. Can we run over your initial observations again?"

The interior of the townhouse is even hotter than last time, but someone at least cleaned out the fridge. It doesn't smell now. And of course, the murdered Mrs. Sloan is not up there anymore.

"Okay," I say. "I entered from the basement door, then went up the steps and onto the main floor."

"No sign of a struggle?" Sammy asks.

"Though the house stunk, nothing alerted me till I went upstairs and found her in the bathroom. She was shot, right where she stood."

"It looks that way. We don't think she caught the robber opening the safe in her library. What did you conclude about that?"

"That she was being robbed never occurred to me. I saw no evidence of that. I concluded she had just come out of the shower."

"Yes," Sammy says. "She was totally unaware. Now, John, when you entered the library, what did you do?"

"I looked over the bills on the desk, called the power company, that sort of thing."

"Did you notice the safe behind the screen?"

"No, I didn't."

"Why not?" Sammy asks.

"I didn't see it."

"That's not possible. Come with me." We walk into the library, and he points to a wall safe, wide open behind a wooden screen.

Sammy says, "It hasn't been touched since we got here."

"I must have missed it. It was dark at the time, Sammy. In that dim light, it wouldn't have been apparent."

Sammy pulls the curtains so very little light illuminates the room. "Was this about like you saw it?"

"Probably. But I can still see that the safe door is open."

"Exactly. So how could you have missed it? Was it possible you overlooked it?"

"I could have, I guess. I mean, it was hot, and I was sort of spooked by the odor in the house. You know…"

"No, I don't know. I don't let any crime scene distract me from making clear observations. Maybe that's just me."

I say, "You're so good you never let your surroundings get to you? Bullet holes in craniums don't bother you?"

"Yes, it affects me…I'm human, but not to the point where I freak. We turn it off when it gets nasty. Or at least, I do. I can handle it, no matter what the circumstances. I don't miss this kind of thing."

"Well, neither do I. Okay?"

"But you just told me you might have missed it, John. That tells me you're not really sure about what you saw. I have a problem with your doubt."

"Well, I'm human too. I never claimed to be perfect. I have good days and bad days. I probably missed it."

"Probably? You're not even sure about that?"

"No! Not probably. I really missed it. Okay? I missed seeing that the safe door was open. Satisfied?"

"I don't understand you today. You are full of doubt when normally you are quite certain. That's what's bothering me. Your uncertainty."

"Well then, dammit, if you really want to know, I did miss it. I was preoccupied with something..."

"Who is it?" Sammy demands.

We move out in the hall.

"I saw Tara the other night."

"We need to talk with her."

"She left town, Sammy."

"It was her landlady that was murdered. You question her?"

"Didn't tell her."

"Christ, John..."

"She'd just come back into town after her father's funeral. She was distraught. I didn't want to further upset her."

"Distraught or not, get her back over here."

"She flew back to San Francisco."

Sammy pauses. "You were falling for her, weren't you?"

"No."

"She give you a piece of ass on the way out of town?"

"Up yours." I walk past him into the library.

I place the back of my hand on the safe door, close my eyes, and exhale. I see nothing. I open my eyes and stare straight ahead. Sometimes, the purple hues of the other world are in my peripheral vision. But they're not there. Only days ago this steel door would have yielded some notion of who touched it last. It refuses me.

I move up the stairs, through the heat to the top of the landing. The closer I grow to Sloan's bedroom, the more my gut churns. The room is bathed with light from open curtains. I look around, avoiding the bathroom, where her body lay. I study instead the swirling pattern on the bedspread. I lift its edge, but there's nothing under there. I look across the floor into the darkened bathroom, its pitch blackness is cave-like. Perhaps a beast is there, with razor talons, awaiting me. I need to place my hand on the cool tile where she lay. I need to place my fingertips on the blood stain.

I kneel there and feel fear creeping up my back. My brain fogs and my breath seizes as I stare deeper into the dark bathroom. I have things buried in me, haunting pieces of other cases. Sammy was right; you must not let death bother other you. Those moments of terror have spilled out now, and all those bodies are coming forth. The young, cold-hearted detective is shaking. I stand up stiffly and see Sammy looking at me. He's not supposed to know I am weak. He sees it.

"We'll do this another time, John," he says.

The lazy turns of the black biplane catch my eye as it climbs and twirls in the blue morning sky above the mountains. Racing along ridgetops, it swoops down to explore the hollows of the Shenandoah Valley. I sit here alone, atop Hawksbill Peak in the Blue Ridge Mountains, watching. At my perch, almost a mile in the air, I am jealous of the freedom the pilot of that fragile, twin-winged plane must feel. I've spent my second night up here, in an old stone camping shelter, and just made the first coffee. My mind is calm, and my ambitions far away. Three hundred miles to the south, along this mountain chain, is the town where I was born.

The valley is green and without movement—except for this solitary aircraft. As if the pilot knew it was empty and decided to inhabit it all for himself. Now a white contrail erupts from its exhaust as the plane roars straight up above me. It pauses at its apogee, stalls, falls back, and then heads straight for the valley floor. Tumbling toward a green collision in the oaks, it pulls back finally, barely clipping the treetops. Barrel rolling its black fuselage in victory, it flies south and vanishes.

I sit back and pour more coffee as the valley grows still once again. I have ten messages on my cell that I have refused to check. There are things I need to do, tasks to accomplish, and details to uncover. Behind that need is an even bigger problem—my continued lack of power. I feel my touch draining away, and I don't seem to care. It's as if I could no

longer drive a car and decided it wasn't really important. Have I identified too much with my special abilities, too little with real detective work?

I retrieve my cell messages. The first four are from Sinclair. He's
elated by a new breakthrough. Then, he's concerns about a sudden
roadblock.

The rest are from Woods, Sammy, Chief Harris, Elizabeth, and a
rare one from Senator Hartner. Not one from Tara, whom I've called
a number of times.

I ring Sinclair.

"John, we got blips yesterday from Aswan's cell phone activity. But
as we were triangulating his location, a nasty virus exploded in my
system."

"You think it was from him?"

"Probably coincidence. But we were literally minutes from determining his locale."

"You have an approximate position?"

"His cell uses satellites in orbit over the mid-Atlantic Ocean. He
could have called from Mexico, Canada, the Caribbean, or anywhere
in Western Europe. We just lack the data to pin it down."

"When will you be back up?"

"A day or two. This bug is nasty."

"If you overcome it, can you get his cell location, Sinclair?"

"Yes."

"Keep it up. I'll call you tomorrow."

I look below and see a convoy of black SUVs down on the highway by the river. They vanish in and out of the dense woods, their
roofs flashing morning sun as they move along the road. I call Senator
Hartner back.

"Detective," he says, "I'm due to vote in a moment. Just wanted to
say again how much your rescuing Elizabeth will always mean to us.
You are remarkable, Mr. Wiley."

"Thank you, Senator. I appreciate your gratitude. But until Gerald
Aswan is stopped, only half the job is done."

"All of the job is done, unfortunately, Detective. I know you will be
missed in this town."

"Senator, I have no intention of leaving until he's captured."

"Then you'll be here a long time. You're not aware of what's occurred?"

"No."

The senator pauses. "I thought Sammy had briefed you."

"No, Senator. Please tell me."

"The formal pursuit of this man who nearly destroyed my family has been terminated. The apprehension of him will continue, but it now belongs solely in the jurisdiction of Homeland Security. And he will not be a prime target for them."

"What does that mean?"

"It means the task force that we put together is being reassigned."

"To what?"

"Back to their normal law enforcement duties. It's over as far as the DC police force and the FBI are concerned. And your work with Sinclair Johnson as well. I'm under enormous pressure to return him to prison."

"He's days from pinning down Aswan's location, Senator."

"I know. Treasury is briefing me. But the global breaching of commercial data systems is growing rampant. Bills are moving through Congress, addressing that very topic. Don't forget, Gerald Aswan and Sinclair Johnson both have a record of cybercrime. I'm having a tough time rationalizing our support of one criminal spying on the other."

He pauses. "What will your plans be?"

I see that the black convoy of SUVs has vanished. "I will return to North Carolina."

"Look me up before you go, John," he says.

I click the phone shut and sit back. A sense of relief comes over me as I search my mind for traces of regret. There are none. Dreams of going home flood me.

That convoy of law enforcement below looks like the FBI detail that backed me up when I brought Elizabeth out here. Why are they returning? I pack, hike down the trail, and reach the parking lot in twenty minutes. I want to see them if they are moving this way.

I head down the winding road. Tourist traffic is picking up. I see the black SUVs moving up a switchback a half mile ahead. I pull over in the grass and wait. Within a minute, they crest the hill. As they grow close, they slow. Two vehicles pull over and stop opposite me. I look in the windshields for familiar faces.

I don't recognize them. They are watching me, waiting for me to emerge. As traffic passes, I get out and walk over. A window goes down.

"Morning, Mr. Wiley. How was the camping?"

"Perfect," I say. "You guys knew I was up here?"

"Sure did."

"Where you headed?" I ask.

"Our mission's already accomplished," he says.

He rolls up the window. I turn around, move back to my truck, and pull away. They're not going to tell me anything.

I call Sinclair back. No answer. As I dip down into the valley, my cell reception dies. When I head down into Sperryville, I see the black convoy following me. As I pull through the tiny village, I stop at the Mountainside Café. There's lots of cars, so breakfast will be good.

I call Woods's cell phone from the café landline to schedule a good-bye dinner. No answer. I eat warm pancakes and watch the morning sun. All the agents walk in as I'm paying the bill. Their black vehicles are parked side by side outside. They are dressed casually, no suits today. The group sits at a corner table, but says nothing.

"Join us, Mr. Wiley," one finally says.

I walk over and sit down, and look over the faces. In the corner seat, with five men on either side, is a man with a shaved head and goatee. He's tanned and serene looking.

It's Gerald Aswan.

CHAPTER TWENTY-SEVEN

I look at Aswan intently, at his bearing, the polished fingernails that lift the menu. He's reading the selections. All is quiet around the table as he decides what to eat.

"Western omelet," he remarks to the waitress.

Normally, a calm comes over me when I encounter a murderer. Not now. I feel a weakness and a lack of concentration. I don't know what tack to take. The waitress takes all their orders, then looks at me.

"Perrier and lime," I say.

They begin talking. Not one face is familiar looking after all the months I've been on this case. They're all new. Aswan eats his breakfast with relish, as do they all. The inn slowly empties of the morning crowd, and soon we are the only party left. The bill arrives. A fresh hundred is placed on the table.

"Ready?" the man beside me asks.

"For what?"

An icy cold spike pierces my shoulder blade. A warm, violent wave hits my brain as I fall into the man beside me. I need to be strong, but nothing's working. I slump all the way over, and I see their feet pushing back from the table. Aswan's polished black loafers walking away are the last images in my mind.

Thank God, I'm back home. Here in the dark, in my swirling head, I know it's home because the silence is the same. The pitch-black darkness of my room is the same. I always went back to my folk's house during rough times. My tiny apartment in Asheville was useful, but never home. I want to sleep some more and wake up and smell Maxwell House drifting though the chilly morning rooms. I want to see the first sunlight in Black Mountain illuminate my bedcovers.

My bed doesn't feel right. I begin to wake up, and open my eyes. I don't see my familiar bedroom. I pull my legs up to my chest and realize I'm lying on a floor. I have pants and shirt on, but no shoes. I lean up and look around. My bedroom ceiling can't be so close. I lie flat on my back and stare straight up. The ceiling is only a few feet away. What has happened to my room? It's a dream. I sleep again, praying that when I awake, I'll be home for sure.

Hours pass, and I feel better.

I reach up and touch the ceiling. It's cold and hard, and the light is so dim I can't tell its composition. I smell my fingertips. Sour. I push my arms out to either side and strike hard surface again. I sit up, and my head hits a damp ceiling. I am in a tiny, dark tunnel. A squiggling image drifts back and forth out in front of me.

I spin around, crawl close to the edge, and look out into the darkness. A rock wall a hundred feet away is catching light from somewhere. Way down below is a pool of water, with its surface undulating, sending up warm light. My eyes focus on the massive cavern in front of me.

I'm not at home.

It must be a full day since I've been in here. I have no way of knowing that is true, but it seems an eternity that I've lain here. I've run out of things to think about. I remember the inn and the breakfast, and seeing Aswan. It took a while to realize that he had done this to me. If I were to be killed, it would have happened already.

I have surveyed the tunnel I'm in. It's two of my body lengths long, three feet high. The big cavern at the end is almost a hundred feet deep. Its walls are slick rock. At the bottom are sharp pinnacles extending upward, at the top, dripping stalactites hanging down. I've seen these underground places before, but never so vast, never without a way out.

On the second day it occurs to me—I may die here. I have no faith they will open a trap door in the wall and push in a hot meal. I crane my head out the tunnel and look up. I see nothing but a slick, dim ceiling. I see no sign it was possible to even climb up here. How did I get here? I feel like I'm in the center of the earth. I fight a panicky feeling the tunnel will collapse—one slip of the world and it will all come down on me.

In desperation, I lick the slick rocks at the lip's edge. I wait, and lick as it grows slick again. I don't want to go back into the tunnel. The dim rocky walls across from me are where I take solace. Notes sung out in the silence are sustained for many seconds. Will anyone bother to look for me? The Aswan case is over, and they will think I went back home.

Was that rope always there?

I stare at it for long minutes before it registers. It's ten feet away, on the dark wall to my right. It extends almost down to the bottom. Perhaps it's a bulging vein of crystal, ribbing the wall, luring me with its shape. Maybe I'm just dreaming about it for such an easy escape. Was it placed here while I slept? I pull off my pants and shirt and tie them together. I sling this clothing rope over at the darkened shape. It wiggles. Its end is pinned into the rock. Perhaps it's abandoned climbing gear left over from a spelunking group.

I form a hook with my belt, attach it to the pants, and swing at the rope. I keep brushing it, but not hooking it. It's too far away to capture. I will have to crawl across the slippery rock and grab for it. But if I miss, I will fall.

I visualize what to do. I will tie a knot in my clothing rope, jam it in this crevice by the lip, and swing over. Once I have the rope, I will swing back, untie my clothes, and slide down.

I peer down to the floor of the cavern. The rope ends two stories up from the bottom. Can I drop from there without breaking an ankle on those stalagmites? No. The solution is to reach the end of the rope, then tie clothes and belt on to form another length that will get me all the way down.

I bitterly curse this wretched place and my growing lack of confidence. I fear I don't have the strength to do this. Yet one thing is certain—I prefer dying while trying to get down than starving to death up here.

Ten minutes later, I drop down to the cavern bottom by the pool, landing barefoot on a slimy rock. I flip the clothes loose and put them back on. I see no sign that anyone's been here, except for the rope. Its ancient twine creaked and nearly broke as I slid down. It may have hung there for years.

A tunnel leads me to another cave where multiple pools lie. Natural fluorescence beams from all the rocks, yet I see no sunlight or manmade illumination. I work back to the main cavern and scour its boundaries. There's no way out. A massive pile of stone blocks what may once have been an exit.

The water here seems to drip from above, collect in pools, then seep away. I drink the scummy water, then lie in the corner of the cavern. I begin to detect evening on what must be my third day here. I feel a kind of dismay I never thought could exist. All the cunning that used to drive me forward is gone, and it all started the last time I saw Tara.

She drained me of my fire, and my touch.

My belt buckle helped me to see the opening above. I was dangling its polished surface in the pool, bouncing light off its face, and shooting it up the walls. That's when I saw it—another tunnel, five feet above the one I awoke in. It's only visible from down here.

I shoot light all around the opening, examining it. There's no way of knowing if it goes anywhere. A trip back up that rope will weaken it, perhaps break it. I could survive down here by the pools for a few weeks. Up there with no water, for only a few days. I tell myself to stay put, yet I stare at the dark, narrow opening.

This place is a paradox for me. I got down from the tunnel above, and yet now I sense I must return back up there. Am I following a course of some kind, where only perfect moves can win? I must climb back up and see where that upper tunnel goes, for to stay down here is hopeless.

I knot my clothes and sling them up through the loop of rope. I pull up. Each pull on that twine creaks its length, echoing in the cavern. As I get halfway up, I rest on a tiny ledge. I pull my clothes up, unknot them from the end, and tie them around my waist. I continue climbing, until the bottom length I'm holding unravels and falls away. I slam face first in the rock, dangling by one hand.

Spinning around, I grab the rope's frayed end and pull myself up. I advance again, taking more care with the rope. A half hour later, I climb back into the first tunnel, sweating and bleeding.

Climbing out onto the lip, I look up. The opening five feet above me is just out of reach. The walls are nearly vertical and super slick, but I see a few shallow purchases that may get me up there. I begin to tie the rope around me when it falls apart in my hands, and its pieces drift away to the bottom.

It's like the last seconds in a long football game, and there's time for one more play. I grab the rocky wall above me, place my foot on the tunnel's edge, and push up. I grab another hold and pull again. I begin to shake with muscle spasms. I scream out, my bellow echoing like a madman's.

Moments later, I pull myself up into the upper tunnel and stare into its darkness.

It's a dead end.

I try not to think about what I've done as I stare down at the luminous pool below. I was down there not long ago, but now I'm perched back up here in an even higher tunnel, with no rope. I've been in control since I woke up a few days ago. Progress was being made. But this cave has no water on its lip, and thirst will come on soon. I also

222

know I can't get back down to the tunnel below me without falling. I am trapped.

That a brown mouse could be cowering here, within this new tunnel, surprises me. But here he is, trembling nearby. He pauses for a while, then proceeds past me toward the dead end of the tunnel. I don't look up, but now patiently wait for him to retreat back out. I will eat him with relish.

He must be asleep? I bring my head up and see a tiny, dark hole at the end of the tunnel. I spin around and poke at the rocky opening. I begin to dig away at the mouse hole frantically now, finding its narrow opening doesn't end.

Within an hour, with bleeding hands, I have scooped out a one-foot hole. I dig for another hour and then see it, the most joyous sight I've seen in a long time.

Sunlight is filtering down the mouse hole.

CHAPTER TWENTY-EIGHT

The earth becomes rocky again, and my hands are growing more bloody, and yet more determined. As hours pass, I push the dirt out of the tunnel to splash in the pool, far below. The light above is growing slightly more brilliant with each inch of progress.

Yet it's hard to judge how far away freedom is. The soil is dense, cold, and filled with sharp rocks. As my hole inches toward the surface, I encounter even more solid rock. Within an hour, it's all stone, yet the mouse tunnel continues all the way to the surface. How did that feeble rodent manage to dig this?

The light in the tunnel dims, then turns black as night falls. Repeated bellowing up the hole gets no response. Impatiently, I lie down and wait for dawn to stream down the tiny tunnel again. I fall into a tumbling dream state, where faces and handguns swirl together in my head. I wake up and look up into darkness.

It seems like an eternity has passed when the mouse hole grows light again, filled with a grayer light than yesterday. Now, I begin chipping away at the rock with a large crystal slab. It helps me cut the tiny hole until it's large enough to stand in. As the sun fades in the hole, I survey my work. I now have a vertical shaft six feet high and two feet wide. There looks to be another four feet to go.

I am dying for water.

I begin to stare at the pool below, wondering how I can get down there, drink deeply, then climb back up. I can't dig for another hour without water. Though it's dark and cool in here, my throat and lips are parched. If I were to get down without smashing my brains out, getting back up here would be impossible. I feel a sense of helplessness again.

Then, a miracle. A thunderstorm hits, its lightning bolts flashing brightly down the narrow hole. For almost an hour it pounds the world above, and then water starts pouring down on me. I hold my mouth open and swallow muddy water as it rushes over my head and shoulders, drinking the warm fluid until I feel sick. The storm finally ends, and the world above begins to grow bright once more. Blue light appears as I look up the opening toward freedom.

I leave small shelves in my shaft so I can climb higher. I get three feet dug during the next day, and slurp all the excess water from the floor around me. The next day, it rains again, and again I drink the stream rushing down on me. The surface now is only a foot away. But the rock seems to know I am almost free, and grows even denser still. That last foot almost kills me, and I begin to fear they will all be waiting for me up there. I must wait till it's night to make the final push, wanting to emerge in total darkness.

When my head and shoulders finally push out through the damp earth, I fill my lungs with warm mountain air, and feel balmy breezes stirring the trees around me. As I climb out into a moonlit pasture, I fight back tears, and wearily walk through the clearing, working my way over toward a nearby cliff.

Below, in a dark valley, is a huge, brightly lit property. Its compound has roads and buildings all around. Behind me is a path leading up the mountain into darkness. I hike it for a hundred yards and sense I can make it all the way, even though I'm barefoot. Dawn begins to brighten the world.

I see a wide mountainous area all around me. Within a half hour I have climbed to the top of the ridge. I stand on the narrow peak and look east. Nothing but mountain ranges as far as I can see. Not one road, not one car. My gaze rests on the big, spacious property, far below. If I follow this trail, it will not lead me out soon. I have only one choice, return down the mountain and approach that home. As I come down the trail, the black biplane I saw days ago is visible in the home's nearby pasture.

I make my way down the slope, then reach an old dirt road. A hundred yards ahead, I see the back of a pickup truck idling in the morning mist. Rifle barrels protrude from the cab's windows.

I approach the truck through dense poplar saplings, and I move up carefully. They could be hunters, but those gun tips look like semiautomatic weapons. I hear the distant crackle of a two-way radio. I throw a rock past the truck, into the woods beyond. Their heads look up.

I run low on the road, straight for the rear of the truck, taking advantage of their distraction. I stop, ten feet back from the cab, out of view of their side mirrors, and lie flat in the dirt. One man gets out and looks ahead, scanning the woods in front of his weapon. I scoot forward in the dirt, slithering ahead till I am underneath the truck bed. I hold my breath until he gets back in. They cut the engine, settle down, open their doors, and sit quietly.

Ten minutes pass. I'm sweating badly.

"Waste of time," one remarks.

"Quiet."

"I'm telling you, he's dead now."

"V's got a way of knowing everything we say."

"The V's got better things to worry about than us bitching, waiting for the fool inside that mountain to lose his mind."

"Shut your yap."

A few moments later I hear his voice over the two-way radio. It chills me, and yet excites me. The man who's done so much damage is still around. The "V" they just referred to must mean the "Vishava." So, it's Gerald Aswan after all.

"How long to remove the stones from the entrance?" Aswan demands arrogantly over the speaker.

"Not long," says one.

"At noon, clear the opening and pull the detective out."

"Yes, sir."

"Regardless of his condition, break both his legs on the ride back over here. I don't want him mobile again."

"Sir, I doubt he's alive."

Aswan says, "I have waited in this region of the world far too long. I have an empire to run. I delayed flying out this morning only because I want to see his face. See his desperation."

"What if he's dead?"

"Don't underestimate Wiley," Aswan spits. "The detective's constant interference makes me suspect he's found a way to survive. But he will be frantic. The US government's intrusion into my network and my banking affairs is lethal for us if it continues. Wiley should be willing to reveal who is hacking us. And if he's dead, break both legs anyway."

"With pleasure," one says.

They hang up and sit quietly. One says, "Get him out now?"

"Yeah, let's get it over with."

The truck starts up, and I grab onto the exhaust pipe and begin grinding along the dirt as the truck moves down the road. We pick up speed to the point where I fear I should let go. But then we slow down, and the truck stops. They get out and walk through the woods to a pile of rocks at the base of the mountain.

They start up a small bulldozer parked there, and begin clearing away the stones piled in front of an opening. One puts on gloves and begins helping by hand.

I slide out from beneath the truck, peer into the cab, and see what I prayed would be lying there. A cell phone. I grab it and slip well back into the woods. I call Sammy in a whisper. "I've been kidnapped for the last week—up in the mountains."

"Who did this to you, John?"

"It's Aswan. He's here, and ready to fly away in a black biplane. We can take him if you can get here quickly. He's staying at the big home at the bottom of the valley. Nothing else around. You can't miss it."

"Christ, John, where are you?"

"Don't know. In the Blue Ridge Mountains somewhere. Can you find my location by using this cell phone as a GPS beacon?"

"Yes, stay on the line. Let me call some people."

Three minutes later, he says, "We've got you located. Just across the West Virginia line. Near Front Royal, Virginia."

How soon till you get here?"

"We'll have choppers out there in a half hour, John. Do what you have to do to keep him from flying away."

"That may be difficult."

"That's why we hired you."

I say, "Call me back when you get close. I'll move down toward the plane."

"Make it happen, John," Sammy says.

I move back through the woods and see the two men have nearly cleared the opening to the cave I was in. They will soon find I am not there. I wait for them to step in with flashlights and climbing rope in hand. They now go in the tunnel.

Two minutes pass. I race over to the bulldozer, start it up, scoop a big load of rocks up, and dump it in the opening. I back up, shove another load on top, then another, and another. They are now in the same position I was in. Trapped.

I drive the pickup back down the hill and into the woods, near the field where the biplane is parked in a deserted pasture. Beyond, the distant, big home has men standing guard all around it. I have little time, and the trapped guards may have tried to radio back to Aswan. I can only hope the cave has shielded their radios.

The sky begins to thicken, and with it, white mist pours down in the valley. Within ten minutes the pasture and plane are nearly invisible. I run toward the old plane now, hiding in the fog as I move up to its structure.

I step up on the wing and peer down into the canvas seats.

Voices cut through the fog.

I jump off and slip away just as two figures approach the plane. They're wearing jackets and leather caps and goggles.

"Climb in," says the voice of Gerald Aswan.

"We need to know about him," a woman replies.

"They will find Wiley and extract what we need to know. We can wait no longer. Another few minutes of this fog and we cannot fly. They will call and tell us what I need to know."

"I understand him well, you know," she says.

"How well?" Aswan says.

"Nothing can be guaranteed about Wiley. He confounded me."

"You performed brilliantly."

"Then mark my words. We should wait for their confirmation. That he has confessed, and then—that he is dead."

"Not this time," Aswan says. "Climb in, Tara."

It cannot be.

I dimly see them climb aboard. The prop fires up, the plane spins around, then it begins to move forward, through the damp grass.

Above, the sound of Sammy's approaching choppers begins to penetrate the fog.

The cell phone vibrates. "John, where are you?"

"Watching him," I say.

"We cannot see you down there," he says. "Don't let him take off. Shoot the frigging plane to pieces. He cannot fly."

I drop the phone and race toward the plane. I catch the wing, pull myself up, and climb up to the fuselage. I reach into the rear seat and slam my fist down on Aswan's arm. The plane bounds violently in the grass. He desperately reaches down for his leather valise.

Tara Chin spins and screams at me, ripping my face with her fingernails. "You are here, you bastard? Why can't you die?" She rises up and tries to push me off. The choppers are near, their blades pounding right above us.

"We must take off," Aswan bellows. "Kill him—shoot him!" She reaches up and fires her handgun, sending a wild shot barking past my head. Aswan is clutching the case to his chest. I grab for it as she slams the gun to my temple. "I will blow you away," she whispers.

I swat her gun away.

Aswan climbs up from his seat in a fury. "Get off my plane, you maggot!"

Momentarily releasing his hold on his valise, he slams me backward. I grab the case at that instant, and fall away with it, off the wing, slamming hard in the wet grass. The plane instantly vanishes off into the fog, with engine running full tilt. I hear a crazy mix of car engines and the roaring aircraft for the next minute. Then silence.

Stunned, I sit up and look inside the case, finding an ornate silver box. I release its latches and lift the lid. Sunk securely in a velvet lining is a shimmering crystal cube.

CHAPTER TWENTY-NINE

Law enforcement's encounter with Gerald Aswan, brief as it was, was a disaster. The fog and the location were blamed for the loss. No one was caught in his group, even the men in the tunnel had dug their way out. Men who should have been captured slipped away in the fog, in cars, and in a plane. With the exception of a few computer terminals, the big home was abandoned. No secret files were found. No big computer servers, no brilliant software guys. There was no evidence he was ever there. We are all looking like fools.

A day later, a black biplane was found abandoned on a deserted sandy strip just over the North Carolina border. Gerald Aswan vanished again, as easily as he had arrived.

During my police physical, ordered as a routine, a discovery was made. In my back, close to my tailbone, the doctor found a tiny sensor lodged under the skin. The same type as the one removed from Elizabeth Hartner's leg. I, too, had been tagged. They had tracked me like a dog, then moved in when they wanted me for kidnapping. I felt different that last night with Tara Chin, and now I know why. The sensor she slipped into me when we were naked immediately dampened my touch. I lost all of my insight, having that thing in me. Now, a day after its removal, I see and sense far more clearly.

I'm back again.

The following day, Sammy drives us out Route 28 in his cruiser, north into Chantilly, Virginia. A long black building allows us

231

entrance through its main gate. A sign on the lawn reads "National Reconnaissance Office." Woods looks caught off guard.

We move through security in this CIA facility until we all are seated in a bright conference room. At the table are a half dozen men. Some were in the Aswan task force. The door opens, and Senator Hartner walks in. A briefcase is set on the table. From it the silver box is removed, and the gleaming cube is exposed.

"Gentlemen, and Ms. Woods," the director says, pointing to the cube, "what you see before you is a perfect marriage of technology, power, and avarice."

Sammy and I are lost.

"In the old days, criminal activities were accompanied by forensics, paper trails, and eyewitnesses. Those days are gone. This extraordinary device is invisibly loaded with more sensitive data than any object on earth. We have examined it, and we have come to some conclusions."

"And we owe a debt of thanks to Detective Wiley for recovering it," Senator Hartner says.

The director agrees. "But we have a problem."

"Yes?"

"John, you must come clean with us about everything."

Sammy steadies my arm as I lean forward. "I've revealed every aspect of what happened to me," I say.

"There is more you haven't told us, Mr. Wiley," the director says.

"What?" I ask.

"John," the senator says, "We have no proof, no eyewitnesses that you were really kidnapped. We have no evidence Aswan was even out there. You show up, lying in a field, with this object." He points to the cube. "You must know more about it. Our discovery of this data storage device is now a matter of the utmost national security."

I say, "Tell me what you've uncovered."

"We can't do that."

Woods says, "But you want him to confess to details he's not supposed to know? Detective Wiley's done his best every day of this investigation. I'm proud to have worked with him."

"Detective Woods, we are not talking about Detective Wiley's success in this case."

"Then what?" Sammy asks.

"We think he's hiding critical details."

"Nonsense," Sammy replies.

The senator says, "We need to know more about Aswan's cube, John. That's the reason I'm present today. To convince you of the seriousness of this inquiry."

"Aswan's people may provide you a better answer," I say.

"You have nothing else to add, Detective?"

"Senator, the fact that I returned this cube is my best defense. Until this moment, I had no idea it was significant."

"We're looking for a much bigger picture."

"I wish I could provide it."

Senator Hartner leans forward. "I'm sorry, John."

"For what?"

"You're being detained, Detective Wiley," says the director. "There may be features of this investigation you have overlooked. You will work with a special team designed to tease out those details. For the moment, you are being placed in witness protection."

"Protection from what?" I say.

"Aswan's remaining network. Surely they know you had the cube at the end. They certainly know where it is now."

"How?" Woods asks.

"Besides the unique properties of data storage, this device has a built-in global positioning system. They can determine the cube's location anywhere in the world."

"Then destroy it," I say.

"We cannot do that," the director says. "For national security purposes, we need to retrieve every bit of stored information in that cube. Many of our top-secret files may reside there. We don't know how to download the cube. That's what this is all about, Detective. We think you do."

❖

Ronald T McMillan

Witness protection is not what it's cracked up to be. The food is awful, and the suspicion is infuriating. I'm in an old brick farmhouse in rural Haymarket, Virginia, with three agents watching my every move. I've spent a full day in another exhaustive debriefing.

Woods and Sammy arrive at 11:00 p.m. We step down into the basement, where the agents hint there are no listening devices.

Sammy says, "The CIA is frantic, John. Senator Hartner's privately sick about all this. But it's out of his control. They want to access the cube before it dies."

"It can drain?" I say.

"Nobody knows. They can detect the cube's structure. They see that it's encoded, but need to know the language and its architecture. They're worried it will soon self-delete as a protective measure."

"Sammy, I wish I knew more. Now I realize why Aswan was clutching it so tightly."

"Exactly, John. That cube may contain all the files Aswan stole from the world's databases. I'm going to share another secret with you. The nanotechnology behind this device is actually a memory storage concept stolen from Lawrence Livermore Labs. They were working on the theory of atomic memory for years. Somehow, Aswan stole that design and made it a reality. He needed a way to store the entire world in a single, portable device. We have to catch up on his technology—quick."

"Then we need to talk to Sinclair Johnson," I say.

Sammy and Woods agree. They make the call down to the prison.

"You've got to understand," Sinclair says to us from his prison phone, "any information that is stored digitally is done so by transforming it into a code, or computer language. If you don't know the language, that's problem number one. And if you don't know the method of storage, that's another."

"Tell me the good news," I say, as we huddle around Woods's cell phone.

"You've got the cube. But the government's so worried about revealing its capability, they're stuck. People who could figure it out may not have security clearances."

"Sinclair, could you do it?"

234

He says, "My 'get out of jail card' expired. Or did it?"

I say, "Maybe we could get another one made up." Sammy's nodding with conviction. "What could you do that all these CIA geeks can't?"

"Get creative."

Within two days, police escort Sinclair Johnson in through the old farmhouse door in Haymarket. Now they have two of us to watch.

We're in the big laser lab in the CIA building, where staff from the FBI, CIA, and NSA are looking over our shoulders. For three days we've been attempting to uncover how the cube works while pumping agency guys to open up a bit. No one's talking.

Sinclair is reviewing what we discovered about the cube and bucking hard for release from prison. His presentation now is critical to that happening.

"The cube's a natural, flawless diamond with an unusual orientation to it," Sinclair begins. "All crystals have a direction that light prefers to go through, and this crystal is polished exactly for that requirement."

He places the cube on a platform and floods it with laser light. "It must utilize a green laser for reading its interior. You all agree?"

A few heads nod.

"So, the laser enters the cube like ones that penetrate the disk in a CD player. But in the case of the cube, the data is stored naturally in the atomic structure, a million times smaller. One needs a special instrument to do that. Agreed?'

"Correct," the director says.

"That instrument doesn't exist. True?'

"Possibly," Senator Hartner says.

"So, you're stumped," Sinclair says. "You don't understand how to scan the cube's atomic structure. You don't know the cube's digital language. Most importantly, you need a critical element that you're missing."

The director says, "Mr. Johnson, before you proceed, I want the room cleared of all level-two personnel."

Half the people walk out. The door is sealed shut again. "All right, Mr. Johnson, tell us what you've discovered."

Part of my dream about Tara dealt with this topic. I told Sinclair what I saw, and he worked on the idea. No one really knew what he was doing, switching lasers, detectors, and lenses around to confuse everyone. In the end, last night, he agreed with me.

Sinclair says, "The cube's atoms are aligned like wood grain on a tabletop. Entering the cube with a laser beam from the wrong side will reveal nothing. The correct access side of the cube is the other way, which we'll call 'the entrance.'"

He turns the cube around to the opposite face. He flips a switch, and the cube is flooded with a scanning green laser. The light passes through the cube, strikes a detector, and is sent to a computer. Gibberish symbols are displayed on a monitor.

"What are we looking at, Mr. Johnson?" the director says.

"This demonstration is crude, but it makes my point. We're looking at the only feature this cube has to offer, the reflected photons that represent the zeros of the stolen data. The 'zeros' are only half of the digital language. To complete the data code, we must add the missing ones."

"How can we retrieve the 'ones'?" the senator asks.

"Find the other cube containing them," Sinclair says.

CHAPTER THIRTY

"Everything Aswan used in his criminal activities was cutting edge technology," Woods says. "The self-deleting e-mail, the body sensors. How clever to divide the data code among two cubes."

Senator Hartner says, "John, any theories on what became of the other cube?"

"Perhaps Tara Chin was carrying it with her at the time."

"Was the abandoned biplane searched?" the senator asks.

"Yes, swept totally," Sammy says. "Where else can we search, John?"

"Agnes Sloan's townhouse, where Tara stayed. I doubt she would keep anything there, but we need to turn over all possibilities."

The director says, "Even the church where Elizabeth Hartner and her captors hid. We must search every location."

"If this cube is detectable with its global positioning system, why not use that same technology to locate the other one?" Woods asks.

"Excellent question, Detective Woods. We cannot determine the beacon signal of this cube accurately enough. Only Aswan's people have the means to detect it."

"And if the other cube is never found?" Sammy asks.

The director says, "By finding the other cube and recovering Aswan's stolen data, we can head off its eventual usage." He pauses. "It must be found."

When Sammy, Woods, and I step into Agnes Sloan's deserted home, the heat still envelopes it on this humid afternoon. I want to leave. Tara's essence is almost suffocating. I move into the den and see Sammy and Woods there, waiting.

"John, hold onto to the safe door. Your touch is back, so tell us what you see."

Last time I was here, I was numb from a psychic point of view. Now, it takes only an instant after I brush the warm steel door. I sense someone's gloved hands opening the safe, removing papers within, then, leaving.

I feel the person who opened this safe.

I move upstairs to Sloan's room. I place my hand on the bathroom tiles where her body lay. A person was here, leaning over her.

I walk over to the bed and lean down like last time. I look across the carpet into the darkened bathroom. With eyes closed, I can see a figure. Sloan's head wound gushes blood on their hands. They are feeling her neck. They move away down the stairs.

"Sloan was murdered by an accomplished killer," I say to Sammy and Woods, standing in the doorway.

"Keep going, John."

"After killing her, they went down and patiently opened the safe."

"Why, John?"

"To throw us off."

"They robbed her to look like theft," Woods says.

"But it was murder. They even knew the combination of the safe." I hesitate. It's clear now what I must do. "Woods, I need a complete workup on Tara Chin. It's time we know who this woman really is."

It's Tuesday morning, and Sinclair is working at the CIA lab in Chantilly with computer technicians on the task of revealing the cube's computer language. Finding all the "zeros" and "ones" is nothing if one can't reassemble them.

Sinclair is also working on other tasks—ones I have instructed him about. When he arrives back at the country farmhouse with his police escort, he joins me in the basement with Woods.

"Dimensions?" Woods asks, jotting some notes on her palm pilot.

"Exactly 20.1 millimeters in length, width, and height," Sinclair says.

"What material will we use—is diamond in our budget?"

"Cubic zirconia," he says. "Unless John lets us use his American Express card."

"CZ it is, guys. How fast can we have it fabricated?"

Woods says, "I found an optical house in Springfield. What should I say is the application?" Woods says.

Sinclair says, "Tell them it's for a laser light show."

Seven days later, Sinclair and I walk into the CIA facility. Aswan's cube has been sequestered in a massive vault. Fearing it will be damaged, the CIA had prohibited us from further testing on it by until the other cube can be recovered. It takes a lot of questions on our part before the director allows us back into the laser lab. A few minutes later, the cube is brought in, escorted by three agents.

Sinclair and I are going over tests he's previously performed, and he's almost ready. My hands have stopped shaking. We rehearsed this move last night, and on his cue, we begin. The cube is secured on a small stage, flooded with emerald laser light. The room is dark. The phony CZ cube we had fabricated is hidden in my cupped palm. Sinclair moves to the end of the big slab surface. He comes around, hits the corner, and stumbles, kicking the power cord loose, and rocking the instruments on this big, air-suspended laboratory table. Lenses fall and shatter. The laser ceases projecting. The engineers rush toward us.

I lean over to stabilize the real cube, then switch it with the fake, returning the real one to my palm, then my pocket. We begin to restore the table's surface, but the testing must now halt. Sinclair apologizes to them. The cube is removed from the table and placed back in its container. I don't look in their eyes. Fifteen minutes later, we are in the unmarked police cruiser heading back to Haymarket.

That night, Woods joins us in the basement, where we unwrap Aswan's real cube. It gleams brightly, like a beacon from hell. Sinclair has calculated there is a 20 percent chance the CIA lab engineers will discover the fake cube by tomorrow. A 100 percent chance by week's end. A technician, fooled by the looks but stumped by its optical performance, may eventually test the CZ cube for resistively—and discover it's not real. We've got to move fast.

"I have no idea how the GPS positioning beacon works in this cube," Sinclair says. "It was shielded at the CIA, but now it's surely sending out its location, John. They will be moving in this direction."

"All the more reason to roll," I say. "Meet me on the road in five minutes, Woods?"

Nervousness has gripped her. "Yes."

With Sinclair distracting the agents upstairs, I slip out the narrow basement window and run across the darkened field. I have only my clothes, my wallet, and the cube.

I reach Woods's idling car. "The flat's ready?" I say.

"Exactly where you asked for."

If you said the Potomac River was wrapped up in this case, that would be true. I have swum it, drunk it, and cursed it for months. Raul Gutab broke his neck in its mud. Elizabeth escaped with me in its brown, crazy waves. 'The Chameleon' met his death there. I find no other fitting place to end all of this than the river. I will use this confounding body of water to my advantage.

It's 4:00 a.m., and I'm standing on Key Bridge in Georgetown, looking downriver into DC. The monuments lie quietly, forcefully built in the distance. I have come here to bring them out. Nothing is stirring yet.

Part of me is skeptical about the existence of the second cube. I need verification. Sinclair can't say with 100 percent certainty that all the information isn't here in the cube now. Aswan and his network were scattered after the raid. But they will have the technology to track its signal.

I am standing halfway across the bridge beneath the tenth streetlight pole, a column ten feet high. I climb up on the wide handrail and steady myself. I unscrew the streetlight's frosted dome and reveal a bright fluorescent lightbulb. I gently place the cube down in the well of the lamp, then replace the dome over the light, and the cube. The bait is prepared.

I look down at the dim green river and wonder if this may be a mistake. But a new dream last night told me differently. I take an object from my pocket and deliberately drop it in the water. I hear it strike the river's surface, then see it vanish below.

I run across the deserted bridge back into Georgetown. Within a few minutes, I am in the efficiency overlooking the river Woods has secured for me. It has a perfect view of Key Bridge. I set up the videotape camera on the tenth light pole, halfway across the bridge, and wait. The trap is set.

CHAPTER THIRTY-ONE

I ask Woods, seated across from me in my temporary Key Bridge flat, "What did Sinclair say to you about my disappearance?"

"The farmhouse agents questioned him for over three hours about your escape. He denied knowing anything."

"And the CZ cube?"

"No one at the CIA knows it was switched with the real one yet. Sinclair also says a very strange thing is occurring in Aswan's banking world. Funds are being withdrawn from hundreds of his global accounts."

"Meaning?"

"Sinclair says it's a reaction to Aswan's legal troubles. It's rippling through the underground banking industry. They must know he's hampered and not sure what to do. They're liquidating fast."

Woods says, "What about the cube—any movements on the lamppost?"

"No one's come near it in the last three days."

"They're cautious."

"I know, and it looks like such an obvious setup. Woods, does Sammy have any idea where I've gone?"

"He didn't ask, and I didn't tell."

"You believe in what I'm doing?"

"Yes, John, but I hope putting yourself in such jeopardy pays off." She sets a folder on the table before she leaves. "And, Detective, you better read this right away—it's Tara Chin's actual background."

I sit back and quickly read Woods's in-depth biography on Tara Chin. A half hour later, I look up, feeling very foolish. I have totally underestimated this woman. She's far older, more educated, and more deadly than I ever imagined.

It's later in the day, and the sun is setting warmly along the Potomac. An old man is pushing a rusted shopping cart across the bridge. He stops often to catch his breath and stare at the river. At the tenth light pole, he pauses and looks around.

Suddenly, a nearby explosion rips the evening air open like the Fourth of July. Two speedboats have collided near the distant riverside restaurants. Their hulls are erupting in the air, raining flaming debris down over the Georgetown waterfront. Within minutes, ambulance and police vehicles are cramming the dock. News helicopters are hovering overhead.

I have swung the camera around to study the explosion scene, and am distracted for many minutes as waves from the explosion slosh the banks on Roosevelt Island. Then it dawns on me.

I swing the camera around back to Key Bridge and see that the homeless guy has vanished. I zoom in on the tenth light pole, and scan it up and down. The frosted dome over the lamppost is in place, but appears slightly ajar. It had been removed during the explosion and has not been reseated. I feel sick.

They *are* here.

Sammy leans back in the chair in my sparse kitchen and stares at the ceiling. I don't know if he's angry, or in shock. The harbor explosion and the now missing cube problem forced me to call him.

"So," he begins.

Woods may be in deeper trouble than I am.

"Which one of you should I fire first? You or Woods?"

"It was all his idea," she whines.

"Me? Just a few hours ago you were backing me up. What happened?"

"You lost the cube—that's what happened!" Sammy bellows. "Did you think they would ring you and ask permission to grab it? It was insane enough that you stole it from the CIA—but to leave the thing hanging out there, with no protection?"

"I don't think all is lost, Sammy," I say.

"What's left to screw up? You stole top-secret government property, jumped witness protection, then got the goddamn cube lifted right before your eyes. You're responsible for that staged boat collision as well. Thank God no one was on board."

"Sammy, we've got a formidable group of Aswan's people still around. They were watching for the cube's movement. They're desperate to get this missing cube."

"Now they have both," Sammy says. "They're back in business."

"Not actually," I say.

"What else do they need?"

"They'll be back."

"Back for what? They've left town."

"Sammy. I don't think so."

"Then what?" he asks.

"The real cube."

"They already have it. You said the streetlight dome was ajar."

"They took it, all right. But that one was a decoy."

"Another CZ cube?" Sammy asks.

"Of course. We had two fabricated. You don't think I would leave the real thing hanging out there in space, do you?"

Sammy hesitates. "Then the real cube is…?"

"At the bottom of the river—right beneath that same lamppost on the bridge. It's sending out its beacon signal in the exact location as the CZ cube was."

"*What?*"

"The first night, I stood for hours on the bridge with both cubes in my pocket. Long enough for them to pick up the real one's signal and determine my location. They watched me place it in the lamppost. But it was dark. They didn't see me drop the real cube in the river as I was getting down."

"That was risky."

"I had to see if they were there. They proved that."

"That's why they'll be back," Woods realizes.

"Exactly. They will determine the lamppost cube is not real, while still detecting a signal in that area. They will conclude it's in the river and return."

"Then, we can retrieve it now…"

"Wouldn't we rather catch *them* doing it?"

"Hell yes. But what's to prevent a scuba diver from swimming in and scooping it up?"

"Because of what lies directly beneath the bridge, on the river bottom."

"And that is?"

"A huge steel cage built back in the 1920s. River water was once drawn through it up to a nearby treatment plant. According to city documents, the structure was never removed. The real cube fell down through its bars and now lies inside that steel-covered cage. The only way to get at it is with heavy equipment. You didn't think I would leave the real thing sitting down there unprotected, did you?"

"How certain are you that the cube fell precisely in that cage?"

"One hundred percent certain," I lie.

Sammy is speechless.

For twenty-four hours, we scan the bridge and the river. Thousands of cars and pedestrians move across. Boats pass beneath; aircraft and helicopters fly overhead. They all move on. If I cannot produce an indication of their presence by tomorrow, Sammy will step in. He will get that cube back his own way.

My problem is, I don't exactly know who or what I'm looking for.

The rain starts to fall in the early evening and settles into a steady pace, pelting the dark river below. Sammy and a special task force are due back at dawn to take over the river retrieval of the cube. Woods has gone home for a few hours, so I put Sinatra on softly and sit back and wait. In the morning, it will all be over. Aswan's men should have appeared by now, but there's nothing.

I doze a bit while watching the video feed on my big monitor. The warm wind blows rain in sideways torrents, swirling around the lampposts along Key Bridge. Traffic begins to slacken. Boats in the river move back to their slips in Old Town, Alexandria. If this is a chess match, I'm about to lose my queen. I can only hope for a mistake on their part. Yet I see no one down there.

I move away from the TV monitor and look south, down the Potomac. Six powerboats are heading upriver, three of which pass under Key Bridge, then stop. Three others stop below the bridge.

Sinclair rings my cell. "Any action over there?"

"Got boats coming up the river in the rain."

"Don't get too excited," he says.

"Why?"

"The agents here just left me. Said they were to report to the Key Bridge area. Some kind of showdown to retrieve the cube."

I ask, "These boats are law enforcement, then?"

"Probably. I think Aswan's group read your setup trap and decided this was too hot a spot. John, they will pass up the chance to get caught."

"You could be right. I could have set the snare a little more deftly."

"You did your best," Sinclair says. "Now, a few more things, John. I must confess to you, I known a lot more about the cube than I've told you."

"What? Then tell me..."

"First, after scanning the cube repeatedly at the CIA lab, I saw a familiar pattern forming. Readout spacings occur every 12.011 spots in the optical output. The atomic weight of carbon is 12.011 on the periodic chart. John, the cube's written code is based on the atomic structure of the diamond itself, which is carbon."

"You lost me," I say.

"The cube's digital language is based on its own atomic structure. A simple design that no one would ever consider. Then, after I determined that, I felt confident enough to temporarily disable the cube by introducing an optical virus into it..."

"You did what?" I ask.

"Before we lifted the cube from the CIA lab, I flooded the cube with a strong UV light—temporarily freezing its interior crystal structure from access. Aswan's cube is now useless to them unless someone heats it up to 100 degrees Celsius. The heating clears the virus from the cube, restoring it so it can be used again. I'm certain they'll not know what happened to it."

"Sinclair, that will come in handy. What's next?"

He says, "Both cubes are oppositely charged, like poles on a battery. That's why one contains only "zeros," the other, "ones." They are cut and polished that way in order to function."

"Yes, okay?"

"The reason both cubes may have been separated by Aswan, besides a security precaution, was the problem of polarity. Both of the cubes' info must be read separately, then recombined to form the final data stream."

"Meaning?"

"If the two cubes were ever to come in physical contact with each other, that would mean…"

"A short?"

"Yes. The result being the total elimination of all the data contained in them. If they ever touch, the electrical short instantly erases every discrete site in the atomic structure. It's the Achilles heel of this design. You're left with two priceless, very empty diamonds."

Dawn comes as dark rain clouds engulf the Potomac. I see law enforcement parking on the bridge and along both sides of the river. I wonder how long till they move in and arrest me.

Sammy rings my cell. "John, we need you to come down here. Walk to the center of the bridge—I'll be waiting for you. Divers are ready to go now. A lot of big dogs are furious about what you've done. If I can retrieve the cube intact, I'll have some pull. But I need that cube."

Five minutes later, I walk up to Sammy, Woods, and lots of police standing on the bridge. Rain's pouring hard as we talk. Below are three harbor patrol boats with teams of divers, waiting on us. I point down from the tenth lamppost to the water's surface.

"You sure that's the spot?"

"Yes. Directly below is the old cage. The cube should be down inside it."

Sammy waves them on. Six divers leap in the churning water and submerge. We get in Sammy's cruiser and cut on the heat. Traffic over the bridge is diverted to one lane, and it's backing up into Virginia. Behind us are three parked black cruisers, full of sullen-faced agents.

After thirty minutes we step out and watch the boats. Two divers are back up now. They're talking with the captain. He radios up to Sammy.

"The cage is down there, all right, but it's mucked up badly. Silt and debris are all over the bars. They tried probing down in the muck but can't find anything. Gonna take down a torch and cut the top off. That's what happening now."

"How soon till they can remove the top?" Sammy asks.

"A good forty-five minutes. The steel bars are two inches thick. They are old, but still tough."

"Any divers seen the cube?"

"Visibility's only a few feet, and the currents are strong. Nothing yet, Detective."

Sammy snorts impatiently.

"Sammy," I say, as we stare down at the rushing water, "Aswan's men are out here somewhere, agreed?"

"They'll have no chance of intercepting us. Don't worry."

"I'm not worried they'll take it away from us. I'm worried they won't."

"John, you need sleep."

An hour later, the divers surface. The captain radios up to us. "Sammy, they cut the top off, climbed in, and searched the entire cage. They sucked up all the silt and searched it meticulously. No cube down there."

I study the river. "Let me get down, Sammy. I'm certified."

"Go," he says.

Soon I am geared up and plunging in the river with a team of divers. The water is turbulent and dim as they escort me down to the bottom. The dreary cage looks like an apparition from the Titanic. We swim around its shape, as big as two SUVs, and I motion them to search outside the cage. We work against the current, searching by hand through the muck. Tree limbs have jammed up in a pile on one side. I break them off, searching the silt. Time passes too quickly.

They signal me to ascend back up to the boats. Watching the other divers make for the surface, I realize I made a mistake when I dropped the cube from the bridge. I didn't account for the powerful currents down here. The cube may have fallen farther downstream from the cage. I swim down and begin searching out in front of the structure.

One lone diver is now back by my side. We begin working farther away from the structure, lifting up rotten debris, letting the current wash it from our hands. If I don't surface, I'll have to decompress soon. I've got two minutes.

Many yards past the cage, we both see the cube down at our feet, sparkling in the darkness on river bottom. In relief, I reach down and retrieve it.

Suddenly, my partner spins and thrusts at me with his gleaming blade, its tip lightly grazing my throat. He wrenches me closer by my weight belt, and I see now he's not one of the law enforcement group. He motions to hand him the cube. As I drop it into his palm, he powerfully shoves me away, and slips the cube into a belt pouch.

Before he can slit my air hose, I back away. He floats there for a long moment, determining my fate, then rapidly paddles off in the current. On his waist is a flashing beacon light.

CHAPTER THIRTY-TWO

The turbulent water gives me no sign of his bubble trail, so the red beacon on his belt is all I have to follow. Its bright flash allows me to paddle well back from him without detection. I am about to surface when the red beacon begins to rise up. He is thirty feet above me, still submerged, nearing a small motorboat on the surface. He's hesitating because another boat is approaching it. Perhaps harbor police are asking questions.

I approach him before he surfaces, rip off his face mask, and yank him backward. His knife flashes out, but unmasked, he cannot see me in the darkness. I swim away, then circle back. I slam my fist down on his wrist, and he weakly drops the knife. He lunges at me, clawing at my face and throat. Spinning him around, I rip his mouthpiece free and slam him in a headlock he cannot shake. He flails and bucks, then begins to loosen his grip on my arm, then begins to relax. He is gone.

I pull his tank and fins free and put them on. I must match his appearance when I surface. The cube pouch he carried is now secured in my vest. The small boat on the surface is sitting alone. I paddle up and break the surface, where a man is waiting. "Do you have it?" he whispers.

"Yes—"

"Stay down there, and let that police launch go off. Hold onto the gunwale; I will motor us farther away."

I grab the lip, and we speed away past the waterfront, out toward Roosevelt Island. I hear him radio to someone and talk animatedly. He stops the boat near the shore, and I jump in with my mask on. In the pouring rain he does not see me. He flips a tarp over me, then we speed away downriver. He says nothing during the half-hour ride.

As the boat slows, he pats the tarp. "We are here."

He lifts the cloth, and I see a big yacht with crew along the decks. We approach its rear landing deck, and then we step aboard, with me still masked up. He gestures for me to hand him the pouch. As I do, a hard blow crushes me from behind, and I fall into darkness.

It's a gray, rainy sky that I now see, with rushing water twenty feet below. My belly is in agony, and my chest is tight. A massive chain is wrapped many times around my chest. I am pinned against the ship's hull, imprisoned by the anchor chain. Men are looking over at me, roaring with laughter.

"He's awake," one screams. "Dump him below!"

The anchor motor engages, and the links shudder. I feel the chain pull me down, inch by inch. The anchor fins carve the water, then submerge. I cannot breathe; I cannot shout. The men laugh madly as I slip closer to the speeding water. My feet splash the surface as waves of salty spray choke me. I see them watching me, like a doomed contestant.

I submerge, pop back up, then go back down. I am gagging and coughing as they yank me back up out of the water, again and again. I hear their hysteria each time I resurface.

"All the way under the water this time!"

I sink below the surface for the last time, dropping under the dark water, pulling away from the ship. I hold my breath in panic, knowing my throat will soon open, and I will swallow death in a cold, dark gulp.

I feel a surge on my chest, as the anchor chain pulls me up toward the ship again. I rush out of the water till I reach the top rail, where men are looking at me.

"What have you done to the cube?" a big one says to me.

Another smaller man rushes over. "What are you doing? I said kill him."

"We've discovered a glitch in the cube. We need to question him."

"Idiot, I am calling the shots, understand? He's lying. Kill him, now."

"No one appointed you the captain. We are a team, remember?"

"Not anymore. Kill him before he causes more problems. He is like a virus—he keeps showing up in mutated forms. Lower the chain!"

Men hesitate.

The big man says, "You're the captain, huh?"

"Yes, I am!"

"Not anymore!" He draws his handgun and shoots the other in the temple. His body slumps to the deck in a pool of blood.

"Draw Wiley back up on board. Take him with us."

I am thrown down hard on the deck and secured. Men stand over me with weapons drawn. I gasp for a long while, shivering, but they do not ask me what I know.

As dusk settles, we near a coastline of green forests and narrow beaches. They lift me up on the rail.

"Can you swim now?" one asks.

"Yes," I say.

"See that vehicle on that road by the shore?"

"Yes."

"Men are waiting for you in the car. You must swim from here, and if you try and escape, we will shoot you."

He shoves me over the side, and I plunge into water, smacking hard in the waves. With weapons brandished, they watch me from the deck. My arms are cramping, and my legs have no power. The current pulls at me as I feebly swim for the vehicle by the beach. Warning shots from them pierce the sloshing waves around me. I reach the sandy bottom and wade ashore through hordes of stinging jellyfish. As I move across the oyster shells and briar, Aswan's big boat motors away to the south. I get to the car, open the door, and find big Asian men sitting inside, with black revolvers drawn. "Get in," one commands me.

I step in, and the vehicle roars off along the shore.

We arrive on a narrow coastline and drive up to a big waterside home. Nearby docks are deserted. A black helicopter lies idle in a nearby field. They yank me from the car and walk me in the house through a basement door. Sullen, armed men are sitting on old furniture, and I am pushed toward a securely locked door. No one has asked me anything. The door is unbolted, and I am shoved in.

Cold concrete and a single light bulb are all there is. A disheveled woman in a dirty dress is squatting in the corner, staring at her bare feet. It's Tara Chin. She turns away from me.

"Why are you here?" she spits.

"Why are you?"

Her slim body looks full of hatred. "Because I didn't kill you when Gerald's biplane took off," she says. "I failed at the most important assignment of all, making you finally gone."

"For a woman who had all the cards, that must be a real disappointment, being a buck private again."

"Perhaps I should be glad you were captured again," she says. "They were about to shoot me in the head just a half hour ago, then hesitated. There are no mistakes with Gerald Aswan. They must want something from you, what?"

"Only my life."

"That they could have had any time they wanted," she replies. "As for me, I know you won't believe me now, but I did care for you. You were different."

"You too," I say.

"Being betrayed by me...was it painful?"

"You betrayed not only me, but the whole world. Aswan's intentions are insane."

"You don't know me, or who I really am. If you did, you might change your mind about why I'm in his organization."

Woods's dossier on her is still fresh in my mind. "Tell me who you are then," I say.

"Remaining a mystery is the way we should leave it. I'll die knowing I did something amazing."

"As you wish, Tara. But you never really fooled me."

"Liar. I had you telling me everything about the Hartner investigation."

"Wrong," I try. "I knew about you the moment I met you."

"Really?" She says. "Where was I born?"

"Born Tarisha Lee Chin, in San Francisco, thirty-three years ago. Parading as a twenty-year-old was your first mistake."

She is silent.

I add, "Then the advanced computer degrees, the activism, the convictions, the jail time. You're far more interesting that your wishy-washy character let on."

"Innocence was necessary for the role."

"Too bad," I say. "I liked the schoolgirl better."

"So you never believed in me?" she asks.

"I believed in your tenderness when we lay together," I say.

"That was genuine."

"But, that is history."

"I'm history," she declares. "They will come for me soon."

"Unless I tell them about the problem with the cube, is that what you're suggesting? Tara, you're quite unconvincing."

She replies, "I know nothing about the cube. Not since you snatched it from Gerald."

"You don't know that cube is now back in Aswan's hands?"

"Certainly not. But if you are telling the truth, he will utilize them very soon."

"What are his plans?" I ask.

"I don't know. I'm powerless now. When Gerald Aswan is done with someone, they vanish."

"No love affair with him?"

"No."

"Convince me you're not tricking me into telling you about the cube's problem."

"I know nothing about it," she says. "The cubes are supposed to be impenetrable. That was the point of them being fabricated from diamond, and the atomic encoding they contain. No one was supposed to be able to scan the cubes, download them, or damage them. You're lying."

"Why would I lie, Tara? I'm as good as dead. I dare say, more than you."

"Well, if you're telling the truth about the cube being disabled, you may be able to broker a deal."

"Perhaps," I say. "But it's strange, finding you conveniently lying here. Convince me."

She pulls aside her dress, revealing fresh bruises around her arms and throat. She's not my friend anymore, nor lover, nor confidante. Perhaps I can finally see into her. I touch her dirty cheek, and what I sense from her is now crystal clear. I pull my hand away after a long pause. At last, I can sense the real Tara Chin.

I feel a murderous woman, bent on revenge and treachery. She provided Aswan with the critical computer skills he needed to make the cubes viable. The bruised, lonely girl next to me is playing the mole, one more time. She is under great pressure to get me to reveal the problem with the cube. I shake my head.

Her eyes grow cold, and, for a moment, she looks terrified, knowing she has failed. She stands and walks quickly from the room.

Soon, footsteps come pounding down the steps. They barge into the room. "Wiley, stand. You're coming up."

They drag me upstairs to a large, well-furnished living room, and seat me in a high-back chair. Three gunmen are standing motionless. Nothing about the cubes must pass my lips. I have won. They must not know the solution to the virus Sinclair put in the cube.

Gerald Aswan steps into the room from the hallway, walks over, then sits in a nearby chair.

"The world is not a good place," he says. "You don't know that, of course, but I do, Detective. If I were to reveal the connections that I have uncovered about countries and their leaders, and murder, and war, and corruption—all of it because of money, you might understand why I am doing this."

"You lost me?"

Aswan says, "No one is beyond corruption, Detective. Your Senator Hartner, certainly not. Nor your parents, nor your president. No one has been able to resist the corrosive lure of money. It weaves itself through banks, and guns, and blood and power. It cuts good men down, and brings bad men up. It's all about the money. And we're all doomed."

"You're lying, Aswan. There're good men and woman who still obey the law."

"Nonsense!" he bellows. "I have seen all the lies, from phony tax returns, to terrorist weapons accounts, to organized hits, to blackmail, to every conceivable illegal transaction you can imagine. I first saw it all when I stole all those files from all those companies, then stored that information in the two cubes. I now want to smash that world, Detective. I want to infiltrate it. I can do it. But not without your help."

"Get it over with, Aswan."

"You mean, shoot you in the back of the head?"

"Yes."

"So," he asks, "you know I am hurt by the cube's inability to transmit its information?"

"Yes."

Aswan says, "Well done, Detective. You did something to it, something subtle, something debilitating. Congratulations."

I say nothing.

"With the click of a mouse," he continues, "I can right wrongs, directing money from a terrorist network to an orphanage on the other side of the world, without detection. I can shrink a tyrant's bank account in the blink of an eye. I can reveal all the lies and corruption that happen every day in the world. And I will. But not without your assistance. You will help me, Mr. Wiley?"

"A change of heart?" I ask.

"It came to me late. At first, I was so intoxicated that I had data on everyone on earth that I went crazy, secretly siphoning billions into my own accounts. I could effortlessly amass all the money I needed. But the more I saw of the real world, the more I began to grow sick at the revelations I uncovered."

"And?" I ask.

"And I came to the conclusion that any man, regardless of his worth, would come to, if he uncovered what I did. I have a responsibility not to sack the world, Detective, but to protect it."

"Sounds wonderful," I say. "I won't buy it."

"Try to believe in what I'm saying. Yet, without both cubes functioning, I am—"

"Impotent."

He freezes. "Aptly put."

Silence lingers in the room. I desperately need more time. I recall an obsession of Aswan's that Woods had uncovered. Will he go for it?

I finally say, "Then let's break the impasse by agreeing to a wager."

"What do you have in mind?" he asks.

"We have been at war with each other for months, Mr. Aswan. The balance of power has tipped many times leading up to this moment. The final victor is still undecided. I propose we end this war with one last battle. I win, you let me walk away. You win, I supply you the solution to restoring the cubes."

"And if I kill you for having the arrogance for even suggesting that?"

I smile. "You stay impotent."

Tara enters the room, sits down, and listens. Her posture is tense. Aswan glances at her with disdain, then turns to me. "What kind of battle, Detective?"

"Any kind of competitive game will do," I say. "You name the game, and I'll play you for my freedom. You'll play for the cube's solution. Winner takes all."

Aswan remains silent. Finally, he says, "You're an idiot."

He walks from the room, then returns with two small cloth bags and a lined wooden board.

"Chess?" I ask.

"Certainly not, Detective Wiley," he replies. "The most appropriate game to end this relationship is a game of Go, the ancient Chinese board game. Are you familiar with it?"

"No."

"Not surprising, judging from your pathetically backward upbringing. Go was always a game for the cerebral aristocrat. To avoid bloodshed, the future of Tibet was once decided by a simple game of Go. The object is to take over territory, either by walling it off, or by completely surrounding your opponent's stones for capture—all while protecting your own. We take turns placing our stones on the intersections of the lines. At the end, the winner is the one who has captured the most territory, plus the number of stones he's captured. Ready?"

I hesitate. "That's hardly a complete lesson," I say. "Proceed anyway."

He pulls a small table between our chairs, places the wooden board down, and hands me a bag of white stones. From his bag, he places a black stone near the corner of the board. I place a white stone in the middle. He shakes his head, and places another piece by his first one. Before I know it, he has captured the upper corner, and thwarted any of my attempts to stop him. He begins another sectional conquest, while preventing me from doing the same.

Aswan smiles. "Detective, you can surrender now; your groups are weak and thin."

"The game hasn't ended yet," I reply.

"Oh, but it has."

I manage to surround a small cluster of his pieces and take them off the board. Unfazed, he captures an ever bigger group of mine. I slow down, taking longer periods of time between each move.

A full hour passes.

Aswan's men and Tara are standing around us, watching as Aswan continues his conquest. I learned from his background that Go was one of his obsessions. But with all his examination of my history, he couldn't have known it was also a recent interest of mine. Since I moved to DC, I have eaten dinner many nights with Sammy and his wife, Yashiro. Yashiro is half-Japanese, has played Go all her life, and is a highly ranked amateur. She and I played this game after we ate. I have never beaten her, but I have become quite competent. More importantly, I have learned her best tricks. She taught me to guard against the greatest threat of all—overconfidence.

Aswan has left his board open to challenge, thinking I won't comprehend its opportunities. But I do. I begin exploiting his positions, slowly gaining on him, strengthening the formations of my stones. The power center of the game is shifting. I see tension in his eyes and hands.

I begin an unhurried attack, inflicting more damage, not allowing him to retaliate in return. He begins to recolonize, to settle a new frontier, but I cut him in two, splitting his forces, swallowing them, thwarting his countermeasures. He changes strategy—wearing me down by attrition, surrounding my white stones, weathering my counterattack, then attacking once again. Clusters of our stones pass from life to death.

As I place each piece down, I intuitively sense his intentions in the wooden board. Aswan's behavior has changed throughout the game—transforming him from a greedy capitalist, to a military tactician, to a sword-wielding warrior. His game mirrors his own hidden desires, revealing a relentless thirst for all things powerful, and an insistent need to acquire them by any means necessary. His Go game is raw brutality over grace.

An hour later, I place my final white stone down, losing to him by three points. There's an emptiness to his expression. "You came very close to winning. How?"

"Beginner's luck."

"That was not the work of a beginner," Aswan says. "You knew I played Go. Obviously, you do as well. You toyed with me, Detective, as if you could have won. Were you trying to show off?"

"I didn't pick the game—you did."

"Then what was the point," he says, "other than to waste hours of my time?"

"There was no other point," I say.

Aswan stands up in a rage and swats the board away, spraying stones across the marble floor. He grabs one of the guard's nine-millimeter pistols and aims it at my head. "Fool, did you think I would abide by your wager, even if you had won? This is your last chance to tell me how to restore my cubes."

He hesitates, then spins the gun on Tara. "I am out of patience. Because this bitch has ultimately failed me today, I will kill her first. Do you want that?"

We hear distant gunshots begin peppering the night. A guard rushes in and warns Aswan, "Coast guard ships and choppers are moving this way."

Aswan curses and orders his men outside into the driving rain. "So, Detective, what is your decision?"

"Murdering Tara buys you nothing," I say.

He screams, "Then, you bastard, give me the solution!"

Tara lunges at him now, slams him backward, then races for the door. Aswan stumbles, then recovers and fires his handgun at Tara, striking her high in the back, slamming her into the wall. She wavers, then slides to the floor, her dark blood streaking the oak paneling.

"Why, Gerald?" she whispers, staring at him.

I move over to her slumped figure and lift up her lovely head. Tara's dilated eyes stare up at me in confusion. I feel the girl I knew, and the angry woman I didn't, both fighting to stay alive. She shudders, then grows still in my arms. I lay her down and look up at Gerald Aswan.

He's vanished.

A fierce gun battle is erupting as I run from the house out into the storm. Aswan's men are on the upper deck of his moored yacht, shooting at the oncoming coast guard ship, whose firing cannon salvoes through the pouring rain. In the distance, two police helicopters are sweeping the yacht with their spotlights.

Rotor blades power up, and the black chopper in the field begins to rise and cant off across the water, vanishing into the rain. Aswan's dark figure is in the pilot's seat.

One of the police choppers lands on the side lawn, and Sammy and Woods frantically wave me over. I race to the open door and jump in. "Dammit, John, what the hell happened? We totally lost track of you until we finally identified Aswan's yacht."

"Grateful to see you both," I say. "But this isn't over. Aswan just escaped in the black chopper, out across the water."

"Where are the cubes?" Sammy demands.

"He must have them."

"Then pursue him," he commands the pilot. "You can continue in this weather?"

"Yes, but buckle up," the pilot shouts. "It's gonna get wild."

As the pilot flies us into the night, chasing Gerald Aswan out into the Chesapeake Bay, Aswan's yacht takes a sudden lethal shelling and erupt in flames.

CHAPTER THIRTY-THREE

Aswan's dim tail-rotor lights are all we see up ahead as we fly through the rainy darkness. We're now gaining on his position, our spotlights illuminating his tiny chopper as it blows back and forth, racing across the bay. The sharpshooter with us is preparing his weapon, waiting for a viable shot to disable the craft.

Another minute and the shooter's ready, sliding the door open, aiming his rifle out into the rain. He fires. Aswan's chopper swerves left, then continues on. Another shot is fired. Then another. Aswan's tail begins to swing back and forth in the storm. His craft dives, then spins around, trying to maintain control. As we grow near, it's buffeted by a massive gust, flips sideways, and spirals toward the water. It slams into the pitching waves, its blades madly slice the swells.

"He's down," Sammy bellows into his headset. Our chopper pilot radios our location back to the trailing coast guard cutter.

We hover over Aswan's craft as it sinks into the churning waters. Within a minute, it has vanished. We scan the area with our spotlights. There's no sign Aswan has escaped, no inflatable rising up from below.

"Coast guard is still ten minutes away," the pilot says.

"He'll be dead by that time," I say. "Let's get a raft down there—now! How deep's the water?"

The chopper pilot releases a container that hits the water and inflates into an orange life raft. He scans a computerized map of the bay. "Shallow right here. About twenty-two feet, but with the storm tide, probably deeper."

"Forget it," Sammy says. "Let the man die like the animal he is."

"We need him alive for a lot of reasons," I say. "Any scuba gear aboard?" I ask the pilot.

"Just mask and flippers," he says.

"Have to make do," I say.

Woods grips my arm. "John, make this your last time in any kind of water, okay?"

I gear up, grab a flashlight, and leap down in the turbulent waves. Swimming to the raft, I get my bearings, look up, and see Sammy pointing farther left. I swim five yards, take a big breath, and dive down into the darkness. The water is chilly, and my clothes feel heavy, and I'm not sure where the hell I am in these currents. Reaching the bottom, I look around and see nothing. I move farther left and spot a dim shape nearby. With my flashlight, I illuminate the black chopper lying on its side in the sand. There's movement inside.

Surfacing, I catch my breath and go back down, locating Gerald Aswan, who's trapped inside the cabin. He's breathing in an air pocket at the top of the glass dome. His arm looks caught, pinned by the collapsed fuselage.

I surface again, and yell to the hovering chopper above, "He's trapped—but alive."

"Hang on, John," Sammy yells. "The coast guard's minutes away."

I dive back down and see that Aswan's air pocket is shrinking fast. He's on his tiptoes, breathing in a narrow gap. I study his trapped arm through the glass. He's holding onto a reinforced aluminum briefcase, crushed in place.

The cubes.

His hand is anxiously clutching the handle. If he were to release his grip, he could remove his arm from the opening it's trapped in. I bang on the glass and motion to him, indicating his fist should release the case. He shakes his head *no!*

I surface, grab air, and come back down again. He's panicking now, coughing in the rising water, his hand still tight around the handle. I dive into the opening and swim inside his watery cabin. Grabbing his arm, I pull hard, trying to get him to release his grip on the briefcase.

He violently fights back, battling me with his free arm. Reaching for my neck, he latches on, crushing my windpipe. I'm not ready for his sudden assault and I tear his hand free and consider retaliation. I could easily kill him now. All would applaud the act. All the death and treachery he's caused the world should rightly return to him, right now.

Yet what I just sensed in his hand was not the darkness of a murderer, which he is. Nor the intolerance of a tyrant, which he would become. All that's left is a powerless little man having a helpless, fearful spasm. He thinks I just want the cubes, and will not surrender them to me, ever. He can't imagine I'm here to help him.

With burning lungs, I back off and swim outside the glass. He's screaming now, in limbo, tormented by his own uncertainty. I motion for him to simply let them go, and swim up to the surface. Gasping, I return to the tossing waves above.

The coast guard cutter has arrived, and its crew is lowering rafts and divers into the waves. Sammy yells at me, "They've got it now. Stay topside—don't go down again!"

I shake my head no.

Taking a final breath, I swim down one more time and shine my light on the man. Gerald Aswan is hovering inside the cabin, wide eyed and motionless. A frozen gaze has claimed his expression. Locked inside this silent chamber, he floats in a dark world of defeat. Gone is the Sumerian god, the Vishava, the invincible global mobster.

His trapped arm now floats freely by his side. He released his grip on the case, but he let it go too late.

CHAPTER THIRTY-FOUR

I t's a very long week afterward.

"Detective Wiley, give me a moment, will you?" Senator Hartner's gaze is earnest and respectful. We are in a National Reconnaissance building in Chantilly, Virginia, awaiting a meeting with the division director. There are a dozen others in the room, including all the top people whom I've worked with over the last months.

Over in the corner, the senator puts his hand on my shoulder and removes a slip of paper from his coat. He places it firmly in my hand. "This is the reward money for saving Elizabeth's life. I know you said we're all clear, but had you not come to town, she would be dead."

I open the check. It's for one million dollars.

"Don't say a thing, Detective. We're all grateful."

The door opens, and the director comes in. "Ladies and gentlemen, please come into the next room. The display is ready."

We all file into a big lab. The table in the middle contains a glass case, and inside are the two gleaming cubes. The director has us move closer.

"From Gerald Aswan's sunken helicopter, dive crews recovered the waterproof case containing the cubes, and, as you can see, they are completely intact. In fact, thanks to Sinclair Johnson's help removing the virus he planted in one of them, they work perfectly."

"Have we accessed the information in the cubes?" Woods asks.

"Yes, Detective Woods. We have sampled it and found that Gerald Aswan had amassed not only banking records and phone numbers, but also medical files, credit card transactions, and every conceivable form of electronic data stored today. And he had gathered it on almost every living person in the world. Inside those cubes are top-secret files from databases all over the planet. Even our own. Gerald Aswan and his team managed to infiltrate and steal more secrets than anyone in history."

"What will become of all those stolen files?" Senator Hartner asks. "Surely they must be deleted for the sake of the world's privacy."

The director shifts gears. "Yes, of course, Senator, but verifying the data, then deleting what parts are not critical to national security will take time. We must painstakingly sift through every file. And there are billions of documents in those two small cubes. Imagine a high-rise building, full of file cabinets, stretching all the way to the moon."

"Who will be in charge of the review of the cube's files?" Woods asks.

He says, "Why, the US government."

Senator Hartner says, "Will there be a review board report on the final determination of the files to be deleted?"

The director smiles. "Senator, of course. But it will take years to know what we've got here. And, besides, the additional private data on every US citizen in those cubes can also help us. We can track down people we never knew about with this new information. We have dental records, medical records, banking records—everything. It's truly a gold mine into the activities of your everyday citizen. Trust us. We will use it with the utmost discretion."

"Any questions?" He pauses. "Then, thank you. Remember, all that you have seen here must remain secret. I've cleared you only because this group was so closely connected with this investigation and the existence of the cubes."

The people there gather in smaller groups and begin talking.

I move to the table where the cubes are displayed and place my hand on the top of the case. This is my first time in contact with them both. Now, as if I too had to have the plus and minus cubes together to make sense of them, I get a clear signal from them. Not names or numbers of anyone, but faces and feelings. I feel chaos, confusion, and panic. I sense the abuse of the data contained in them. I see the world's privacy intrusively exposed. It's clear that no good will come from knowing the information they contain.

Sinclair's been watching me. He knows what I've just sensed, because he's deciphered the language and glimpsed into Aswan's cubes as well. The US government has rescinded his jail time, and the CIA has hired him. He's one of them now. He's giving me a strong "no-go" glance.

I look up to the ceiling and see a big array of chrome sprinklers. I turn my back to the table, touch the cube's glass case, and gently move the cover ajar, exposing the cubes to the air.

I announce warmly, "Ladies and gentlemen, can I have your attention, please? In all good conscience, I cannot take this reward money from Senator Hartner for the recovery of his daughter, Elizabeth. I am on salary with the DC police department. My association with them forbids officers making any financial gains from any case they work on."

I hold up the check, and everybody freezes. I pull a butane lighter from my pocket and light the check on fire, holding it high for all to see.

For a moment, right before the smoke from the senator's flaming check sets off the ceiling sprinklers, dousing the room and the cubes with cold water, their smiles at my gesture are supportive. Then, all turns to panic. As the room empties out, I slide the glass cover shut over the wet cubes. Out of the corner of my eye, I see the two diamonds brightly arcing as they make electrical contact with the thin layer of water around them.

All of humanity's secrets—the joys, horrors, and mysteries—are now instantly erased.

The investigation is brief and tortured. A major find in criminal data acquisition is sadly lost for the US government. I am admonished for destroying the cube's stolen data, removed from the DC police force, and told that such careless behavior around government property is unprofessional and bordering on treason. I keep my mouth shut, nod a great deal, but never apologize.

A week later, the senator throws a quiet Sunday afternoon party for me at his house. The events surrounding the climactic end of Aswan's cubes are blowing over. No one was injured, none the worse for wear, nor apparently angry. Except, of course, a few of this country's National Security Agency employees.

I skip the party and meet Sammy outside for a quick handshake in the senator's sun-splashed driveway. "No one wants you to leave, John."

I smile. "That was a good one, huh, Sammy?"

A rare grin from him crosses his face. "A memorable case, indeed, young man. But we still need you here. Everything's cleared to bring you back in. DC police want you around, John. You've seen this city now, and you know it's full of trouble. Trouble we can knock down together."

"Thanks for the offer," I say. "But it's time to ride away from here."

I pat Sammy, my godfather, on the shoulder, climb in, and drive my old Landcruiser out onto Reservoir Road, with its summer air beckoning. I see Elizabeth in the silver BMW coming up quickly behind me. She waves sadly as I turn onto Key Bridge toward Virginia.

I take Highway 81, driving it south down through the Shenandoah Valley. The Blue Ridge Mountains come and go, like so many big, silent faces.

When I cross into North Carolina, it's like I've been gone forever. Home is not far away. I can smell my mother's coffee, and feel my father's handshake. I'll bush hog his back fields tomorrow morning. I'll let it all go.

But in the back of my mind, I'll miss DC. That wild Potomac River, that crazy, confounding city. I'll be back. Someday.

The End

Made in the USA
Charleston, SC
16 November 2014